To Ela

May you always be blessed.
Hope you enjoy the book!

Sincerely,
David Isbell

THE
TRUE LOVE
MESSIAH
An Adventure of Biblical Proportions

TLM Press

We want to hear from you about this book. Please send your comments to us in care of www.thetruelovemessiah.com/Contact.html. Thank you.

Copyright © 2008 by David Isbell
All rights reserved

This title is also available as an audio product.
Visit www.thetruelovemessiah.com for more information.

Library of Congress Cataloging-In-Publication Data

Isbell, David
    The True Love Messiah: / David Isbell.
      p. cm.
    ISBN: 978-0-9815348-3-1
    LOC number is available upon request

All scripture quotations, unless otherwise indicated, are taken from the *Holy Bible: New International Version*. NIV. Copyright © 1973 by International Bible Society. Used by permission of Zondervan. All rights reserved.

This book is printed on acid-free paper.

Printed in the United States of America

All rights reserved. No part of this publication may be reproduced, stored in a retrieval system, or transmitted in any form or by any means- electronic, mechanical, photocopy, recording, or any other- except for brief quotations in printed reviews, without the prior permission of the publisher.

To Jacinda Kaialani and Eden
For the glory of God

Acknowledgements:

This project would not have been possible without the blood, sweat and tears of the Messiah and the steadfast prayers and support of the following miracle workers: Peggy Smith, Peggy Odam, Mildred Goldthwaite, Dr. Jim Jackson and the members of Chapelwood United Methodist Church, Rev. Conrell Lockett and the Touch Tobago mission team, the many friends and family members who encouraged and inspired in so many ways and all those who believe in True Love and the Messiah.

My son, if you accept my words
and store up my commands within you,
turning your ear to wisdom
and applying your heart to understanding,
and if you call out for insight
and cry aloud for understanding,
and if you look for it as for silver
and search for it as for hidden treasure,
then you will understand the fear of the Lord
and find the knowledge of God.
For the Lord gives wisdom,
and from his mouth come knowledge and understanding.

-Proverbs 2:1-6

INTRODUCTION

The Lord instructed Moses to write the book of Genesis and other books of the Old Testament. John was instructed to, "Write the things which thou hast seen." Books and instructions about writing are mentioned no less than 175 times in the Bible and the urge of prophets and patriarchs to write down the words that came to them is illustrated in the book of Job.

> **"Oh that my words were written! Oh that they were printed in a book! That they were graven with an iron pen and lead in the rock forever!"**
> **-Job 19:23**

I feel obligated. I am compelled. I have a need to put to paper the story which you are about to read. The fact you are reading these written words signifies that you are seeking knowledge and insight, none of which I claim to have, other than the wisdom that manifests itself from trusting in the God of the Universe with all your heart and loving the Lord, God, your Creator, above all else.

King Solomon once said in Ecclesiastes 12:12 "Of making books there is no end..." But, like Moses and John, Matthew, Mark, Luke and Saint Paul, I intend to record that which I have seen and heard and, thus, that which I have witnessed for myself. By the act of writing and recording, I will share these events with all those who seek truth and affirmation of faith. We are encouraged to continue our search for answers and to seek ultimate truths. It's clear what the Bible has to say about our quest...

> **"What was hidden from the wise and the learned is now revealed unto the babes and the suckling."**
> -**Matthew 11:25**

That's us, no matter young or old.

God promises to…

> **"Pour out my spirit upon all flesh; and your sons and your daughters shall prophecy, your old men shall dream dreams, your young men shall see visions."**
> -**Joel 2:28**

I want to share with you my visions.

CHAPTER 1

*"So God created man in His own image,
male and female he created them."*
-Genesis 1:27

The first time I saw her was by chance. Or was it fate? We were at the school cafeteria, a popular place for most students to casually drop in for lunch. Just a glimpse of her caused me to stop and pause. A more prolonged view of her shimmering smile and soft flowing hair enticed me to approach. Sweet and demure, yet athletic and fit, I felt an instant attraction to her charm. Usually shy and somewhat reserved, a brief moment and some slight self-encouragement was all it took for me to engage her in conversation. This was our first encounter. Ten years ago to the day, I can still smell the distinct aroma of the most fragrant of flowers that surely blossomed during that springtime in Texas. I was in love.

At our private Christian university, certain theological studies were mandatory. However, with just two required classes, one focusing on world religions and another on the Bible, it was hardly an in-depth probe into the subject. For someone with such an unquenchable thirst for truth and certainty, it was necessary to research and investigate on my own. Though not the most decorated of students, I was more than apt at uncovering secrets, solving mysteries and delving into the unknown. My grades began to suffer. Instead of late nights studying economics and English literature, I couldn't help but to read from the I Ching, The Quran, The Torah and the Bible. The Rig Vedas, The Book of Mormon and Popol Vuh, The Mayan Book of Creation, held my interest. Hours of studying for final exams were traded for burning the midnight candle in hopes of uncovering some hidden, ancient truth.

Like I said, I was drawn to her. It was a magical time for both of us. We were young. We had so many questions with answers that seemed so attainable. How was it all created? Is there a God? Are we Christians? We talked about ecology, the environment and saving the

Earth. We were two hopeless romantics, a couple of dreamers. I'm sure you have known the type. Perhaps you are one of us, too. It is a quest; as much a dream for a better world as a search for enlightenment and truth. Starting down this path, the answers seemed so very clear. I would soon come to find out I didn't even know the questions. *Am I a Christian?* I thought.

I stared into her eyes and began to speak, "I do have an earnest desire to save the world, but what does that mean, Kari?"

"It means you want to accomplish some good. You want to serve others. You want to make the world a better place. You know, I did read the book you suggested to me."

"<u>Ishmael</u>?" I had mentioned to her that I read it a couple of weeks prior.

"Yes. <u>Ishmael</u> by Daniel Quinn. And thank you for recommending it! I know I definitely want to be a leaver and not a taker. I realized that I can actually make a difference!"

"But, did you learn how to save the world?"

"From a book? Really, David?"

"Yes, really. From a book."

"Well, no…I guess I didn't. I wish there was some kind of guide book on how to save the world, but that's just wishful thinking."

Maybe not, I thought. *Maybe the world has already been saved.*

"Not necessarily a book that tells you how to save the world, Kari, but how to save yourself."

"How to save myself? Come on, now. Everybody has to die sooner or later."

"Do they?"

"Certainly. It's called life and death. Haven't you heard of it?"

"Yes. Well, according to this book, there is a way you can avoid death."

"And save yourself? Yeah, yeah, you must be talking about the Bible. I did go to Catholic school, you know. This is pretty basic stuff."

"Yes, but important stuff!"

"I guess you're right. But, do you truly believe that Jesus Christ was born of a virgin? That He did miracles? That He came back from the dead? That He came to..."

I quickly finished her thought…"That He came to save the world? That He came to save you and me? So many people around here question whether or not Jesus even existed, whether He ever lived or came to Earth. They want evidence, facts, proof."

"Proof? They want proof? How can you prove faith?"

"I'm not sure, but I want to do it."

"In a book? You can't be serious? That's very ambitious, David!"

"Well, thanks. But, I can't even prove there is a God. I can only tell of my experiences, give my testimony so to say, influence and…"

"And, perhaps, write a book that will save the world…by convincing people to save themselves? Good God, where would you start?"

CHAPTER 2

My thesis was due later that afternoon. With only one elective and an Astronomy class remaining for me to graduate, this paper had only two requirements. It had to be turned in on time and it had to be good. A "C" average and a degree in Latin American Studies would be the outcome of my four years at the university. I had already signed up for the last elective of my undergraduate career, Mysticism 101. It sounded interesting and fun. After ingesting all that material from so many different religious texts, it seemed only natural that I register for this class. It was surprising that such a class even existed and was offered at my school. The truth is, I was just happy to be getting a diploma. After seven months and a full course load of accredited hours in Mexico, I was about to receive a degree in what was, essentially, Spanish.

Almost a year had passed since I said "adiós" to Kari and left for my studies at La Universidad de Las Américas near Puebla, Mexico, about 60 miles east of Mexico City. We were 30 miles from the massive steam-producing volcano, Popocatepetl, aptly named by the Aztecs, "smoking mountain." A summer session in Puebla and another six weeks in Guanajuato, home of the Cervantino (a non-stop three week party in October celebrating author Miguel de Cervantes and his famed novel <u>Don Quijote</u>) and I had decided to stay in Mexico for at least another semester.

On weekdays I spent time with my *cuates, mis amigos mexicanos*, going to class most of the time and drinking *cerveza* and *tequila* any chance I got. On weekends we would travel. Oaxaca, Acapulco, Cuernavaca, Vera Cruz, small little *pueblitos* and beach towns. I studied the culture of Mexico, the history. I learned of the Aztec empire and read the writings of Bartolome de Las Casas, chief priest of the Spaniards, and those of the famed *conquistador,* Hernán Cortés. De Las Casas would dedicate his life to improving the conditions of Native Americans everywhere. He wrote…

An Adventure of Biblical Proportions

"These Indians can bring near the redemption. Their conversion is apt indeed, as I am convinced the Indians originate in Ancient Israel. Indeed, I can bring proofs from the Bible that they are of the Lost Tribes."

In fact, because of the many similarities to Christianity which the Spanish priests found in the native religion, they thought the Devil had attempted to build a counterfeit church in America. Father Duran in his <u>Historia Antigua de la Nueva España</u> wrote in 1585, "I verily believe that the evil spirit himself must have somehow supplied these poor people with a spurious edition of the Bible."

Immense masses of documents were stored in the archives of ancient Mexico. Unfortunately, most all of them were destroyed. Torquemada wrote that five cities alone yielded to the Spanish governor no less than 16,000 volumes of scrolls of which every leaf was burned. Indeed, *Tor* in Hebrew means 'the law' and *quemada* in Spanish means 'burned.' Torquemada is 'the burned law.' Hernan Cortés would say of Tenochtitlan, the capital city of the Aztecs…

"We saw so many towns and villages. Everywhere were great towers, temples and pyramids. You find apothecaries, where you can buy medicine, barber shops, bath houses, restaurants. A city of 300,000 residents. Many roof gardens, clean streets, pipes carrying drinking water from the mountains to the city, granaries, an aviary, zoo, fountains, fish ponds, schools." Cortés wrote, "There is still another market twice as large as Salamanca's. Jewelers, potters, painters, goldsmiths, stone-cutters, weavers, fisherman, florists. You could buy bronze axes, razors, mirrors, swords, animals, and much chocolate." He continued, "I said everything to them I could to draw them to a knowledge of God our Lord. Moctezuma replied that they were not the aborigines of the country, but that their ancestors had emigrated to it many years ago; and they fully believed that after so long an absence from their native land, they might have fallen into some errors; that I having more recently arrived must know better than themselves what they ought to believe; and that if I would instruct them in these matters, and make them understand the true faith, they would follow my directions, as being for the best. I answered that they must learn there was but one God, the universal

Lord of all, who had created the heavens and earth, and all things else, and had made them and us; that He was without beginning and immortal, and they were bound to adore and believe Him, and no other creature or thing."

Like I said, sometimes I would travel alone. I walked alone that night to the little *tienda* around the corner. This particular store sold semi-cold Negra Modelo, a Mexican beer that would surely whet my palate. I paid 10 pesos and quickly left. However, I wasn't ready for what followed next. In spite of not having received any mail for nearly half a year, earlier that very afternoon I decided to stop in at the school post office. Surprised it was postmarked four months prior, now arriving in my mailbox was a letter from an old flame, someone I had loved. After dating for the better part of a year, circumstances caused her to move back to Salt Lake City. We drifted apart. I met Kari. Now, a few months later, here I find myself staring at the smoke rising from El Popo volcano and walking to the store to get that beer.

> **"Be not forgetful to entertain strangers, for thereby some have entertained angels without knowing it."**
> **-Hebrews 13:2**

I had always believed in God and had some noteworthy things happen to me in the past, but this was out of the ordinary. This was different. This was strange. I started to tremble when he suddenly grabbed me by the shoulders. Although he did shake me slightly, I was more startled than scared.

"*Por qué estás aquí?* Why are you here?" he said in Spanish. "*Hijo, por qué estás aquí? Vete a tu país, enamórate.*" Go back to your country and be in love. He repeated it once more in his native tongue.

Maybe it was the way he said it, the certainty in his voice? Maybe it was the crazed look in his eyes? It was sort of biblical, certainly mystical from my point of view.

As I left the old man standing there, maybe a beggar, maybe an angel, I turned the corner and there was a sight to behold. Illuminating the *camino al Norte*, lighting the way home (or at least the road back to my apartment) was the most spectacular vision of the moon in all its fullness and grandeur that my eyes had ever seen. What did the *viejo* mean by what he said? To whom was he referring? Who could be my true love? Does such a thing exist? I thought of the letter I had received that day. I thought of Kari and our time together, our long talks on philosophy and religion. I thought of a girl whom I had yet to meet, my soulmate, my *alma gemela, mi verdadero amor.*

CHAPTER 3

I took final exams, spent a week or so in the Yucatán, left Mexico and headed back to Texas. Arriving in Ft. Worth, I was ready to start my last few classes at the university. I was also excited to see Kari again. God she was beautiful. After a few unsuccessful tries to contact her, I heard through the grapevine that she was, indeed, gone. She had left for Spain for the entire spring semester and would not be returning until the end of May. *That's what I deserve for not writing her*, I thought. Long distance communication has never been easy and has probably cost me more than a few friends.

Right now, I'm worried about other things. I need to graduate and I'm in a rush to turn in this paper. My professor, Dr. Frischmann, is a bit eccentric, smart and very likeable. He has done a good deal of work with the *Zapatistas,* a self-proclaimed liberation movement of indigenous peoples in Chiapas, Mexico. He has also shown quite a bit of patience with me, as my thesis has already changed once. Originally planning to report on the Tarahumaras, the native people of the *Cañon del Cobre* in Northwest Mexico, I visited Copper Canyon by train, gathering lots of interesting facts and information, but ultimately deciding at the last minute to change topics.

This research paper had morphed into a sort-of scientific, theological hodge-podge of information with an intended purpose of which I wasn't quite sure. In theory, it was to trace the population of the Americas by our early ancestors down to the tip of South America, the Tierra del Fuego. *Maybe I had a hidden agenda?* Was the intent to show a possible co-existence of Creationism and evolution theories? Maybe, it was to show that all people are related to a common ancestor- a mitochondrial Eve? Or, maybe, just maybe, it was to prove to myself that I really am a Christian? More than likely it was just a simple search for knowledge and truth. I proof-read the final copy once more as my grade depended on it. Of the important parts I took mental notes and highlighted their scholarly significance. Would my professor be impressed? Would he believe the premise? Would I graduate? *Am I really a Christian?*

An Adventure of Biblical Proportions

I studied Astronomy and the Big Bang Theory, the scientific dating of the Earth at 4.6 billion years. I studied paleoanthropology and wrote about supposed early human ancestors, the hominids of East Africa and the Great Rift Valley around 3 million years ago. I wrote about the supposed appearance of *Homo erectus* 1.6 million years ago, pin-pointed scientific data supporting the first appearance of fully capable modern humans, *Homo Sapiens Sapiens,* and the out-of-Africa theory, a mass migration that may have taken place 100,000 years ago. I researched about Neanderthals, a branch of primate relatives that became extinct around 30,000 years ago. (Although, from time to time I think, perhaps, some of them are still around!) Soon after their extinction, I discovered that the Ice Age was upon us. Climatologists will say that from 22,000-11,600 B.C. most of the Earth was covered in ice. Most anthropologists will then say that a mass migration took place from Siberia over the Bering Strait land bridge that, due to Ice Age conditions, temporarily connected the two continents, Asia and North America. They'll say that these people came in waves as hunter-gatherers living side by side with wooly mammoths, saber-toothed tigers and other large game animals. Carbon-dating places these nomadic human ancestors of ours in the farthest reaches of South America by 13,000 years ago. The whole world was now populated.

Our "human story" continues. Many scientists will agree that the Ice Age climate ended around this time, 11,500-10,500 B.C., and that the Earth had warmed abruptly by 20 degrees or more. Some say there was a temperature increase of more than 50 degrees in the North Polar Region within a 50 year period. In the last years of the Ice Age, warming caused the sea level to rise 150 feet. Huge floods occurred in wide swaths of land and altered the landscape. The Great Lakes, The Grand Canyon, the Mississippi River Valley, the world is full of wonderful geological relics and reminders of what remain as the climate of the Earth shifts. Large-scale weather changes occur during both the beginning and, now, the end of an Age of Polar Ice. As the glaciers retreated and temperatures rose, the climate became more humid and the rains began to fall….and fall….and fall. A global Ice Age civilization, according to many "creation stories" from cultures around the world, was destroyed by water, by a "Great Flood." In

Quechua, the native language of the Incas of Ecuador, the word Quito (also the name of the capital city) signifies a rebirth of life after a flood.

The Bible has this to say about life <u>before</u> the Flood.

> **Cain was then building a city, and he named it after his son Enoch.**
>
> -Genesis 4:17

> **Tubal-Cain forged all kinds of tools out of bronze and iron.**
>
> -Genesis 4:22

What's that? Iron tools? Apparently, before the melting of the glaciers and the end of the Ice Age and before the Great Flood, there was the knowledge of metallurgy. *What kind of tools would they need? Hammers, screwdrivers, wrenches, nails?* Much construction was going on. Cities were being built. Life was being lived.

> **For in the days before the flood, people were eating and drinking, marrying and giving in marriage, up to the day that Noah entered the ark.**
>
> -Matthew 24:38

Whatever the exact date of the Biblical flood, the Bible has this to say of the surviving family.

> **Noah became the father of Ham, Shem and Japheth.**
>
> -Genesis 5:32

Noah and his family were the only ones to survive the deluge, riding out the storm on the Ark. And the Lord promised...

> **Never again will I destroy all living creatures as I have done.**
>
> -Genesis 8:21

God told Noah to…

> **Be fruitful and increase in number and fill the earth.**
> **-Genesis 9:18**

The sons of Noah who came out of the ark were Shem, Ham and Japheth. These were the three sons of Noah, and from them came the people who were scattered over the earth.

In ancient Sanskrit, *nau* is boat. Interestingly enough, in the Nahuatl language of the Meso-Americans, ancestors of the Aztecs, *Nahua* is what they called themselves, meaning "the people." Could this, in fact, mean "the people of Noah" or "the people of *nau*", the people of the boat? (*nau*tical = of, or relating to a boat, astro*naut* = one who pilots a starship!)

If the world was destroyed by a universal flood, if Noah's three sons and their wives began to repopulate the entire world, shouldn't there be evidence of these events recorded in the languages which have come down to us? The Bible clearly says that...

> **Now the whole world had one language and a common speech.**
> **-Genesis 11:1**

Just as ancient artifacts, bones, pottery and fossils have been preserved for millennia, it is not surprising to find equally ancient and impressive linguistic "artifacts" if we look closely at languages.

> **From Noah's grandson descended maritime peoples.**
> **-Genesis 10:5**

Did Noah teach his grandkids how to sail?

I took walks to Kathryn's house over on Hemphill Road. She was cute, someone interesting to talk to. She would tell me her theories, share her ideas. She told me that "Hemp can save the world," that "until the propaganda and prohibition of the Civil War, it was grown all over the south. Just outside of Houston, Texas, the fourth largest metropolis in the United States, there's a town called Hempstead, so named because it was at the heart of the Cannabis cultivation. From *cannabis* we get the word *canvas*, the material used to make the first sails." She went on and on, "fuel, food, paper, clothing."

> **Then God said, "I give you every seed-bearing plant on the face of the whole earth and every tree that has fruit with seed in it. They will be yours for food.**
> **-Genesis 1:29**

I turned in my thesis. Do we humans of the Earth share the same origin in that we are descended from the sole surviving family of the last Ice Age and the great floods that followed? Are we all descendants of this Noah or *Nahua*?

With my final paper completed and handed over to Dr. Frischmann, I definitely needed a break, so I thought, *maybe just to clear my mind a little*. After all, I lacked only two more classes in order to graduate, one of the classes being Mysticism. Go figure. I decided to make the most of the short time remaining until the summer session began.

CHAPTER 4

We hit the road and soon left Texas. Exactly where we were headed, we weren't really sure. With only four or five days to travel, we figured to make a straight path toward Utah, or as straight a path as Interstate highways and a 2-door Corolla would allow us. It was early May and made for a nice springtime drive. Having recently quit smoking and drinking, I wanted to clear my mind *and* my lungs. This proved difficult as Paul's incessant chain-smoking filled up the car with thick clouds of stale second-hand smoke. Empty bags of potato chips, Styrofoam cups and coke cans littered the floorboard of his vehicle.

We talked of many things, Paul and I. Our discussions and debates broke up the grueling monotony of the West Texas plains. Paul was adopted, raised by two loving parents in a Christian home. His mom was a deacon in their church back in Mississippi. He knew the Bible well and had much insight into religion and philosophy.

After God knows how many hours with Paul behind the wheel and me navigating, we finally crossed through New Mexico, Colorado and into Utah and began to notice many towns and places with names seemingly related to people or locations mentioned in the Old Testament, many Biblical place names.

"It's because of the Mormons," Paul said.

"I know. My mom is from Carthage, Illinois. That's where their leader Joseph Smith, the author of the Book of Mormon, was shot and killed just before Brigham Young led them here to Utah, to the Salt Lake Valley."

"Doesn't your ex-girlfriend live there?" Paul asked me, "in Salt Lake City? Do you miss her?"

"Sure. But she's not my true love, not my twin soul."

I told Paul about the man outside the store in Mexico, about how he ordered me to go home, to be in love. I told him about the brightest moon I had ever seen leading me in a certain direction. The moon was shining like a beacon that night as well. We kept driving.

"I've enjoyed spending time with Kathryn." She and Paul were good friends. "I've enjoyed our discussions and long talks. She understands things." I said.

"She told you *all* about hemp, right? She *is* kind of a hippie."

"Yes. And she helped me with my thesis. Have you read it, Paul?" He didn't answer.

"So you want to marry her?" Paul asked inquisitively, trying to pry a little more deeply into my personal life.

"To tell you the truth, I don't know. I do know that someday I want to get married, to have a wife. Only one, though. One is enough for me!" We passed a sign that said Moab 42 miles. We were on our way to the Canyonlands.

"The purpose of the Book of Mormon is to convince the world that Jesus is the Christ, Our Lord and Redeemer." Paul had a way of being very blunt, and I wasn't sure if he was being factual or opinionated.

"So Joseph Smith wrote the Book of Mormon in 1830, right?" An ex-girlfriend had taken me to see *Legacy*, a historical Mormon narrative produced by the LDS church and shown there in the movie theater at the Tabernacle.

"Yes, it was written in 1830," Paul replied.

"And the intent was to prove that Jesus really existed?" I mumbled to myself, assuming Paul was listening as well.

"Funny," I said. "That's what I'm trying to do, too. Have you read my thesis?" I was hoping to get an answer this time.

"Yes. It's good. But, what happens after the flood? After Noah?"

"You grew up in the church, Paul. You tell me!"

"Okay. Where do I start?" I could tell he was serious.

After spotting a place called Heber City on the Utah state map, I continued to navigate using the Atlas, but Paul was in control of both the car and the conversation.

"Heber City?" I said along with a puzzled expression.

"I guess we better start with the Hebrews," Paul quickly decided before proceeding to explain…

"A few thousand years before Christ, a people of Neolithic culture settled in the Nile River valley in a sedentary lifestyle. Skeletal remains suggest a blending of Negroid and Mediterranean populations during this period that has remained constant until the present time. Notice the word *Hebrew*. You'll see the root of the words *hybrid* and *brew*, both of which mean a mix, a blending together."

"Fair enough," I said. "So you're saying the Hebrews came to signify a hybrid or a mixed breed."

"I'm saying that in ancient Egypt they are clearly depicted as Caucasian-Semitic types. Yet, as late as the Roman period there are references to Hebrews being compared to Ethiopians and Egyptians. It is most likely to conclude that the ancient Hebrews derived from diverse groups."

"Okay. I'm following you. What next?"

"Next you get out your Bible. You did bring it with you, didn't you?"

I unbuckled my safety belt, reached around the seat to my duffle bag in back and grabbed my New International Version. "Any old Bible will do," he said.

"The land the Hebrews dwelt in was named for a people called the Canaanites. Canaan was a son of Ham," Paul began. I glanced down at the map, reminding myself the sun would soon be rising and we had no place to stay. We passed another sign that said Moab 22 miles and had an arrow pointing south. "Ham's remaining sons were all linked to nation groups in Africa: Cush in Nubia, Mizraim in Egypt and Punt in Somalia." Paul told me to read the following passage:

> **The sons of Ham: Cush, Mizraim, Put and Canaan. The sons of Cush: Seba, Havilah, Sabtah, Raamah, Sheba and Dedan. Cush was the father of Nimrod. Nimrod was the first king of Babylon. The first centers of his of kingdom were Babylon, Erech, Akkad and Calneh, in Shinar. From that land he went to Assyria."**
> **-Genesis 10:6-10**

"We are told in the Book of Genesis that a river watering the garden flowed from Eden, a second river winds through Cush." He continued, "Cush is modern day Ethiopia and Sudan."

I felt the need to stop him here. "This is great and all, but I need some more background. What was going on in the world around this time?"

"About 3100 B.C., Egypt was unified under Menes. Commerce and writing developed there. Pyramids were being built on the Giza plateau. 2681-2181 B.C. is known as the Old Kingdom and is appreciated as a famous epoch of pyramid building. Egyptian caravans carried grain to Ethiopia and returned with ivory, incense, hides, gold and slaves. King Sneferu sent a fleet of 40 ships to the city of Byblos to obtain cedar and other woods."

"Ships?" I questioned. "They were sailing ships at this time?"

"Yes, of course. You do remember Noah and the Ark, don't you? What makes you think they forgot how to build boats?"

"I mean, I guess they didn't forget," I quickly said, trying to appease Paul.

He continued the history lesson. "Around 2340 B.C. Sargon the Great of Akkad conquered Sumeria in modern-day Iraq and built an empire. In the city of Ur, there rose up a revolt and the empire fell."

"Abraham, the Patriarch of the Judeo-Christian-Islamic religions, was from Ur, wasn't he?" I interjected, quite proud for having remembered.

"Whoa, slow down! Don't get ahead of yourself," Paul cautioned. "But, yes, you are correct. During Ur's supremacy, around 2100 B.C., Sumerian culture reached its highest development. Sumerian tablets reveal that kings took voyages to the 'land beyond the Western Sea.' King Shulgi of Sumeria wrote, 'Where people do not have the use of paved roads, where they have no access to the written word they shall witness that I am a fashioner of words, a composer of songs, a composer of words, and they will recite my songs and heavenly writings.'"

"Okay, Paul. Can we get back to the Hebrews? I recognize it's almost time for Abraham to leave his country."

"Yes, of course. First let's look at Shem, Noah's son and Ham's brother."

Shem was the ancestor of all the sons of Eber.
                                           -Genesis 10:21

"From Shem we get *Semitic*, the Semitic people, the Semitic languages. In Hebrew *Shem* means 'name.' From Eber we get *Heber*, the root of the Hebrew people. Eber was the great-grandson of Shem."

"Now we're talking!" I said excitedly. "So the Hebrew people are the descendents of Eber. And the Semitic people are the descendents of Shem!"

> **Now the Lord said unto Abraham, "Get thee out of thy country, unto a land I will show thee: And I will make thee a great nation: and in thee shall all families of the earth be blessed."**
> **-Genesis 12:1-3**

"Abraham received the covenants which appear in Chapter 12 of the Book of Genesis. 'I have made you a father of many nations, I will make nations of you and kings shall come from you.'"

> **I will greatly increase your numbers**
> **And he blessed Abraham again**
> **And again.**
> **-Genesis 17:1, Genesis 24:60, Genesis 18:18**

"Pharaoh Sesostris III, of Kushite decent, dominates Europe and Asia and has extensive military, trading and fort networks in Kush and Upper Egypt. His African military garrison stationed on the Black Sea coast at Colchis, in modern-day Georgia, becomes the main center of trade and government in the Caucasus region. The garrison does not return home. Colchis would be regarded as an African colony. Pharaoh Sesostris builds a canal that connects the Mediterranean to the Red Sea. This is the original Suez Canal. Stonehenge in England begins its construction. In Iraq, between the Tigris and the Euphrates, Hammurabi was administering rules through his code of ethics. He builds roads, creates a postal system and sees himself as conqueror of the world."

"The Lord also blessed Abraham's son, Isaac. He tells him…

> **In your seed all the nations of the earth shall be blessed.**
> **I will make your descendants as numerous as the stars**

> in the sky and through your offspring all the nations of the earth will be blessed.
> -Genesis 26:5

"Isaac's son Jacob, Abraham's grandson, receives the birthright and the blessing. And the Lord makes him a few promises, too...

> *Descendants will come out of Egypt with great possessions
>
> *Unto your seed I give this land from the Nile River to the Euphrates
>
> *Your descendants will be as numerous as stars in the sky
> -Genesis15:13, Genesis 15:18, Genesis 22:17

"Excuse me Paul, how about a time-frame here?"

"Oh, yes, of course...Jacob had a dream around 1750 B.C. at a place called Beth-El. His head rested upon a stone pillow. In his dream he wrestled with God, who, in turn, changed his name to Israel."

"So, first we had Noah, then the Semites, the Hebrews, and now we have...

"Israel," Paul said, cutting my revelation a bit short. "The Israelites are descended from Jacob whose name was changed to Israel."

> Thy name shall not be called Jacob, but Israel. Be fruitful and multiply; a nation and a company of nations shall be of thee, and kings shall come out of thy loins.
> -Genesis 32:28

A company of nations? Kings? "So you're saying not just the nation of Israel, but the descendents of Jacob, the Israelites, would build other nations as well?"

"True," Paul confirmed. "The Lord had said to Jacob...

Your seed will be like the dust of the earth, and you will spread abroad to the west, and to the east, and to the north, and to the south. Through your offspring all families and peoples on earth will be blessed.
-Genesis 28:14

"All the families of the earth are blessed? Is this true Paul?"

"Yes, it is if you're a Christian."

"O.k., I think I'm starting to understand the meaning of all this."

"If not, I'll be glad to tell you more. Do you know about the Beth-el stone?" Paul questioned, "Also known as Jacob's Pillar or the Stone of Destiny?"

"No. Can you fill me in?" Now I was curious.

"It's the stone that Jacob placed under his head during the night while he dreamt."

"Why is *that* important?" I wondered.

"You want to know why?" Paul said, surprised I didn't already know. "I'll tell you why it's important. In 1296 A.D., King Edward I of England placed the stone in Westminster Abbey. The Abbey, in London, is a famous sanctuary and burial site. It is here where the bodies of many of Britain's kings and queens have been laid to rest. Jacob's Stone upon which he rested his very head while God gave him the name Israel has long been used for the coronation of royalty. For nearly eight centuries Jacob's pillar was cradled in the lower portion of the St. Edwards Chair, the British coronation chair specifically built to house the stone. After having been invested the emblems and insignia of royal dignity, the King, while seated over Jacob's Stone, receives the crown. The Imperial crown is placed only after the King submits to the King of Kings. From the time of King Edward onward, all the Monarchs of England have been crowned on the Stone of Destiny and on the Coronation Chair, the only exception being Mary I, whom we know as 'Bloody Mary.'" *Hey, at least she has a drink named after her!*

Paul continued, "King Edward is said to have declared this stone, Jacob's Stone of Destiny, to be 'the one primeval monument which binds together the whole empire.' Kings and Queens are still consecrated with the same recipe of sacred oils and, upon entering the coronation church, one will notice the large stained glass window identifying the twelve sons of Jacob."

"Does this have something to do with why the British flag is called the Union Jack?" I wondered. "Does it refer to the Union of Jacob, to the 12 tribes of Israel?"

But, how? Why? "When was the Bethel stone taken to England?" I had so many questions.

Paul didn't answer them. "Let's get back on subject," he said. "About Jacob and his descendants, the Hebrew Israelites...

Jacob had twelve sons:
-Genesis 35:22

"All twelve sons of Jacob Israel are Hebrews, descendents of Judah are Jews. Jacob's two sons, Judah and Joseph, are selected for special inheritance."

The scepter will not depart from Judah nor the ruler's staff from between his feet until Shiloh.
-Genesis 49:10

"I notice that Zebulon was a haven for ships," I casually blurted out after reading a little bit ahead.

Paul ignored me and continued, "Judah held the 'scepter' or rod of office significant of leadership. Judah was being singled out as a ruler, though the throne was not to be established in Israel until many years later."

I chimed in once more with what I considered very knowledgeable and pertinent information, "The tribe of Judah provided the kingly House of David, to rule over the people of Israel forever."

"And to provide kings of other nations, too!" Paul commented. "During a great famine, Jacob and his family moved to Egypt to escape starvation. They bought food and shelter by selling their services. It was there where they met their brother, Joseph, who had been appointed Prime Minister by Pharaoh. As you probably know, Joseph had been previously sold into slavery by his brothers and, now, they didn't even recognize him. Two great pyramids and the

Egyptian labyrinth were constructed at this time, all probably built with hard labor or rented labor that quickly turned into slave labor for the Israelites. That's why some of them left Egypt."

The Israelites left Egypt? "Before Moses was born?"

"Yes, of course. Before the labor got too harsh, before slavery, they left. Let's follow the Jews."

"Wait! I thought we were learning about the Israelites?"

"We are. Now we're focusing on the Jews, the descendents of Judah, son of Jacob whose name became Israel."

"The descendents of Judah, yes, yes," I conceded. "Okay, go ahead."

And he did.

"God had disinherited Judah's first two sons because of wickedness for which they were punished by death. Judah's third son, like his brothers, was the child of a Canaanite woman."

> **Judah got a wife for his son, her name was Tamar.**
> **-Genesis 38:6**

> **After Judah's daughter-in-law Tamar was unable to produce royal offspring because her husbands were wicked, she dressed as a prostitute in order to trick Judah into impregnating her with his royal seed.**
> **-Genesis 38:13**

> **And it came to pass, that, behold, twins were in her womb. And during birth one put out his hand: and the midwife tied upon his wrist a scarlet thread, saying this came out first. And, as he drew back his hand, behold, his brother came out: and she said, how hast thou broken forth? This breach be upon thee: Therefore his name was called Pharez. And afterward his brother came out, that had the scarlet thread upon his hand: and his name was called Zarah.**
> **-Genesis 38:27**

> **Judah the father of Perez and Zerah, whose mother was Tamar.**

-Matthew 1:3

Tamar bore Perez and Zerah for Judah.
-I Chronicles 2:4

"The Bible places great importance on the birth of these twins. The genealogical line of the Kings of Israel descended from Pharez. From Exodus onward, the Biblical story of Judah is concerned particularly with the family of Pharez. It is from this family that King David descended and, eventually, Jesus Christ. We know what happened to the Pharez branch of the tribe of Judah that settled in Jerusalem."

> **Ira was of the tribe of Judah since Jair was the son of Segub, son of Hezron, son of Pharez, one of the twins born of the union of Judah with Tamar, his daughter-in-law. It was from Pharez that King David also descended.**
> -Samuel 20:26

> **King David, the greatest King of Israel was descended from Pharez in this manner: Pharez was the ancestor of Boaz, who married Ruth and gave birth to Obed, the father of Jesse, who was the father of King David.**
> -Ruth 1:1

> **May your house be like the house of Perez whom Tamar bore to Judah.**
> -Ruth 4:2

I was curious, "Did the Israelites go down into Egypt before or after the twins were born?"

> **Store grain was kept by pharaoh for food. -Genesis 41:35**

> **Storehouse opened. -Genesis 41:56**

> **Israelites to buy grain. -Genesis 42:5**

Names of sons of Israel who went to Egypt. -Genesis 46:8

And the sons of Judah (included in the group of 70); Er and Onan, and Shelah, and Pharez and Zarah (Jacob's grandsons).
-Genesis 46:12

I tried to get it straight, "So the twins were born, there was a famine, the 12 sons of Israel went down into Egypt to where pharaoh had stockpiled grain and…"

"Not 12 sons. Joseph was sold into slavery, remember? He was now Prime Minister of Egypt. It was his idea to stockpile the grain. And it's here where we witness an interesting turn of events. After years in Egypt, the descendants of Zarah decide to leave in a massive migration."

"*Before* the Hebrews were enslaved?"

"Around that time, yes," answered Paul. "Greek Historians talk of two exoduses out of Egypt, one by sea and one under Moses. Various groups managed to leave Egypt and cross the Mediterranean Sea. These descendants of Zerah started kingdoms of their own. They were led by Zerah's two sons, Calcol and Darda."

The sons of Zerah: Calcol and Darda.
-I Chronicles 2:6

"They were very wise. They are referred to in the book of Kings…

Solomon wiser than Calcol and Darda.
-I Kings 4:30

"The origin of the words *calculate* and *calculus* comes from Calcol, descendant of Judah. The city of Troy, in modern-day Turkey, was located on a body of water named after Darda, called the Dardanelles. Some regard Calcol as the first King of Athens. Another descendant of Zerah, Gathelus, the son of Calcol, led a group of Hebrew Israelites across Europe."

THE TRUE LOVE MESSIAH:

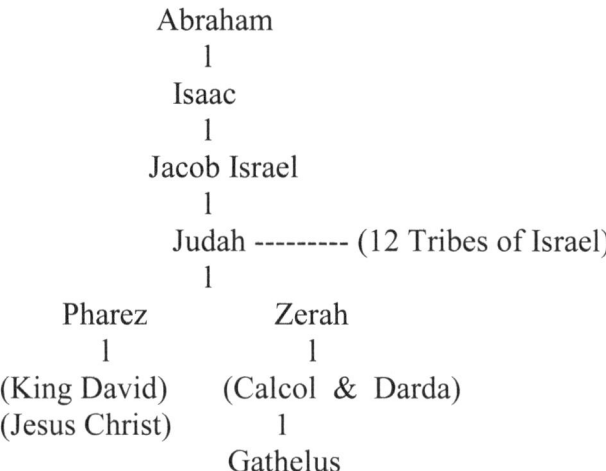

I found this difficult to believe. "Are you telling me the truth?"

"Yes. In Spain you can visit the city of Zaragoza, named after these first colonists. It means, 'the stronghold of Zerah.' As descendants of Zerah, their heraldic emblem was symbolized as a red hand bound by a scarlet cord. This is in reference to the Biblical story of the birth of the twin sons of Judah. To this day, in Ireland, there is a people and a region represented by a flag bearing this same image. It's called the Red Hand of Ulster."

"That's interesting, Paul. But, what's more interesting is that we're about to run out of gas. Where *are* we anyway?"

"I don't know. You've got the map don't you?"

"Yeah, but…" I really hadn't been paying the slightest bit of attention to the road or where we were going.

"Let's stop here for some gas. I'll ask for directions." Paul stopped the car, got out and headed inside the station to pay. I continued to pump the gas as I noticed Paul having a conversation with a bearded older gentleman who was dressed in what looked like something Abraham Lincoln would have worn. *Must be one of the locals*, I thought.

Soon the tank was full and Paul was back in the driver's seat. "Who was that man you were speaking with?"

"Oh…that was Jacob. He's Mormon."

"I figured that," I said, waiting for him to continue.

"I had a question for him...I couldn't remember the name of the city the Israelites built in America."

"Israelites? A city in America? What are you talking about?"

Paul informed me, "According to the Book of Mormon, a group of Israelites came to the New World and built a city. I couldn't remember the name of the city."

"And?"

"*Zarahemla.* They named it Zarahemla."

A few seconds ticked off the clock and then it hit me. "Wait! We were just taking about..."

"I know. I can't believe I've never put two and two together."

"Paul, you know I speak Spanish and that I study Linguistics. Do you know what *gemela* means?"

"I do. That's why I can't believe it."

"It's pronounced with an *h,* he-me-la, and it means twin," I said. "Zarahemla is named after Zerah, the twin son of Judah. It's the city of Zerah *gemela*!"

"You know...you just might be right!" Paul seemed more shocked than I did.

"Alright," I said. "Let's keep going. I don't want to be lost." *Not here, not now.* "Please tell me you got directions, Paul?"

"No, but I think we're headed the right way."

"If you say so." But, I had my doubts.

Paul continued to teach me things I never knew about the Israelites. "The bondage in Egypt was gradually getting more strenuous for the Hebrews. Different groups managed to escape and flee to other areas. The Tribe of Dan founded cities in Greece, Spain, Britain and Ireland. Their migration was so important that the Greeks called themselves Danoi for centuries."

"So there was a lot of colonizing going on by the Hebrews," I concluded.

"Yes. In fact, we find signs of their colonization all over Europe. You've heard of Iberia?"

"Of course. Doesn't the Iberian peninsula refer to Spain?"

"Sure does, Spain and Portugal. It was the Hebrews who settled there. Remember Eber, father of the Hebrews? Well, these early settlers were called Hibernians, 'nians' being a Latin suffix meaning 'people of, or descendants of.'"

"They were descendants of Eber?" I was astonished. "The Hebrews settled Iberia! They settled Western Europe!"

"That's right! You're getting pretty good at this. The name was carried by the Hebrews from Spain to Ireland. They called their island home Hibernai. Ireland was called Hibernia by the Romans, the 'Land of the Hebrews.'"

Amazing! "So Spain and Portugal make up Iberia, which is named after Abraham's ancestor Eber, the father of the Hebrews and Zaragoza was named after the descendants of Zarah." I also knew that the town of Zaragoza was built on the banks of the Ebro River. Considering the Hebrew migration through Spain, the name Ebro would appear to be of the same origin…"And the Hebrides islands off the coast of Scotland?"

"Yes. Linguistically, Eber is an ethnicon, a family, tribal or racial designation. Genesis 14:13 speaks of Abraham the Ibri (the Hebrew), Joseph is known as an Ibri in Genesis 39:17 and Moses saw an Egyptian smiting an Ibri in Exodus 2:11."

"Okay, so let's get back to the story now."

"What story?"

"You know…the Bible."

"Oh, well, it's not a story. But, I'll be glad to share a little history with you." Paul knew I wanted to continue. And he did.

"The Hebrews had been slaves for quite a few generations in Egypt.

> **(Now Joseph and all his brothers and all that generation died, but the Israelites were fruitful and multiplied greatly and became exceedingly numerous, so that the land was filled with them.)**
> **-Exodus 1:7**

Pharaoh and the rulers of Egypt became worried.

> **Look, the Israelites have become much too numerous for us.**
> **-Exodus 1:9**

> **So they put slave masters over them to oppress them with forced labor, and they built Pithom and Ramses as store cities.**
>
> **-Exodus 1:11**

It was Moses' job to lead the Hebrews out of that "iron-smelting furnace." He was a Hebrew himself and quite a scholar…

> **Moses was educated in all the wisdom of the Egyptians.**
>
> **-Acts 7:22**

He couldn't stand by and watch his people being mistreated and, one day, he up and killed an Egyptian who was whipping a Hebrew. He was forced to leave Egypt in a hurry. At the time, Egypt was in a battle with Cush, modern-day Ethiopia and Sudan. It was there, while in exile, where Moses found his wife.

> **Miriam and Aaron began to talk against Moses because of his Cushite wife, for he had married a Cushite.**
>
> **-Numbers 12:1**

Why they didn't approve of her at first, who knows? But, God was not pleased.

> **The anger of the Lord burned against them, and he left them.**
>
> **-Numbers 12:9**

The Lord actually gave Miriam leprosy and healed her after one week.

As most of us know, Moses would soon be called upon to rescue his people from captivity and lead them to freedom.

> **I am sending you to Pharoah to bring my people the Israelites out of Egypt.**
>
> **-Exodus 3:10**

> **The Israelites set out from Ramses in view of all the Egyptians.**
> **-Numbers 33:1**

> **Israel counted 600,000 men on foot.**
> **-Exodus 12:37**

Moses raised his staff and parted the waters. The Egyptian Army was drowned in the Red Sea. Thousands of Cushite Ethiopians joined the Hebrews as they left Egypt; among them were Moses' wife and his father-in-law, Jethro. And look…they carried the bones of Joseph with them!

> **Moses took the bones of Joseph with him because Joseph had made the sons of Israel swear an oath. He had said, "God will surely come to your aid, and then you must carry my bones up with you from this place."**
> **-Exodus 13:19**

In the desert, this same staff of Moses was used to strike a rock so that water would flow from it. The Lord says for Moses to tell the people of Israel…

> **You will be for me a kingdom of priests and a holy nation.**
> **-Exodus 19:5**

> **The Lord said to Moses, "I am going to come to you in dense cloud."**
> **-Exodus 19:9**

In Exodus chapter 20, Moses receives the Ten Commandments.

> **The Lord Your God has increased your numbers so that today you are as many as the stars in the sky.**
> **-Deuteronomy 1:10**

> **So at the Lord's command Moses sent out leaders of the Israelites to explore the land of Canaan.**
> **-Numbers 13:1**

An Adventure of Biblical Proportions

From the tribe of Judah, he sent Caleb
                                                    -Numbers 13:6

When Moses took the second census the descendants of Judah by their clans were: through Selah, through Perez, through Zerah."

"Time for a break," I admitted to Paul, "We've been driving for hours and I'm ready to get out and walk, maybe explore a little bit."
"Just like the Israelites, huh?"
"Like Caleb from the tribe of Judah!"

We were in the middle of nowhere. Somehow while I had been listening intently, Paul had managed to drive down a severely bumpy and extremely dusty, unpaved dirt road not even remotely located anywhere on the map as far as I could tell.
"Do you know where we are?" I asked, knowing he was just as disoriented and lost as I was.
"Zion?" he replied.
"Funny. But, I would think we're closer to Moab, somewhere just outside Canyonlands National Park."
It seemed like some sort of pre-historic landscape, as if we had somehow gone back in time. We took a look around, checked out a few small caves, hiked up some hills and slung a few rocks. Then...there it was! I pointed in the general direction as I couldn't believe what I seeing. *My Lord!* "Is it on fire?" It was somehow burning, but not being consumed, not really *on* fire.
"That's interesting." Paul didn't seem as impressed. I mean, we *were* just talking about the Hebrews. He *was* just talking about Moses.
"It's a burning bush!" I exclaimed, trying to warrant a response.
We approached cautiously and carefully touched the lightly charred ground around it. A few ashes lay at its base. A warm temperature emanated from its core. Maybe Paul wasn't surprised, maybe he was more inclined to be a little scared.
"Do not fear," something inside of me whispered.
We got back in the car and proceeded back down the dusty dirt road, through the town of Moab and out of Utah. We were headed back to school. I had to go to class.

CHAPTER 5

Mysticism and Astronomy were the final two classes I needed to graduate from this private little Christian university of mine. A better script could not have been written. *Or could it?* Though our short trip to Utah had lasted only five whole days I was feeling rejuvenated both physically and spiritually. I had quit drinking, quit smoking and had cleansed my temple. I was feeling quite good.

The first few days of class were fine as I enjoyed the extra reading. A steady stream of homework assignments included the study of Buddhist texts, Hindu philosophical writings and early Christian manuscripts. I was ecstatic. This was right up my alley. I couldn't have been more interested in the course material. Finally, a class I truly enjoyed!

After just a few days of Mysticism class, it happened. The night before, after a time of intense research, I thought I found the answer I so desperately sought, the key to the universe, some secret code or feeling. I'm not sure you can experience God in a piece of paper, but I thought to have done it. The following afternoon, while stretched out on the couch with some of my assigned reading, I wondered. I became doubtful. I began to question. *Why am I here? Why was I born? I need a sign*, I thought. *If God is really listening, why can't He give me a sign?* I shocked myself, never having before posed the question, never having asked for a sign. Did I doubt God? Was I testing the Lord? Something told me it more than likely would not be a lightning bolt sent through the roof. How, then, would I receive this Divine Communication?

Suddenly, the most incredible urge or power came over me. *I must look at the television!* There was no volume. It was normal in the house I shared with my two college roommates that the television would be blaring at extremely high decibels, as loud as technologically possible. However, now it was mute. Only flashing images of light from the screen were visible as I lay prone, facing the opposite direction, innocently reading my class materials. I turned to look, surprised at what I saw. It appeared to be a Bible verse.

Job 3:14

I was startled, slightly scared and happy at the same time. It was a sign. *Ask and you shall receive!* I thought. It was hard to believe, but there it was right there on the screen. *A sign!* I ran to my bedroom, grabbed my Bible and, hurriedly, turned to the book of Job as it was necessary to re-familiarize myself with the story. *And, oh yes, what a miraculous and truly perfect answer it was!* I felt a deep sense of purpose, a peace within, wanting to tell all of my friends as soon as humanly possible. *Let it be known…*the Lord has sent me a sign!

After slipping a thin-layered jacket on over my t-shirt, I exited the front door and started down the sidewalk. Not 100 yards into my trek, I noticed a group of young students crossing the street, all blessed with smooth dark skin and possessing an unusually white glow to their eyes, all of them wearing similar clothing, grey pants and white shirts, the sort of dress that you generally see worn by a Jehovah's Witness. They strolled across the street and approached, laughing and giggling.

"He's a witness! He's a witness!" they said in unison while pointing in my direction. Their smiles were comforting. Although a bit surprised, I felt very much at peace. I smiled back as my feet went numb. Surely I was floating on a heavenly wisp of a cirrus cloud, a gentle gust of wind. *Were they apparitions? Were they angels?* I continued walking, a little uneasy at this point and somewhat confused as well. *Was I alive?*

After stumbling down the sidewalk for a few more minutes, I made it to an outdoor café area where picnic tables were set up and students were enjoying lunch. Scanning the crowd, I couldn't help but notice a cute, blonde girl from Mysticism class sitting alone at one of the tables. *I'll sit next to her.* As a cackle of crows produced a cacophony of sound from the trees above, I sat down beside her and we began to talk. Not reluctant to open up to interesting conversation, she was receptive to what I had to say. Therefore, I recounted to her my day.

"It's all very strange," I pondered as she listened quietly to my thoughts and concerns. "I'm not sure if I haven't died. Maybe something has happened to me? I can't figure out for certain if I'm in heaven or hell or, perhaps, some type of purgatory. I *could* be dead." She sheepishly smiled back at me, clearly not having made up her mind quite how to answer.

As my gaze turned toward the doors of Sadler Hall, many students and teachers were now exiting the building as classes had now ended. Out walked one of my instructors. She fixated her eyes upon me and calmly asked, "How's life?"

Sure enough I had my answer! "How's life?" she said. What a reassurance, a feeling of relief! I was alive, not dead! I was not yet in heaven, however grand that time might be! I was comforted to be here on earth, alive, my heart beating regularly. It may have been palpitating somewhat rapidly and skipping a beat here and there, but it was sure as hell beating, thank God.

"Life is good!" I responded.

Sometimes I wish it had all ended there. I wouldn't be sitting here today feeling the burden of writing this book. But, what happened next is truly amazing and I must let you know, I haven't been the same since. Some say it's what we're called to be…a new creation; that we're to be born again. I don't know about that, as I simply felt bewildered, confused and a little uneasy.

I agreed to meet some friends for the weekend, maybe take my mind off things for a while. The state capital of Austin is only about a three hours drive from Fort Worth, but I honestly don't remember how I got there, neither do I have much recollection as to what happened there. A few friends hung out, laughed, talked, had fun and did what college kids do. I, admittedly, wasn't much fun that weekend, didn't really talk much. To tell the truth, I hardly uttered a word. I did my best to try to relax and enjoy myself, but found it very difficult to calm the nerves.

Soon, however, the party was over and it was time to head back to school. From this point forward, I remember everything as clear as a bell, as if it were just yesterday. In fact, I'll never forget what happened that afternoon during our drive up Interstate 35 North. I hitched a ride from Sarah, a Religion major at Pomona College in California where she attended along with a good friend of mine, Ben, whom she dated. They had both been visiting for the weekend and, now, Sarah was headed up to visit her family in Oklahoma. She would take me along for part of the way. Somewhere along that stretch of road, as we passed discount outlet malls and dozens of little Baptist churches, I began to ask her questions. She was, after all, a religion major and, well, I needed answers, at least *some* kind of explanation. At one point I inquired about her belief in angels.

"What about angels, Sarah?" I asked. "What do you think about angels?"

I have no idea as to what her response might have been. At that exact moment I turned my head and looked out the passenger side window at the scenery that was quickly passing by. I glanced to the right, stunned at what I beheld. A car was driving beside us in the other lane and the driver, well, the driver was wearing sunglasses and flashing the hugest, bright white Colgate smile you could ever imagine and…on top of the driver's head…on top of the drivers head...were google balls. I mean those fake, toy antennae things, those silly looking springy things that are attached to a headband and, well, what else can I say except that is what it was. I know it's strange. It was an odd sight. But, I'll never erase that image from my mind because what I saw next was even more incredible. On the back of that car was a bumper sticker. It was no ordinary bumper sticker. It read…

I BELIEVE IN ANGELS

I turned to Sarah, "Did you see that?"
"See what?"
"Did you see that bumper sticker?" I tried to articulate. "It said…I believe in angels. You didn't see that?"
"No."

After quizzing her about theology and after all my inquiries into her thoughts on religion, now she really must have thought I was crazy. I didn't bother to tell her about the driver, the smile, the glasses…and the google balls. She dropped me off at the house I shared with my two college roommates. I had to attend Mysticism class the following morning.

CHAPTER 6

Trey is a good friend of mine. We've known each other for years and had planned to take this trip after graduation. It was a little whimsical, somewhat spur of the moment, I admit. We were to set out on this adventure and learn as much as possible about an interesting part of the world. Both Latin American Studies majors, as well as old friends, we had a mutual interest in *la cultura, la historia y el lenguaje*. Trey knows almost everything about me and I certainly didn't neglect to inform him of all the recent strange occurrences. We were on a similar path and would share part of our spiritual journey together. Trey's good friend Buck was to accompany me on the first leg of the trip as we crossed the border down into Mexico.

It was mid-July as we loaded up onto the Estrella de Oro bus and started south from Nuevo Laredo. The sun was intensely hot, the clouds were sparce and low and eagles filled the skies. Trey was waiting for us down in San Luis Potosí where he had studied two years prior and was now visiting his host family and friends. Buck and I had time to chat as we rode the Gold Starliner through the North Mexican desert states of Tamaulipas and Nuevo León. Out of the blue, Buck asked me about my thesis. I willingly and excitedly told him of the premise, of Noah and the Ark, and I shared with him some of what I'd learned about the Hebrews.

"The Tribe of Dan, one of the Twelve Tribes of Israel, left Egypt and migrated to Greece, Ireland and other countries in Europe. At this point, a people called Danoi colonized Hellas (modern-day Greece) and organized a Navy. Since Hebrew was written with only consonants and no vowels, Dan would be DN. All over Europe you will find many cities, towns and rivers containing the name Dan."

I grabbed my Bible in order to show him some verses.

> **They settled and named the town Dan after their forefather.**
>
> -Joshua 19:47

"Dan was given territory along the Mediterranean Sea and the busy port city of Joppa, Israel, next to modern day Tel-Aviv. In Judges 5:17, the judge Deborah asks, 'Why did the tribe of Dan remain on their ships while the Israelites were in battle?' It's no coincidence that the Irish Gaelic word *Dun* means 'judge', just as it does in Hebrew. During the Trojan war…

"Stop!" Buck interrupted, seeming just a little annoyed, "Wait…the Trojan War? Slow down man, we haven't even finished discussing the Ark, yet."

"Of course we have," I said. "I told you my thesis. I told you about the flood, about Noah, the Hebrews…Abraham, Jacob, Moses and how the Israelites are colonizing…"

He stopped me again, this time dead in my tracks. "You told me about Noah's Ark. You told me all about Moses leading the Israelites in their Exodus out of Egypt, but you failed to mention anything about the Ark…the Ark of the Covenant." Buck continued, "God told them to construct this Ark as well."

> **Have them make a sanctuary for me and I will dwell among them.**
> **-Exodus 24:8**

"The Lord was to reside in the Ark in the form of a cloud. He gave them instructions on how to build it."

> **Make a chest. Overlay it with pure gold. Insert the poles into the rings on the sides of the chest to carry it. The poles are to remain in the rings of this ark; they are not to be removed. Put in the ark the Testimony, which I will give you. I will meet with you and give you all my commands for the Israelites.**

"God had them make a sanctuary and He commanded them to put the Ark of the Covenant inside, in the Most Holy Place."

We reached San Luis Potosí and after the long, dusty bus ride, I felt it to be a most holy place. Buck and I hopped into an old Volkswagon Beetle driven by experienced *taxista* and wannabe mariachi singer José María de la Rosa and over to the house where Trey was awaiting our arrival. In a splendidly beautiful and very comfortable home, the widowed señora made our stay in San Luis a special one. Her son Alejandro showed off his deceased father's study. The library boasted a full collection of Spanish and Latin titles, tomes of information about the history of Mexico, politics, archaeology and medicine. With a little elbow grease and some fiddling around, we managed to coax into operation an antique movie projector which had lay dormant for at least a decade and watched an old film about the ancient Mayans. We admired the family's pet falcon, Mr. Aguilar, and the sharp talons which he used to strongly grip onto his perch as the moon hanging over San Luis shone bright; encircled, even, by a halo of rainbow-colored light. After a few days rest in this mystical retreat, we boarded another bus and headed further south.

The clock on the wall struck midnight without making a sound. Stuck in this terminal on the north side of Distrito Federal awaiting the early dawn departure of a southbound bus to Oaxaca, my friends were kind enough to remind me that it was, now, officially my birthday and give me a congratulatory pat on the back. It turns out we would do some celebrating later in the day. I stepped onto the Estrella de Blanco, found an empty seat and tried desperately to go to sleep. After a few light snoozes, two punctured tires and a rough eight hours ride, we finally arrived in Oaxaca.

The central plaza was brewing with tables and people. It was the 23rd of July and the Guelaguetza Festival was in full swing, although I'm not sure what we were celebrating. As far as I was concerned, it was my twenty-second birthday party. Just now 12 o'clock noon, on a Sunday no less, and everybody was forming line after line at each table tasting free samples of Mezcal, the euphoric, mind-altering, body-numbing alcoholic beverage of indigenous Mexico made from the cactus plant. There was your regular run-of-the-mill Mezcal, a delicate chocolate flavored Mezcal and a refreshing mint flavored Mezcal. I tried them all. What a fiesta it was! *Feliz cumpleaños, indeed!*

I woke up the next morning pleasantly surprised that I wasn't suffering from a hangover. There was research to do. Buck had started me off hot on the trail of the Ark of the Covenant.

When Moses brought the Ark to the tabernacle, a cloud began to fill the room.

> **The glory of the Lord filled the tabernacle.**
> **-Exodus 40:24**

The Ark of the Covenant resided in the Holy of Holies, the innermost room of the Tabernacle. Access was permitted once a year on Yom Kippur, the Day of Atonement, and was restricted to only one person, a Levitical priest who was required to come into the Holy of Holies with the blood of a goat on behalf of his sins and those of the people of Israel. The ark was God's throne, His dwelling place within the Tabernacle.

"The ark had incredible powers." Buck enthusiastically pulled up a chair, sitting down beside me on the patio of the Grouchy Gringo Hotel & Bar. He showed me a few verses from the Book of Joshua to illustrate the power of the ark.

> **As soon as the priests who carry the ark of the Lord-the Lord of all the Earth-set foot in the Jordan, its waters flowing downstream will be cut off and stand up in a heap.**
> **-Joshua 3:13**
>
> **The priests came out of the river carrying the ark of the covenant of the Lord.**
> **-Joshua 4:18**
>
> **...priest in front of the Ark. The city was destroyed.**
> **-Joshua 6:4**

"Moses died and was succeeded by Miriam, Aaron and Joshua."

> **The sons of Moses the man of God were counted as part of the Israel tribe of Levi.**
> **-1 Chronicles 23:14**

"They were designated as priests and were in charge of carrying the ark."

> **The Israelites took 60 cities.**
> **-Deuteronomy 3:4**

"After the death of Joshua, the Lord says that Judah will be the ones to first fight the Canaanites."

> **The men of Judah attacked Jerusalem also and took it.**
> **-Judges 1:8**

> **The descendants of Moses' father-in-law (the Cushites) went up with the men of Judah to live among the people of the Desert of Judah.**
> **-Judges 1:16**

"The Ark of the Covenant was indeed incredibly powerful. It caused tumors among the Philistines after they captured it." Buck suggested I read a few more verses.

> **Samuel 5:11 "send the ark of the god of Israel away; let it go back to its own place or it will kill us and our people."**

> **Samuel 6:7 Ark returned to Israel**

> **Samuel 6:19 God struck down 70 men because they looked at the Ark.**

Buck finished, "You were going to mention something about the Trojan War?"

"Well I was just going to say that, according to many sources, Brutus went from Greece to London in 1074 B.C. During the reign of King Edward I of England a parliament was held, letters were sent to the Pope sealed with a hundred seals and witnesses, declaring that, 'in the time of Samuel the Prophet, Brutus, a Trojan, landed here, in Britain, and called the country Britannia.' Before, it was named Albion. Some people even think the word 'British' originates from *Brit-ish*, meaning 'covenant man' in Hebrew."

An Adventure of Biblical Proportions

We continued talking as Buck lifted his backpack up and onto the shuttle bus, wedging it between two other suitcases on the metal luggage rack. Arriving at the airport with no time to spare, I showed him the terminal where he was to depart. We quickly said our goodbyes while Buck added, "As for the Ark of the Covenant: know its importance…trace its movements…find its location…solve the mystery."

"A mystery?" I was confused. Was I supposed to solve a mystery?

Buck left me hanging. He left a carrot dangling right in front of my nose as if I were a hungry rabbit willing to shamelessly hop through hoops just for a little taste of knowledge and insight. He was right. I would do anything at this point to gain a little wisdom. I watched him disappear down the walkway as he boarded his flight back to the States, non-stop on Aeromexico from Cancún.

CHAPTER 7

The speedboat couldn't go any faster. Already moving at a decent clip, maybe 50 or 60 knots per hour, displaced water was sent splashing, lapping up against the mangled mangrove trees and roots left in our wake. Whether this was a river, a bayou or the Caribbean Sea, I didn't know for sure. The map showed it as the Río Dulce, but it looked more like a swamp to me. We were fast approaching the large sandbar that separated the brackish river water from the warm and salty Gulf Stream waters of the Caribbean. This tiny forgotten backwater hideaway where our boat would soon dock is Livingston, Guatemala.

Most people don't realize Guatemala even has a Caribbean coastline, and it really doesn't, not besides this alluvial flood plane of a town where enough mud and silt have been clumped together over time to now support a healthy population of 20,000 souls. Most everyone here is Garifuna, an ethnic mix of African, native Arawak and maybe some Moskito Indian blood. They speak a sort of *patois*, a mix of Spanish, English and perhaps French melded together with a long lost African dialect. Whatever the language, it was difficult for the average visitor and for me to understand. We had been informed to ask for Phillip upon our arrival as he had some *palapas* or basic, low-budget cabins for rent. He could at least provide us with a cheap place to stay for awhile. Although at the outset I had no idea why we were here, it didn't take long to find out.

We asked around down at the busy marketplace trying locate Phillip.

"Phillip you say? You all are looking for Phillip? Come. I'll show you where he stays." We followed a sun-baked barefoot man with long dreadlocks through the streets of Livingston.

"He must be at the field playing soccer. I mon will take you there," he said in a thick Caribbean accent.

We introduced ourselves. "So you are David? Like King David of Israel? What a positive vibration. Ya mon! So tell me why you are here? Are you a representative of His Majesty?"

"His Majesty?" I questioned rather confusedly as to whom he was referring.

"Ras Tafari. His Majesty, Emperor Haile Selassie I of Ethiopia, the conquering lion of the tribe of Judah."

The tribe of Judah? Rastafari? "Well I *am* studying about King David and the Ark of the Covenant in Israel."

"No, no, no. You have it all wrong. Everyone knows dat de ark is now in Ethiopia," responded our Rasta friend in his rhythmic lingo that sounded more Jamaican in origin than Guatemalan. He, like most everyone else here, was probably descended from marooned slaves who had escaped during the hellacious days of pirates, plantations and human trafficking. "But, I mon will let brother Phillip tell you more 'bout dat. Natty!"

He whistled towards a crowd of men who had gathered at the local field for a soccer game. An older black man, short in stature with a wiry frame, came trotting off the field towards us.

"Natty...these young men here was looking for you. Guys, dis is Phillip. Natty, meet David and Trey. They be needing a place to stay."

"Well if you guys is staying with me, you best come now and help I and I cook some lunch. You guys know how to cook, right?"

We looked blankly at each other and followed him up the hill.

"They call you Natty, huh? Is that a nickname?"

"Short for Natty Dreadlocks. That's it." Apparently this is a common term of endearment for Rastafarians, referring to the dreadfully matted clumps of hair which they proudly refuse to cut, citing the "Nazarene vow" found in the Old Testament of the Bible.

> **The LORD said to Moses, "Speak to the Israelites and say to them: 'If a man or woman wants to make a special vow, a vow of separation to the LORD as a Nazirite...During the entire period of his vow of separation no razor may be used on his head. He must be holy until the period of his separation to the LORD is over; he must let the hair of his head grow long.**
> **-Numbers 6:1-2, 5**

Natty's tangled locks hung down out the back of an old sailor's cap, covering what I suspect was a balding head. I have no idea as to his age. His physical prowess successfully hid his many years of toilsome labor and experience. There was not an ounce of fat on his dark, thin body. Small, but firm muscles balled up and flexed as he walked, his calves like tennis balls and his biceps like tangerines.

"Are you a Rastamon?" Trey asked, not quite sure what that meant.

"I am an Israelite," he replied.

"Yeah sure, Natty. And the Ark of the Covenant is in Ethiopia! Your Rasta friend already told us." I was being a little sarcastic. I never actually believed that he could be an Israelite. Or that the Ark really was in Ethiopia.

"Good. Now, what then do you want from me?"

"Well…you can start by telling us what you know about the Ark. Explain what you mean by being an Israelite."

"Okay, my friend." He looked at me with a wide, bright, pearly white smile that reminded me of an angel I had once seen. "I'll start with your namesake…King David. You brought your Bible, did you?" And reaching into his knapsack, he extracted a well-worn copy of the King James Version looking, like its owner, a little rough around the edges. "First you guys need to collect some firewood. We're gonna cook a little food. You guys like to eat, right?"

We arrived at a concrete house in the woods. Directly behind it, and hardly worth noticing, was a little bamboo shack, almost hidden by the jungle vegetation.

"I'm gonna put you guys to work. You guys do know how to work, don't you?" Without verbally answering we simply nodded our heads and began gathering kindling from the thick forest surrounding the hut. Natty helped us light a fire and then showed us how to make what he called a Caribbean ital naturally prepared meal.

"Breadfruit soup and saltfish. Not a ting mo bettah!" Natty was enthusiastic. Trey and I especially enjoyed the coconut bread we devoured for dessert; the thick and heavy loaf now weighing in my stomach like a cannonball lodged somewhere within the digestive tract.

It wasn't until after our bellies were stuffed completely full that Phillip would begin to teach. By the flickering light of the campfire and the dull beams of a new quarter moon, we opened up our Bibles and began to follow along.

> **David was 30 years old when he became King, and he reigned for 40 years.**
> **-2Samuel 5:4**

"David fulfilled the prophecy that the royal family of Israel would come from the tribe of Judah. The Lord communicated to David that He would, 'make his name like the names of the greatest men on Earth.' He declared to David, 'I will build a house for you. I will raise up your offspring to succeed you, one of your own sons, and I will establish his kingdom. He is the one who will build a house for me. I will set him over my house and my kingdom forever; his throne will be established forever.'"

> **Then David comforted his wife, Bathsheba, and he went to lay with her. She gave birth to a son, and they named him Solomon.**
> **-2Samuel 12:24**

> **David assembled all Israel in Jerusalem to bring up the ark of the Lord to the place he prepared for it.**
> **-I Chronicles 15:3**

"He declared that none other than the Levites from the priestly tribe of Levi would be allowed to carry the Ark. David summoned the priests, talked to leaders and organized musicians."

> **David brought together out of Israel chosen men, 30,000 in all to bring up the ark of God.**
> **-2Samuel 6:2**

"We must realize that during this time David was collecting a lot of iron ore and much copper."

> **He provided a large amount of iron to make nails and more bronze than could be weighed.**
> **-I Chronicles 22:3**

"During the Bronze Age, 250,000 tons of copper ore was removed from the Great Lakes region of the United States. Radio carbon dating tells us that between 1500-1000 B.C. it was mined from this area. Interestingly enough, the state of Michigan sounds very similar to the Hebrew word *Mishkan* which means 'place of dwelling' and refers to the Tabernacle, temple or sanctuary built by the Israelites to house the Presence of God. Was copper mined from the state of Michigan used to build the *Mishkan*, the dwelling place of YHWH in Israel?"

> **To David my servant, I will set his hand also in the sea.**
> **-Psalm 89:20**

> **Others went out on the sea in ships; they were merchants on the mighty waters.**
> **-Psalm 107:23**

"Whoa! Wait a minute!" I insisted that Natty stop for a moment and clarify. "Are you implying that the Israelites traveled to the Northern United States during the reign of King David?"

"Israel worked closely with the Phoenicians," Natty responded. "They provided David with lumber for the temple."

> **He also provided more cedar logs than could be counted, for the Sidonians and Tyrians (Phoenicians) had brought large numbers of them to David.**
> **-I Chronicles 22:4**

> **Now Hiram king of Tyre sent messengers to David, along with cedar logs and carpenters and stonemasons, and they built a palace for David.**
> **-2Samuel 5:11**

"The Phoenicians were sailors and merchants, seafarers and traders. They developed the keel, streamlined their ships, covered the decks and improved the sail. Their ships were from 80-100 feet long and could easily travel 100 miles in a day. During this time there was much need for copper, a bronze and tin alloy, as this was, in fact, the Bronze Age. So many useful things were made of the metal that a civilization could not survive long without a good supply of it. The Phoenicians are believed to have played an important role in spreading the early bronze culture through their trade in tin. The tin mines in England had been productive ever since pyramids were being built on the Giza plateau. These Phoenician traders established many successful trade routes and built many ports."

"That's Phoenicia, not Israel," I countered. "And besides, I don't think it's true."

Trey confronted me, "What makes you think it isn't true? You know that after leaving Egypt, the Israelites traveled to many far away lands, to Greece and Spain, to England and all over Europe."

"But to the New World?" I questioned, "To the Americas? Is this true Natty?"

"The kingdom of David spread far and wide. In Ireland there is an ancient Celtic kingdom of Dyfed, named after King David. Remember, only consonants were used to write Hebrew. David would have been DVD. We'll get to that later." Natty sternly reminded us, "I was teaching you about David's plans to build a temple."

> **King David said to Israel, "I had it in my heart to build a house as a place of rest for the ark of the covenant of the Lord. I made plans to build it. But God said to me, you are not to build it, because you are a warrior and have shed blood."**
> **-I Chronicles 28:2**

"King Solomon would be the one to build the temple, instead."

> **When David was old and full of years, he made his son Solomon king over Israel.**
> **-I Chronicles 23:1**

"God had promised to David, 'You will have a son who will be a man of peace and rest. His name will be Solomon. I will establish the throne of his kingdom over Israel forever.'

> **I have appointed him ruler of Israel and Judah.**
> **-I Kings 1:35**

"David blessed Solomon, 'I have taken great pains to provide for the temple of the Lord gold, silver, quantities of bronze and iron too great to be weighed, and wood and stone. And you may add to them. You have many workmen: stonecutters, masons and carpenters, as well as men skilled in every kind of work, in gold and silver, bronze and iron- craftsmen beyond number. Now begin the work, and the Lord be with you.'"

Then David ordered all the leaders of Israel to help his son Solomon.
-I Chronicles 22:17

"The Lord said to Solomon, 'Wisdom and knowledge will be given you. And I will also give you wealth, riches and honor, such as no king who was before you ever had and no one after you will have.'"

Solomon made an alliance with Pharaoh king of Egypt and married his daughter. He brought her to Jerusalem until he finished building his palace and the temple of the Lord.
-I Kings 3:1

"Indeed, Solomon was wiser than the sons of Zerah, Calcol and Darda, and the kings of Europe."

Solomon's wisdom was greater than all the men of the East, and greater than the wisdom of all of Egypt.
-I Kings 5:30

"He spoke proverbs and sang songs. He was a botanist, a biologist. Men of all nations came to listen to Solomon. They were sent by the kings of the world who had heard of his wisdom."

I interrupted, "Surely the Bible is referring only to the kings of the Middle East? People didn't really travel to Israel from *all* over the world, did they?"

"Believe it or not, they did," Natty replied. "This was a time of peace and prosperity during the reign of King Solomon. Israel made an alliance with the Phoenicians and they traveled the world over. They were merchants and traders, remember? Seafarers and sailors."

> **There were peaceful relations between King Hiram of Phoenicia and King Solomon of Israel and the two of them made a treaty.**
> **-I Kings 5:12**

> **When Hiram King of Tyre heard that Solomon had been anointed king to succeed his father David, he sent his envoys to Solomon.**
> **-I Kings 5:1**

"A common misconception is that, although the Phoenicians traded and established colonies throughout the Mediterranean, their Israelite neighbors never set foot on a boat or visited distant lands in ancient times. The truth is that the Israelites, along with the Phoenicians, imported materials from around the globe."

> **King Solomon made silver and gold as common in Jerusalem as stones.**
> **-2Chronicles 1:15**

"He had his own royal merchants. Can you believe it?"

> **The people of Israel and Judah were as numerous as sand on the seashore; they ate, drank and they were happy.**
> **-I Kings 4:20**

> **Solomon had four thousand stalls for chariot horses and twelve thousand horses.**
> **-I Kings 4:26**

> **His horses were imported from Egypt and all other countries.**
> **-2Chronicles 9:28**

"Tell us more about the construction of the temple!" we demanded. "Was it anything like the temples we see around here?" I told Natty we soon planned on heading into interior Guatemala with the hopes of visiting some of the most fascinating Mayan ruins.

"You guys want me to finish?" Natty snapped back. "In that case, you must stay a few more days. That is enough for tonight. Try and get some rest, there's work to do in the morning."

Sleeping in an undersized hammock in a moist, tropical humidity which can smother you like a wet blanket wasn't really enticing me to hit the sack, to say the least, so I stayed awake reading for a while. Lucky for him, Trey was out like a light. Trying not to disturb him, I kept a small paraffin candle lit beside me on the bedside nightstand. (Or I should say the old piece of wood next to my hammock.) I quietly thumbed through the pages of my Bible wondering, *how was the temple in Israel built? How were these temples here in Central America built?*

> **He inscripted 153,000 men to carry and cut stones.**
> **-2Chronicles 2:2**

Solomon sent a message to king Hiram asking him to send cedar logs as he did for David when he built his palace.

> **Hiram had the logs floated on rafts.**
> **-I Kings 5:9**

> **No tools were used at the temple site.**
> **-I Kings 6:7**

> **He prepared the inner sanctuary for the Ark of the Covenant. The Levites took up the Ark and brought the ark to its place in the inner sanctuary of the Temple.**
> **-I Kings 6:19**

> **There was nothing in the ark except the two tablets Moses had placed in it, where the Lord made a covenant with the Israelites after they came out of Egypt.**
> **-2Chronicles 5:10**

> **Then the Lord said to Moses, "Write down these words, for in accordance with these words I have made a**

> covenant with you and with Israel." Moses was there with the Lord for forty days and forty nights without eating bread or drinking water. And he wrote on the tablets the words of the covenant- the Ten Commandments."
>
> -Exodus 34:27

> The priests then brought the ark of the Lord's covenant to its place in the inner sanctuary of the temple, the Most Holy Place, and put it beneath the wings of the cherubim.
>
> -I Kings 8:6

> They raised their voices in praise to the Lord and sang. "He is good; his love endures forever."
>
> -2Chronicles 5:13

Then the temple of the Lord was filled with a cloud, for the glory of the Lord filled the temple of God. Solomon said, "I have built a magnificent temple for you, a place for you to dwell forever."

> "The Lord has kept the promise he made. I have succeeded David my father and now I sit on the throne of Israel, just as the Lord promised, and I have built the temple for YHWH, the God of Israel. There I have placed the ark in which is the covenant of the Lord that he made with the people of Israel."
>
> -2Chronicles 6:10

> I will establish your royal throne, as I covenanted with David your father when I said, 'You shall never fail to have a man to rule over Israel.'
>
> -2Chronicles 7:18

A faint light was beginning to shine through the bamboo walls of our tiny shack. I blew out the candle, for it was no longer necessary, the sun was slowly starting to rise. I had been reading all night and hadn't slept a wink. Trey began to toss and turn restlessly in his hammock as I listened to the sound of footsteps squeak across the wet morning grass. Someone was walking around outside our cabin. *Who could it be?*

"Good morning! Give thanks and praise! What a beautiful day it is! You guys are ready to work?" *Natty.*

Trey was awake now and wearing the same dirt-stained jeans and filthy t-shirt he wore the day before. Our backpacks were nearly empty as the weight of carrying too heavy a load had caused us to discard most of our belongings at random locations along the way. I rose up reluctantly from my hammock with a stiff lower back and clothes so damp and dingy they stuck to my body like a Curad band-aid.

"We're ready," Trey answered back. Seemingly, a good night's sleep had done him well. I was a bit more laggard and looking pretty haggard as I followed him out to where Natty was waiting.

"Very good. I thought we would have an early study session. You guys get de fire going. I'm gonna mek some tea."

A few minutes later, with the tea brewing and the three of us huddled together around the fire on the two rocks and a tree stump we used as chairs, Natty began to speak, "Well, you see, now it's clear how Hiram and the Phoenicians helped King Solomon and Israel build the temple of the Lord, which housed the Ark of the Covenant. You guys go ahead and read some more from de Bible. Start with this verse here…

> **Then Solomon went to Ezion Geber and Hiram sent him ships commanded by his own officers, men who knew the sea. These with Solomon's, sailed to Ophir and brought back gold, which they delivered to King Solomon.**
>
> **-2Chronicles 8:17**

"In Kings 9:26 we see that the port of Ezion Geber was on the shores of the Red Sea. The Phoenicians served in this fleet with Solomon's men."

Wait a second. "So Israel had ports on both the Mediterranean AND the Red Sea? Incredible!" I was amazed. *Maybe the Israelites really did travel the world?*

Natty continued, "They sailed with the Phoenicians who were well known for building numerous and powerful fleets of ships. They built marts, *bodegas* and warehouses along their routes. The Phoenicians were not interested in conquering lands, but in acquiring exotic native products and exportable resources. They built anchorages and stations along the trade route from Phoenicia to Spain, which was quickly becoming a prime source of silver and tin. From the Phoenician city of Cartago, or Carthage, on the North coast of Africa, we get the root of the word *cartography*; hence, the Phoenicians were mapmakers. They were known to guard the secrets of oceanic navigation from other nations."

Natty proceeded to teach, "King Solomon of Israel grew in fame and fortune."

> **The king had a fleet of trading ships manned by Hiram's men. Once every three years it returned carrying gold, silver and ivory, and apes and baboons. King Solomon was greater in riches and wisdom than all the other kings of the earth. All the kings of the earth sought audience with Solomon to hear the wisdom God had put in his heart. Year after year everyone who came brought a gift- articles of silver and gold, and robes, weapons and spices, and horses and mules.**
> **-2Chronicles 9:21**

"It also says in Kings 10:22 that Solomon had a fleet of trading ships along with the ships of Hiram. And, yes, once every three years the fleet returned, carrying gold and silver, apes, baboons and peacocks."

Trey astutely reminded us, "Three years is the same time it required Ferdinand Magellan to circumnavigate the globe. And peacocks are native to India and Sri Lanka."

> **Solomon received 25 tons of gold yearly, not including revenue brought in by merchants and traders.**
> **-I Kings 10:14**

> **Men of all nations came to listen to Solomon's wisdom, sent by all the kings of the world, who had heard of his wisdom.**
>
> **-I Kings 4:34**

"In the book of Ecclesiastes, King Solomon writes, 'I know there is nothing better for men than to be happy and do good while they live. That everyone may eat and drink, and find satisfaction in all his toil- this is the gift of God.' He adds, 'There is not a righteous man on earth who does what is right and never sins.'"

"Check out this verse!" Trey was poking a little fun at me. He knew it was my intention to someday author a book.

> **Of making books there is no end and much study wearies the body.**
>
> **-Ecclesiastes 12:12**

I have to confess, I'm exhausted. Do I really want to continue writing this book? It would be much easier to conclude this story right here, quote the wise King Solomon from the book of Ecclesiastes and just end it now.

> **'Now all has been heard; here is the conclusion of the matter: Fear God and keep his commandments, for this is the whole duty of man. For God will bring every deed into judgment, including every hidden thing, whether it is good or evil.'**

Great advice and worth adhering to, but alas, all has not been heard! We shall seek more truths, solve more mysteries, learn more history and weary our bodies with much study! Of making books there is no end, yet this one has just begun!

Maybe you already know the answer. God bless you. Congratulations, that's great! Some of us, however, are on a quest and will keep on searching, trying to piece together the world's largest jigsaw puzzle, wind our way through the tricky maze and uncover the half-buried secrets that will allow us to answer that impending question. Does true love really exist? *Am I really a Christian?*

CHAPTER 8

"Yes mon, I am an Israelite." Natty had me almost convinced. After the next three days of listening to him teach, I was quite sure of it.

"The Hebrew Israelites sailed to Brazil," he told us. "The name Brazil comes from Hy-brasil, which was noted on early maps. Hy-brasil is 'Hebrew's isle.' Brazil was named after the Hebrews. The Brazilian flag has a circle with a channel across the center of it. This was the symbol for Hy-brasil or 'Hebrew's isle' on these early maps. The Irish, too, believed in a paradise across the ocean called Hy-breasail. The word for iron in the Hebrew language is BRZL. The word brass also stems from this root!"

> **Zillah bore Tubal-Cain, he was the forger of all instruments of bronze and iron. In Hebrew, Tubal-Cain is also known as Bar-Zillah (the son of Zillah.)**
> **-Genesis 4:22**

Natty taught us that Brazil is full of vestiges pointing to the presence of Phoenicia and Israel in its lands. Inscriptions found in the Amazon reference many kings of Sidon and Tyre. In the Louvre museum archives, also in Vatican documents, it is stated that the original name given to the Amazon River was the Solimoes, perhaps named in honor of King Solomon.

In the National Museum in Rio de Janeiro there exist other ancient relics. An inscription found in Brazil in 1872 translates:

> 'We are Sidonian Canaanites (Phoenicians) from the city of the merchant king. We were cast upon this distant island, a land of mountains. In the nineteenth year of our mighty King Hiram we embarked from Ezion Geber into the Red Sea. We voyaged 10 ships and were at sea together 2 years around Africa. Then we were separated by the hand of Baal.'

An Adventure of Biblical Proportions

Herodotus, the famous Greek historian, tells of a decree published by the Carthaginian senate that forbid, under the penalty of death, that anyone take trips from the port-city of Carthage to the other side of the Atlantic Ocean. The frequent coming and going of men was emptying this Phoenician capital located on the north coast of Africa, less than 10 km from present-day Tunis, Tunisia.

"Yes mon, both the Romans and the Greeks knew of a western continent across the Atlantic Ocean called Epeiros Occidentalis, or 'The Hebrew's Western Land.'"

Trey wondered aloud in sheer disbelief, "How did Plato, born in 4th century B.C. Greece, first come to write about the lost city of Atlantis? Was this a folktale? A legend? How did he have knowledge of the Nahuatl language of Mexico from which the word 'Atlan' originates? You know…" he said, "I have heard of this thing called Inscription Rock. It's somewhere in New Mexico, I think. Some sort of Hebrew writing carved on a rock. Natty, do you know anything about this?"

"Do I know anyting 'bout dis? Ya mon, of course, I and I know all about it. The American Indians call it 'Cliff of Strange Writings.' Also called Phoenician Rock or Commandment Stone, you'll find it along a tributary of the Rio Grande. The writing on the stone is Semitic in origin and preserves an abbreviated form of the Ten Commandments." The inscription on the stone reads:

> 'I (am) Jehovah (the eternal) Eloha (your God) who brought you out of the land of Mitsrayim (Egypt) out of the house of bondages…'

"Phoenician artifacts have been found in Tennessee, Alabama, Georgia and other areas of the United States."

As Natty continued, I was about to be shocked even more. "In fact, the name Alabama is Hebrew in origin. The Israelites built a special type of outdoor altar called a *bamah*, which can be translated as a 'high place.' Alabama, or *Al-bamah*, means 'the high place'…probably because it was not in the massive flood plain along the Southern Gulf Coast. Perhaps, also, because of the bamah or 'high places' that native peoples built in the area, such as the ones found in Moundville, Alabama. This same root is found in the Spanish word *alaba*, meaning 'to praise God.' In Arabic *al-Abba* means 'to the father.'

As you sail around the tip of Florida to Louisiana and to Texas, the entire coastline is low and flat with the exception of inland Alabama being a 'high place' or bamah. The Bahama Islands were also named because of this Hebrew meaning. Of course, this land was the first 'high place' or *bamah* to be seen by explorers after making the long Trans-Atlantic voyage and just before entering into the present-day Gulf of Mexico."

Natty challenged us, "There are other U.S. states with names in Hebrew, some in Greek and Arabic as well. But, I'll leave that up to you guys to figure out. You *can* think for yourselves, can't you?"

Another mystery? C'mon, am I really supposed to be solving puzzles? I remembered what Buck had said about the Ark of the Covenant...*Know its importance, trace its movements, find its location, solve the mystery.*

"What about the Ark, Natty?" I felt the need to investigate. "What happened to the Ark of the Covenant? Did it remain inside the Temple?"

"Know the answer to that," he informed us, "and you will know how I am an Israelite! From the Tribe of Judah, yes mon!"

"So, you're a Jew?" Trey couldn't help but to ask.

"I am a Christian. An Ancient Christian, descended from King David of Israel, through the lineage of King Solomon and the Tribe of Judah!" Natty seemed to know what he was talking about. He was also very animated. I couldn't help but to believe him and I certainly tried not to interrupt his speech.

Trey was a little more skeptical, "Really, Natty? I could've sworn you were African."

"Precisely," Natty replied. "Are you guys gonna let me finish? Man you guys is antsy. Patience is a virtue, mon. You want to know about the Ark, don't you?"

Trey backed off a little and let Natty proceed. "During the time of King Solomon, in the 10th century B.C., Ethiopia was ruled by a line of virgin queens."

"We do know how Solomon liked women!" I half-jokingly commented.

It's true. He had over 700 wives. But, most of these marriages were for political purposes. They were alliances with other rulers and other kingdoms. Such was his alliance with the Pharaoh Shishak of Egypt.

> **Shishak sends his daughter off with 80,000 builders and 1,000 musical instruments.**
> **-2Chronicles 7:18**

> **King Solomon brought Pharaohs daughter up from Jerusalem to the palace he built for her, for he said 'my wife must not live in palace of David king of Israel because the places where the ark of the Lord entered are holy."**
> **-2Chronicles 8:14**

"So the Ark of the Covenant was still in the Temple," Trey said quietly.

"True," Natty whispered, "And there was one woman who *was* allowed to stay there, in the Temple." He continued, "Like I was saying, 1000 years before the birth of Christ, an Ethiopian King appointed his daughter Makeda to succeed him on the throne. After her father's death, she became the matriarchal ruler of Kush at age 15, the virgin Queen of Ethiopia. She became known as the Queen of Sheba."

I knew the story fairly well. "And she traveled to Jerusalem to visit King Solomon, right?"

"That's right." Natty smiled like an overly-excited child. "Word came to Sheba in Ethiopia concerning Solomon and Israel…"

After reading 2Samuel chapter 18 we know there was a Cushite in the palace at the time of King David who would have delivered the message to the Queen.

> **When the queen of Sheba heard about the fame of Solomon and his relation to YHWH, she came to test him with hard questions. Arriving at Jerusalem with a very great caravan- with camels carrying spices, large quantities of gold, and precious stones- she came to Solomon and talked with him about what she had on her**

> mind. Solomon answered all her questions; nothing was too hard for the king to explain to her. When Sheba saw all the wisdom of Solomon and the palace he built, she was overwhelmed. She said to him, "the report I heard in my own country about your achievements and your wisdom is true. But I did not believe these things until I came and saw with my own eyes. Indeed, not even half was told me; in wisdom and wealth you have far exceeded the report I heard. Praise be to the Lord your God, who has delighted in you and placed you on the throne of Israel. Because of the Lord's eternal love for Israel, he has made you king, to maintain justice and righteousness." And she gave the king gold, large quantities of spices and precious stones.
>
> -I Kings 10:1-10

What Natty claimed that occurred next was news to me. I was simply amazed.

"Queen Sheba stayed with Solomon for six months while he taught her all that he knew. He loved her very much. And when it became time for Sheba to go, she was with child."

> **King Solomon gave the queen of Sheba all she desired and asked for, besides what he had given her out of his royal bounty. He gave her more than she brought to him. Then she left and returned with her retinue to her own country.**
>
> -2Chronicles 9:12; IKings10:13

"Queen Sheba was carrying in her womb the child of King Solomon of Israel, impregnated with the seed of the descendant of the Royal bloodline of Judah."

I couldn't believe what I was hearing.

"You can read more about their encounter in the Kebra Nagast, The Glory of Kings, a holy book of Ethiopia...

'The following morning as Sheba prepared to leave Israel, King Solomon placed a ring on her finger, engraved on it was the seal of the Lion of Judah. 'If you have a son, give him this ring,' he said to her. After returning to the throne of her kingdom in Ethiopia, Sheba gave birth to a boy. She named him Menelik, Son of the King. Thus was the beginning of the Solomonic Dynasty of royal Kush, modern-day Ethiopia.'

"There you have it! Now you know how I am an Israelite from the tribe of Judah! Yes mon! Respect! Oh, but you are curious about the Ark, aren't you? In that case, let me continue…"

"Yes Natty. I mean, ya mon! Please do. Did Sheba take the Ark back to Ethiopia?"

"No. Be patient and I will tell you." His look became more intense. "You see, when Menelik, the son of Sheba and prince of Kush, was 18 years old, he came to visit his father, King Solomon of Israel. He made the trip in a large caravan just like his mother the Queen had done. As he rode into the city of Jerusalem, people greeted him with sounds of cheering and applause, for they knew he was coming to learn the Mosaic Law and to be anointed by his father. After a visit thought to have lasted three years, Menelik, son of the King of Israel, was anointed King of Ethiopia, first in the line of the famous Royal Solomonic Dynasty."

"So Menelik took the Ark!" I exclaimed loudly, hoping I had come to the right conclusion.

"But…how? Why?" Trey was puzzled. "The Ark went before the Armies of the Israelites and helped win battles against the Philistines. It destroyed 53,000 people when they looked inside. It held back the waters of the River Jordan. It was, after all, the dwelling place of God! Why would King Solomon allow the Ark to be taken from the Temple?"

"The kingdom of Israel was in grave danger," Natty replied.

> **So the Lord said to Solomon, "Since you have not kept my covenant, which I commanded you, I will most certainly tear the kingdom away from you and give it to one of your subordinates."**
> **-I Kings 11:11**

"He broke the covenant?" I wondered aloud.

"Yes," Natty informed us. "As Solomon grew old, his wives turned his heart to other gods. He followed Ashtoreth, the goddess of the Phoenicians. On a hill east of Jerusalem, Solomon built a high place, a bamah, for the god of Moab. He built more of these altars, these bamoth, for all his foreign wives."

Moab? I had flashbacks to the desert, the drive to Utah with Paul, the burning bush we witnessed there. Nightfall was upon us here in Livingston and as we sat around the raging campfire, I felt the intense, scorching heat from the flames would consume me.

"Should we keep going?" Natty noticed the streams of sweat pouring off my forehead and rolling down my cheeks. "It's getting late. You guys need some rest?"

"No," Trey and I replied in unison.

> **The Lord became angry with Solomon because his heart had turned away from the Lord, the God of Israel, who had appeared to him twice.**
> **-I Kings 11:9**

Had I turned away from the Lord? Had the Lord appeared to me? I was now drenched in perspiration as Natty continued the lesson.

"The Lord said to Solomon in Kings 11:12…

> **Nevertheless, for the sake of David your father, I will not do it during your lifetime. I will tear it out of the hand of your son. Yet I will not tear the whole kingdom from him, but will give him one tribe for the sake of David my servant and for the sake of Jerusalem.**

Jeroboam was an official in Solomon's army. He rebelled against the king.

> **About that time Jeroboam was going out of Jerusalem, and Ahijah the prophet met him on the way, wearing a new cloak. The two of them were alone out in the country, and Ahijah took hold of the new cloak he was wearing and tore it into twelve pieces. Then he said to Jeroboam, "Take ten pieces for yourself, for this is what the Lord, the God of Israel, says: 'See, I am going to**

> tear the kingdom out of Solomon's hand and give you ten tribes. But for the sake of my servant David and the city of Jerusalem, he will have one tribe. I will do this because they have forsaken me and worshipped the god of the Phoenicians.'"
>
> -I Kings 11:29-33

"Pay attention!" Natty ordered. "God says that He has made Solomon ruler all the days of his life, but that upon his death, Jeroboam will become king of Israel and rule over 10 tribes. This is the beginning of a Civil War, the division of Israel! What do you think King Solomon will do?" Natty asked. "Jeroboam had already started the rebellion. Solomon was fully aware that upon his death, war would ensue. His political alliance with Egypt was disintegrating and many were plotting against him. He knew they wanted the treasures kept in the Temple of God in Jerusalem. Solomon *knew* they were after the Ark."

> Solomon tried to kill Jeroboam, but Jeroboam fled to Egypt, to Shishak the king, and stayed there until Solomon's death.
>
> -I Kings 11:40

"It was during this time that King Solomon's firstborn son, Menelik, son of the Queen of Sheba, came to visit him from Ethiopia." Natty was as excited as a wide-eyed kid opening gifts on Christmas morning, "This is what we've been waiting for! After being instructed in the Mosaic Law and being anointed King of Ethiopia by his father King Solomon, Menelik was given charge of the Ark of the Covenant of the Lord containing the Ten Commandments, the Manna the Israelites ate in the desert and Aaron's staff that budded.

Accompanying Menelik on the journey back to Ethiopia were the first-born sons of the wise men of Israel, the caretakers of Ark, the priests from the tribe of Levi, the descendants of Moses and Aaron. Solomon sent the sons of the Levites with Menelik to be counselors and teachers of the Hebraic Law in Ethiopia. These priests of Levi, wise men of Israel, placed the heavy poles on their shoulders and carried the Ark of the Covenant as prescribed by law. This is the origin of the word 'levee', meaning 'to raise or to lift up', also the words 'leave, left, level, leaven, levitate and Levitical.' LVT.

The Levites, the priests of Levi who carried the Ark, stole away from Jerusalem at night, in secrecy, escorted by King Menelik and his Cushite caravan as they headed south into the desert. All of this is in accordance with the prophecy of King David...

> **Envoys will come from Egypt; Ethiopia shall stretch forth her hands unto God.**
> **-Psalm 68:31**

"Unbelievable Natty, you did it!" Trey said. "You actually proved to me that you *are* an Israelite and the Ark of the Covenant *is* in Ethiopia!"

"Don't be surprised," Natty responded rather bluntly, "You guys are probably Israelites, too."

I wasn't real sure what Natty meant by that comment, but I think I have a pretty good idea now. Natty had proved so much to us by teaching straight from the Bible. He said that all Rastafarians are encouraged to read a chapter a day. Although it was already late, I would continue reading in my hammock.

King Solomon dies and his son Rehoboam becomes King of Israel amid civil unrest. The Ten Tribes of Israel rebel and they retain the name ISRAEL, while the remaining two tribes, Judah and Benjamin, form the House of DAVID.

> **When Jeroboam heard this (he was in Egypt where he had fled King Solomon) he returned from Egypt. He returns to confront King Rehoboam about the harsh labor put on Israel. Rehoboam refused to lighten the heavy labor and threatened to make it harder.**
> **-2 Chronicles 10:2**

Rehoboam threatened to scourge Jeroboam and the people of Israel with scorpions. Oh, the nerve! Can you believe it? And to think, I've spotted two or three of them inching up and creeping around on the bamboo walls of this poorly-constructed hut. Occasionally, one could be seen hanging, suspended from the ceiling, tail cocked and ready. Secluded in this jungle locale, miles from civilization and a decent hospital, I wondered as to the potency of the venom. They were slightly large and rather stealthy, these behemoths of the insect family.

> **When Israel saw that the king refused to listen to them, they answered the king, "What share do we have in David, what part in Jesse's son? To our tents, O Israel! Look after your own house, O David."**
> **-2 Chronicles 10:16**

The ten tribes of the House of Israel made Jeroboam their king.

> **Only the tribe of Judah remained loyal to the House of David. When Rehoboam arrived in Jerusalem, he mustered the whole house of Judah and the tribe of Benjamin- 180,000 fighting men- to make war against the house of Israel and to regain the kingdom for Rehoboam, son of Solomon.**
> **-I Kings 12:20**

It was told to Rehoboam son of Solomon King of Judah and to the whole house of Judah and Benjamin…

> **'This is what the Lord says: Do not go up to fight against your brothers, the Israelites. Go home, every one of you, for this is my doing.'**
> **-I Kings 12:24**

Jeroboam King of Israel was worried. He thought, "The kingdom will now likely revert to the House of David, the people will give their allegiance to Rehoboam King of Judah." Jeroboam lived in the hill country where he built high places and set up idols so the Israelites wouldn't worship at the Temple in Jerusalem.

On the other hand…

> **Rehoboam lived in Jerusalem and built up towns for defense in Judah.**
> **-2Chronicles 11:5**

The priests and Levites throughout Israel sided with Rehoboam. The Levites came to Judah and Jerusalem because Jeroboam had rejected them as priests of the Lord and had appointed his own priests for the high places, the *bamah*.

> **Those from every tribe of Israel who set their hearts on seeking the Lord, the God of Israel, followed the Levites to Jerusalem. They strengthened the kingdom of Judah and supported Rehoboam son of Solomon.**
> **-2Chronicles 11:16**

The Lord says that, because of the sins that Jeroboam has committed and has caused Israel to commit, He will "uproot Israel from this land and scatter them."

Unwisely, Rehoboam and Judah also began to set up bamah and worship in the ways of the Phoenicians.

> **After Rehoboam's position as king was established and he had become strong, he and all Israel with him abandoned the law of the Lord.**
> **-2Chronicles 12:1**

> **Judah did evil in the eyes of the Lord.**
> **-I Kings 14:22**

Because they had been unfaithful to the Lord, Shishak king of Egypt attacked Jerusalem in the fifth year of King Rehoboam with 1,200 chariots, 60,000 horsemen and innumerable troops that came with him from Egypt.

> **When Shishak king of Egypt attacked Jerusalem, he carried off the treasures of the temple of the Lord and the treasures of the royal palace. He took everything including all the gold shields Solomon had made.**

-2Chronicles 12:9

This is confirmed in the Talmud, "The Great Treasure which Joseph accumulated in Egypt returned to Egypt." Pharoah Shishak was on the throne from 945-924 B.C. Upon his return, he constructed a large festival court in front of the Temple at Thebes. This project was almost certainly financed by the plunder from Judah and Israel.

Wait a second! I thought to myself. *Pharoah Shishak stole everything in the Temple of the Lord in Jerusalem. Could it be that the Ark was still there? Could he have taken it back to Egypt with the other treasures of the palace?* I blew out the flame as the candle was now merely a few drops of wax with a small burnt wick sitting precariously on the makeshift table beside the most uncomfortable of hammocks. Daybreak was approaching and we were scheduled to catch a boat out of Livingston in few short hours. Our time at Natty's was almost up.

Trey spoke my name a few times before I found the will to open my eyes and the strength to lift my body up from the awkward position in which I had become accustomed to sleeping. It was the crack of dawn.

"You were up for a while reading last night, weren't you?" Trey asked. "Anything interesting you care to divulge?"

Well, yes. "Now that you mention it...just that, you know, maybe the Ark *was* still in the Temple when Pharoah Shishak invaded Jerusalem? Maybe he really did take *all* the treasures back to Egypt?" I raised the questions while haphazardly reaching down into my unzipped backpack in order to grab a shirt not quite as dirty as the one I had on.

"Ouch!" A sharp pain. A sting!

"Ahhhh..." I screamed so loud that mangoes began to fall from a nearby tree onto the top of our cabin. "A scorpion!" I saw it briefly as it scurried from out of my bag and across the dirt floor of the shack, disappearing into the shadows.

"Let's get out of here," I muttered to Trey as we hoisted our packs onto our shoulders and headed out the door. I contemplated waking Natty to thank him for his hospitality and exchange our goodbyes.

"Hey guys, what's all the fuss?" Too late, Natty was already up. He must have heard my high-pitched yelp, as much a result of me being surprised by the scorpion as to the pain it had caused to my right hand. "You guys is leaving?" he asked, already certain of the answer.

Natty wished us luck as we made our way down the jungle path towards the town of Livingston. "And by the way, the Ark was already gone. I told you guys, the Ark of the Covenant is in Ethiopia. Go and see it for yourselves if you want. In fact, maybe I mon will see you there! Rastafari!" he shouted out to us as we continued walking.

Beads of sweat were welling up on my forehead and I was already beginning to pant and breathe heavily. Was my throat closing? Were my airways being restricted? Not knowing whether it was due to the intense tropical heat and early morning humidity or the lethal injection of poison that might possibly be circulating throughout my body, I decided to keep on moving. Besides, the only doctor I could be in hopes of finding around here was a 'bush doctor' who would probably prescribe some sort of natural herbal remedy. There were certainly no medical clinics nearby.

Trey encouraged me all the while, "Come on, dude, we've got a boat to catch!"

> **So Israel has been in rebellion against the house of David to this day.**
>
> **-I Kings12:19**

CHAPTER 9

"Hear me, thou Jeroboam, and all Israel; ought ye not to know that the Lord God of Israel gave the kingdom over Israel to David and his descendants forever?"
- Abijah, King of Judah, 2Chronicles 13:4


```
        KINGDOM OF ISRAEL
            David                    PHOENICIA (Tyre & Sidon)
            Solomon                        Hiram

HOUSE OF DAVID      HOUSE OF ISRAEL
Rehoboam                Jeroboam
                        Nadab
Abijah              -------------------
                        Baasha (kills Nadab)
                        Elah
                        Zimri (kills Elah)
                    -------------------

Asa                     Omri
Jehoshaphat             Ahab   <<<married to>>>   Jezebel
    l                                  l
Jehoram  <<<married to>>>   Athalia---Ahaziah---Joram
            l               --------------------------------
         Ahaziah            Jehu (kills Ahazia and Joram)
            l
         Joash
```

I told her I was an Israelite, but she was reluctant to believe me. Her name was Yael, from Tel-Aviv, an Israeli citizen. She had just completed her mandatory stint in the Army and had somehow ended up in this place.

"Whose idea was it to get off here anyway?" Trey complained, only after we had lugged our backpacks about three miles down a seemingly endless dirt road. We had exited the bus somewhere along the Hummingbird Highway, a verdant stretch of road between Belmopan, the capital, and San Ignacio, a border town.

It was Regina's idea.

Why had we listened to a 16 year old from Santa Cruz? What was she doing here traveling alone through the jungles of Belize? Was she naive to the dangers? Probably not, which is more than likely the reason she had latched onto us. It's safer to travel in groups, especially for women.

Just then a bright yellow truck pulled up beside us, stained red with dust and mud. Trey flagged down the driver with a slight wave. It was the only gasoline-powered vehicle we'd seen on this road, although we had noticed a few horse and buggies parked in the far-off fields in the distance. Men with long beards dressed in overalls swung machetes and carried shovels as they worked alongside one another tending the land.

"Need a ride?" said an older gentleman with a German accent as the truck came slowing to a stop. He and his passenger, a fellow Deutchlander sitting shotgun in the heavy-duty pick-up, were working on a solar and wind energy project in the area.

"We're looking for a place to stay." Trey spoke for the group.

It had been recommended that we come here to Mountain Pine Ridge to get a taste of the incredible bio-diversity of the region, supposedly home to the highest concentration of Jaguars in all of Central America. By this time, I was more concerned with getting a taste of some beans and rice, maybe a piece of fruit, something to appease the hunger that was wrenching my abdomen like someone would do a wet towel before hanging it up to dry. We would have to wait to eat, however.

"We'll take you half way," they offered. We hopped into the bed of the truck, squatting down as the driver accelerated stirring up a summer squall of magenta-colored funnel clouds and fumaroles back behind us.

After continuing down the bumpy road a few more miles, the German informed us, "There's a place to stay a short distance down this road here. You'll have to walk the rest of the way. We would have to go very slow due to all the wagon ruts and...I have a meeting to attend." A meeting in the jungle? *Hmm?*

"That's fine." We jumped out and started down the rough path through what appeared to be Amish country. Yael and I walked ahead while the others followed closely behind, giving us an opportunity to get to know each other a little better.

"Are you Jewish?" I asked her, not sparing any time to strike up a conversation.

"Not really," she replied, matter-of-factly.

"Not really?"

"I mean I'm not a follower of Judaism."

"So you're a Christian?" This inquiry garnered a stern response.

"I'm Israeli. And as far as my religious beliefs go, I am Agnostic. I don't pretend to know the answer."

The question seemed to surface again inside my head as a wave sent undulating almost unnoticeably from a distant coastline announcing its arrival with a crash upon a newfound shore. *Am I a ....*

"But, your parents are Jewish, right?"

"My last name is Bukowski. My grandfather was in Auschwitz. I come from a long line of Polish Jews. *And you?* Please humor me. Tell me how you think you are an Israelite."

"Get them to stop!" I yelled back to Trey.

A mestizo man with a thick mustache pulled alongside us. His wife and young children sat silently next to him in the cab of the old Chevrolet.

"We heard there was a campground near here. Could you give us a lift?"

"Sure thing," he answered, "But, I wouldn't call it a campground. An investor from Canada bought the property recently and has plans to turn it into an eco-tourist resort. I work for him. Project Coordinator Pedro Pérez-Sosa, *a su servicio*. My crew and I are scheduled to be here for the next couple of weeks commencing with the construction. You're certainly welcome to stay in the old cabin as well."

After passing half a dozen wooden farmhouses along the way, the rusty Chevy came screeching to a halt at the end of the road in an area of thick jungle growth. A small clearing had been hacked out of the tangled vegetation, presumably the future location of the new lodge. The "old cabin", as Pedro had referred to it, was just that, if you could call it a cabin at all. To warrant the consideration, wouldn't it be necessary that the decrepit structure have four walls and a roof? This open-air, leaky building looked more like a haven for rodents and bugs and every other creature that lurks in the dense forests of Western Belize.

"I'll be back later with my crew." Pedro had spent the last half hour sharing with us some useful information about the area. The cave found on the property was an ancient burial place for his Mayan ancestors. Because it was part *cenote*, a Spanish word denoting an underground river system, a canoe was necessary to enter the gaping aperture in the side of the vine covered, rocky outcropping.

"If you're really daring," Pedro told us, "it is possible to swim past the entrance and into the mysterious macabre darkness that hides many fossilized bones, bats and miles of uncharted tunnels and crevices."

After a quick dip in the almost still lagoon, our group finally realized the magnitude of our predicament. We were hungry. We had no food, nor any potable water. The problem of thirst was easily resolved by carrying an empty Ozarka bottle down to the nearly stagnant river and filling it up with water, a decision that a week later I would painfully come to regret. Centuries-old decaying Mayan bones and the millions of parasites and amoeba contaminating the only water source was a likely cause of Giardia, causing my stomach to bloat to the size of a pregnant mother carrying a late-term baby.

The problem of hunger was met with more success. A group-decision was made to head back up the road and visit some of the old farmhouses in search of something to eat, desperately hoping the Quakers didn't own any guns and, if they did, wouldn't be frightened enough due to our disheveled appearance to use them. *Surely they might have a few morsels of food to share with some hungry travelers in need?*

An Adventure of Biblical Proportions

Little blue-eyed children with snowy white hair scurried back towards their houses as we made our way down the road. Some chose to stop and stare at the passers-by from behind the cover of an old fruit tree.

"That must have been Rachel and Isaiah," Roger told us. "They're not used to seeing strangers around here just yet. You all are a bit out of the ordinary."

He wasn't a Mennonite as far as I could tell. It turns out these people around here are neither Amish, nor Quakers, but a group a Swiss-German immigrants that are commonly referred to as Mennonites. Roger had left his home in Florida and integrated himself and his family into the community, citing Big Brother, the excessive control of the government and the invasion of privacy as the reasons for his exile. His five daughters, Freedom, Liberty, Sarah, Leah and Rebecca would all be given in marriage to upstanding young Mennonite boys in due time. There was a shortage of properly raised females fit for wedlock in this particular community.

"You're from Israel?" He looked at Yael in astonished disbelief. Roger was fascinated that someone from Israel was actually standing on his doorstep. "Do you know what is going to happen? You know about the war?" He was concerned about a war to end all wars, an apocalyptic battle that was to take place in Israel and the United States. He wanted to be assured that we heed his warning. We spoke for a minute longer and were soon on our way, not before gladly accepting hand-outs of freshly baked bread, a large jar of fruit and a container of wildflower honey harvested from hives located around back of the house. Content and appreciative, we thanked Roger immensely for the supplies and headed back to camp.

"So are you going to tell me?" Yael and I strolled along leisurely. We had about a mile to go until we would reach Barton Creek and the old cabin where we were to stay the night. The sun was beginning to set and the wind had calmed down. The screeching and buzzing and croaking of hundreds of species of insects and a plethora of amphibians could be heard all around us as we walked.

"Tell you what?" I replied.

"Are you going to tell me how in God's name you think you're an Israelite?"

"Certainly, my dear."

After leaving Natty's, I had spent half a day at a local library in Belize City doing nothing but research. "One of my distant relatives married into the royal family of Israel." This was sure to draw a much anticipated reaction from Yael.

"Royal family? There is no royal family in Israel."

"There was at that time," I informed her. "The kingdom of Israel, divided after the death of King Solomon, was now split into two. The war between the House of Israel and the House of David (Judah & Benjamin) continued."

> **In the thirty-first year of Asa king of Judah, Omri became king of Israel.**
> **-I Kings 16:23**
>
> **Omri did evil in the eyes of the Lord and sinned more than all of those before him.**
> **-I Kings 16:25**

"King Omri moved Israel's capital to the city of Samaria, which he built. The capital of Judah was Jerusalem. Asa was King of Judah at this time."

> **Asa did what was right in the eyes of the Lord**
> **-I Kings 15:11**

"The Spirit of God communicated to Asa…

> **'The Lord is with you when you are with him. If you seek him, he will be found by you, but if you forsake him, he will forsake you. Be strong and do not give up, for your work will be rewarded.'**

"When they saw that the Lord was with Asa, large numbers of people from Israel came over to live among the tribe of Judah."

I could tell by the way her ears perked up like those of a kitten that all of this had undoubtedly peeked Yael's interest.

"I'm waiting," she said with a slight smile on her face.

"Yes, of course." I continued…

> **In the thirty-eighth year of Asa king of Judah, Ahab son of Omri became king of Israel, and he reigned in Samaria over twenty-two years. Ahab son of Omri did more evil in the eyes of the Lord than any of those before him.**
> **-I Kings 16:29**

"King Ahab of Israel married Jezebel, a Phoenician princess who, after becoming Queen of Israel, promptly began killing off the prophets of the Lord. Together, Ahab and Jezebel became known as the wicked royal family of Israel. At this time, the prophet Elijah foresaw a drought for Samaria and Ahab. Not a drop of rain would fall for three years."

> **While Jezebel was killing off the prophets of YHWH, Obadiah had taken a hundred prophets and hidden them in two caves, fifty in each, and supplied them with food and water.**
> **-I Kings 18:4**

"Although Obadiah worked in the palace of Ahab in Samaria, he did believe in YHWH, the God of Israel. The prophet Elijah had gone into hiding for three years, only to return and present himself to Ahab. As Obadiah was walking along, Elijah met him. 'Go tell your master King Ahab that I, Elijah, am here.'

> **As surely as the Lord your God lives, there is not a nation or kingdom where my master has not sent someone to look for you. And whenever a nation or kingdom claimed you were not there, he made them swear they could not find you.**
> **-I Kings 18:10**

"Ahab King of Israel, because of his alliance with Phoenicia, had the ability to send search parties wherever their fleets sailed and traded in both the Old World and the New World."

This would open the floodgates of interest and Yael, I could tell, was very intrigued. We arrived back at camp and enjoyed our manna sent from heaven, a simple meal of wholegrain wheat bread and raw, unfiltered honey. The mangoes would have also been a nice addition if my avaricious appetite had not let greed get the best of me while walking down the peaceful country lane. I didn't think anyone would notice as I attempted to sneak just a few feet off the road and into a nicely kept orchard where the juiciest of grapefruits could be seen hanging from the trees. What an appealing delicacy, mature and ripe, ready for the picking! As I hastily reached up to grab the forbidden fruit, the entire contents of my backpack spilled to the ground striking a rock, the glass jar breaking into pieces. The mangoes were wasted.

I quickly left, banished from the garden feeling ashamed, knowing that I had been scolded and reprimanded as was well deserved. Yael, doubled over with laughter, continued the chastisement all the way back to the cabin where she informed Trey and Regina of my most unfortunate mishap. Fortunately, the bread and honey sufficed and filled our bellies; mine not yet having been affected by the parasites. I grabbed a flashlight and led Yael out to a spot beside the water where we sat down on a half-rotten log and continued our discussion.

> **Jehoshaphat son of Asa became king of Judah in the fourth year of Ahab king of Israel. In everything he walked in the ways of his father Asa and did not stray from them; he did what was right in the eyes of the Lord. "He sought God and followed his commands rather than the practices of Israel."**
>
> -I Kings 22:41

"Jehoshaphat king of Judah went to visit Ahab king of Israel in Samaria. For a short time they were united in battle. While sitting in his chariot, Ahab was hit with an arrow, died, and was brought to Samaria where they buried him. They washed the chariot at a pool where the prostitutes bathed, and the dogs licked up his blood, as the word of the Lord had declared. When Jehoshaphat king of Judah returned safely to his palace in Jerusalem, it was said to him because of his alliance with Israel, "Should you help the wicked and love those that hate the Lord?"

"Ahazia son of Ahab and Jezebel became king of Israel in Samaria."

> He did evil in the eyes of the Lord, because he walked in the ways of his father and mother. He served and worshiped Baal and provoked the Lord, the God of Israel, to anger, just as his father had done.
> -I Kings 22:52

"Jehoshaphat, King of Judah, made an alliance with Ahazia the King of Israel who was guilty of wickedness. He agreed with him to construct a fleet of trading ships."

> Now Jehoshaphat built a fleet of trading ships to go to Ophir for gold, but they never set sail-they were wrecked at Ezion-Geber.
> -I Kings 22:28
>
> (This port was constructed on the Red Sea. Remember, the Suez Canal was already in use at this time!)

"Ahazia son of Ahab said to Jehoshaphat, 'Let my men sail with your men,' but Jehoshaphat refused."

> Then Jehoshaphat rested with his fathers and was buried with them in the city of David. And Jehoram his son succeeded him (as King of Judah.)
> -I Kings 22:51
>
> He walked in the ways of the kings of Israel, as the house of Ahab had done, for he married a daughter of Ahab and Jezebel.
> -2 Chronicles 21:6

"And guess what? I am related to the wicked Queen Jezebel!" I admitted to Yael, to which she half-jokingly snarled back at me, "You must be very proud."

"No, really, I am."

> **She wrote letters in Ahab's name, placed his seal on them, and sent them.**
>
> -I Kings 21:8

Jezebel had a seal of her own, too. Many artifacts have been found and linked to the Phoenician-born Queen of Israel, among them are stamps made of the seal of Jezebel, written in the Hebrew-Phoenician alphabet of consonants and no vowels as YZBL. Jezebel is YZBL. My surname, Isbell, is derived from this spelling. And it is from this *same* derivation in which the name of the famous Queen Isabella of Spain finds its origin! Is it merely a coincidence that Isabella expelled the Jews from Spain? Evidence of Queen Jezebel can also be found in the name of the organization founded by her Phoenician descendants of Lebanon, the Hezbollah. YZBL, the wicked Queen of Israel.

Jehoram king of Judah marries Athalia (daughter of Ahab & Jezebel). Their son Ahaziah (nephew of Ahazia King of Israel) reigns for one year as King of Judah. He too walked in the ways of Ahab, while his mother, Athalia, encouraged him in doing wrong.

Jehu kills Ahaziah king of Judah AND Joram king of Israel. After the death of her son and her brother, Athalia proceeded to destroy the whole royal family of the House of Judah, including the attempted murder of her grandson Joash, son of Ahaziah king of Judah. He is hidden by an aunt on the Judah side of the family. Young Prince Joash remained hidden at the temple of God for six years while Athalia ruled the land. **At age 7, Joash, the male descendant of the royal bloodline of Judah, becomes king.** His great-grandparents include Jehoshaphat King of Judah, Ahab king of Israel and Jezebel, the Phoenician princess. He is the offspring of the Judah-Israel-Phoenician alliance.

HOUSE OF DAVID		HOUSE OF ISRAEL
Joash		Jehu
l		Jehoahaz
Amaziah	(major prophets)	Jehoash
l	Amos	Jeroboam II
Uzziah	750 B.C.	Zecharia
l		Shallum
l		Menahem
Jotham		Pekahiah
l		Pekah
Ahaz	Isaiah	Hosea *722 BC
l		
Hezekiah	*701 B.C.	

"**King Amaziah, son of Joash** found there were 300,000 men of Judah and Benjamin ready for military service. He also hired 100,000 men from Israel."

> **But a man of God came to him and said, "O king, these troops from Israel must not march with you, for the Lord is not with Israel."**
> **-2 Chronicles 25:7**

"He sent them home to Samaria. The troops of Israel were furious and attacked King Amaziah and Judah. **King Jehoash of Israel** took all the gold and silver located in the temple of God and returned to Samaria.

> **Tyre and Sidon (Phoenicia), you sold the people of Judah and Jerusalem to the Greeks, that you might send them far from their homeland.**
> **-Joel 3:6**

"**Uzziah became king of Judah** and reigned fifty-two years in Jerusalem. He did what was right in the eyes of the Lord, just as his father Amaziah had done. He sought God. Uzziah had an army of over 300,000."

> Uzziah provided shields, spears, helmets, coats of armor, bows and slingstones for the entire army. In Jerusalem he made machines designed by skillfull men for use on the towers and on the corner defenses to shoot arrows and hurl large stones.
>
> -2 Chronicles 26:14

"The famous Homer, who lived in Greece around this time, wrote the *Iliad* and the *Odyssey* about the Trojan War. And Jonah of the Bible was alive at this time…"

> Jonah ran away from the Lord and headed for Tarshish. He went to the coast and found a ship headed for that port. After paying the fare, he went aboard.
>
> -Jonah 1:3

"He boarded a passenger ship that would ferry him across the Mediterranean Sea all the way to Spain. It was commonplace to find vessels coming and going from different ports located along the coastlines of the Mediterranean. The Phoenicians, along with Israel, established these trade routes more than 300 years before Jonah's lifetime. By 770 B.C., Barcelona, Spain was already well-known as the capital of the iron and tin trade. Barcelona, like Brazil, comes from the Hebrew word BRZL (pronounced Bar-cel) which means iron. Barcelona is the 'place of iron!'"

The prophet Amos was a herdsman in Judah at this time. He was sent to announce God's judgment on the House of Israel. Amos calls for social justice and condemns those who make themselves rich at the expense of others.

> Assemble yourselves on the mountains of Samaria; see the great unrest within her and the oppression among her people…the houses adorned with ivory will be destroyed and the mansions will be demolished…Seek good, not evil, that you may live. Then the Lord God Almighty will be with you, just as you say he is.
>
> -Amos 3:9

> **"Are not you Israelites the same to me as the Cushites?" declares the Lord.**
>
> **-Amos 9:7**

Yael looked like she was hit with a ton of bricks. Confused, she asked, "What does *that* mean, the same as the Cushites?"

I told her about Menelik, son of Solomon and Sheba. I informed her about the sons of the Levites leaving with the Ark of the Covenant and going to Ethiopia.

"Surely you're joking, aren't you?" she asked. "I'm pretty sure the Ark of the Covenant was in Jerusalem around this time."

Uh oh, I thought, *here we go again*.

"You're right Yael!" I said to her. And she was.

However, the mystery of how and why the Ark actually made it back there would soon be revealed. I would have to wait for the most opportune time to tell her.

> **The Lord declares, "For I will shake the house of Israel among all the nations as grain is shaken in a sieve."**
>
> **-Amos 9:9**

"In 722 B.C., Assyria, led by king Shalmaneser, attacked Samaria and deported the Israelites away from their homeland. The 10 tribes of Israel were scattered throughout the nations. Only the tribe of Judah remained."

> **In king Hezekiah's fourth year, which was the seventh year of Hoshea king of Israel, Shalmaneser king of Assyria marched against Samaria and laid siege to it. At the end of three years the Assyrians took it.**
>
> **-2 Kings 18:9**

> **The king of Assyria brought people from Babylon, Cuthah, Avva, Hammath and Sepharvaim and settled them in the towns of Samaria to replace the Israelites. They took over Samaria and lived in its towns.**
>
> **-2 Kings 17:24**

THE TRUE LOVE MESSIAH:

"Sepharvaim is Spain. Is it possible that Avva refers to Avalon or England, as it is known today?"

[The Ten Tribes of Israel were known to the Assyrians as the Khumri due to pronunciation of the first letter, *ayin*, of the name of King Omri. During the years 690-650 B.C., the Greeks called them the Kimmeroi, and in Britain they are still known today as the Khumry, or the 'Welsh.' The Khumric language prevailed in different dialects throughout Europe and over a large part of Asia. It is the Substructure of all Celtic tongues and the archaic element found in Greek, Sanskrit and hieroglyphic Egyptian. Both the Khumry and the Egyptians called their language 'the language of heaven.' Sir Walter Raleigh in his <u>History of the World</u> mentioned that the Indians he encountered used many Welsh words long before the Welsh were known to come to America. The Ten Tribes of Israel were called Bet Khumir, 'the House of Omri', in part because, as the King of Israel, Omri moved the capital of the northern ten tribes to Samaria. They have since been called by many names: Ombri, Ghomri, Khumri, Humri, Gimiri, Gimarrai, Kimmerioi, Cimmerians and Cimbri. The Cimmerians or (Samarians) have also been known as the Keltai, Geltae, Galatae, Galatians, Goidels, Gauls and Gaels. Some Samarians migrated further east into Central Asia, some as far as China. It has been claimed that the Chiang-Men Jews of China are descended from the ancient Israelites. The Chiang-Min live in fortlike villages high in the mountains of the China/Tibet border. There is even a resemblance in Japanese word *samurai* to Samaria, the capital of Israel. One of the most common names in Japan is Sakai, like the House of Isaac. The first known king of Japan was said to be Osee around 730 B.C. This king has been identified with Hosea.]

Yael was tired, and I was pretty exhausted myself. We joined the others in the cabin, laying our sleeping bags beside theirs on the few solid pieces of flooring that we could locate. A few holes pervaded here and there in the floorboards giving access to the thousands of spawning mosquitoes using the damp, dark area below as a fertile breeding ground. The serious infestation of these pesky blood-suckers made for a rough night's sleep and a cause for legitimate concern due to the possibility of acquiring the dreaded Dengue-fever virus so common in these parts. If suffocation could have been avoided, I would have slept entirely covered, my head buried deep within the sleeping bag.

Unfortunately, an air hole was necessary and I was forced to leave my face exposed, my nostrils and mouth inhaling loads of fresh oxygen while filtering out tiny little insects. Needless to say, after laboring through the early morning hours fighting off broods of the buggers and waking to a bloody forehead and bloody palms, we decided that was the last night we would subject ourselves to such utter discomfort.

> **And the Lord will strike Israel, so that it will be like a reed swaying in the water. He will uproot Israel from the land which He gave to their fathers, and will scatter them beyond the River...**
> **-I Kings 14:15**

We scattered like the Israelites. We scattered past farmhouses, past Mennonite farmers working in their fields, past gardens and orchards supporting the most tempting of fruits. We scattered and didn't stop until we felt safe from the army of mosquitoes left in our wake. With our arrival in a new nation only came the realization that the persistent little persecutors were in hot pursuit.

CHAPTER 10

Yet I will show love to the house of Judah; and I will save them- not by bow, sword or battle, or by horses and horsemen, but by the Lord their God.
-Hosea 1:7

There must have been an equal number of poultry being transported as there were people on the bus. I made my way down the aisle, wading through elderly Guatemalan women in traditional dress who really didn't seem to mind the clucking chickens. They, the old women *and* the chickens, frantically cleared a path for me to the front of the rickety, run-down vehicle. Spitting out feathers and swallowing small particles of dirt, I descended down the steps and onto solid ground. The bus pulled away in a thick, noxious cloud of dust and exhaust.

The smell of fumes and manure lingered in the air, but soon the fragrances and sounds of the rain forest would overcome them and overtake the senses. We had been warned that this was guerilla territory; not *gorila* as in Spanish for gorilla, the large primate animal, but *guerilla* as in the armed bandits that inhabit the region. This was El Petén, a dense jungle area of Northeastern Guatemala. Here, friendly *Chapinos*, or residents of the country, greet you with a seemingly misplaced "adiós", which upon further inspection means "to God."

I must state that we had come not without a purpose. This is a familiar journey for those intrepid pilgrims intent on exploring the vast complex of pyramids that dot the landscape. This was the road to Tikal. It's said that the Maya settled here around 700 B.C., which conveniently coincides with the period in which Israel was **"scattered throughout the nations"** and the Israelites were **"sifted through the nations as grain is shaken through a sieve."** This was a useful reminder that we would soon continue our discussion.

For a small pittance of a fee, Trey, Yael and I would hang our hammocks at El Mirador del Duende, a small eco-lodge/bed & breakfast on a hillside overlooking Lake Pétén-Itzá. As we planned a visit to the ruins the following day, our short stay here became an eventful one. A familiar sight around the hotel grounds was a pregnant female spider monkey (a correctly identified species, as she had a peculiar affinity for capturing and, then, allowing long-legged arachnids to crawl and maneuver all over her furry body) who innately prepared for her upcoming motherhood by lovingly cradling in her long, gangly, hairy arms a large and spotted toad. She carried it around, caressing and squeezing the poor, unfortunate frog, until it could no longer survive her constant, overly-anxious affection and soon, literally, croaked. Upon realizing her "baby" was now deceased, the doting primate became emotionally distant and distraught, mourning the loss of her "child."

The following morning as we gathered around a common table for breakfast, the grief-stricken monkey sat perched upon a ledge behind us, inconspicuously eyeing a plate of pancakes belonging to a fellow traveler. In an instant, the soon-to-be mother impulsively stretched out her arm in a daring grab for the breakfast she had been silently craving. Certainly due to first reaction and without giving it much thought, Jim from Louisiana reached out in an attempt to defend his plate and save his precious stack of pancakes. Very carelessly, Jim blocked the hungry monkey by placing his hand across her swollen belly, thus causing the impregnated female to become fiercely enraged.

Quickly grabbing hold of his forearm, and while wrapping her long fingers and strong hands around his lily-white, brown-freckled flesh, she flashed a fearsome display of large, sharp fangs and locked down with a savage bite. An unsuspecting Jim, surprised and unable to react at first, didn't delay too long in wrestling loose from her grasp.

It wasn't until after the two were separated and the initial shock of the incident wore off that we were fully able to appreciate the humor in witnessing such an event. Our good-natured friend was not harmed, and Jim only suffered a minor injury!

This, however, would not be the end of all the 'monkey-business.' A young male of a different species, slightly smaller and darker in hue, came swinging down on cue from an overhanging vine.

"Hola Pedro!" I called to him as the cute little fellow latched onto my arm as if it were just another tree branch to aid him in his descent from the upper reaches of the well-developed jungle canopy. He must have noticed I was holding a banana in my hand. *A friend in need is a friend indeed!*

He sat down beside me, put his arm around my shoulder and gave me such a pitiful look, that I couldn't help but to feel sympathy for the creature. Naturally, both of us lovers of bananas, we harmoniously shared together the tropical treat while enjoying a sort-of brotherly comraderie. We had instantly become good friends, *mi compadre y yo*. As another old, dilapidated bus came skidding to a stop on the road down below, Pedro very amicably waved goodbye, more than content to have received the remaining portion of the shared meal.

I carefully traversed the precariously placed stair-steps along the moist and rocky hillside in order to reach the idle vehicle. My friends were already on board saving me a seat as the conductor revved the unimpressive engine of the outdated machine. With good reason, we would reach the gates of Tikal National Park within an hour of its scheduled closing time. We had planned for this. It was the best and, perhaps, only way to experience a night spent amongst some of the largest and most impressive pyramids of the Western Hemisphere and amongst the jungle creatures and spirits that inhabit such a place, especially during this phase of the lunar cycle. Tonight there would be a full moon.

After entering the park and studying the layout and placement of the ancient structures for the better part of an hour, we crept quietly, unnoticed by the guards, down a lightly-worn path on the outskirts of the ruins. Here we would stay until the machine-gun toting vigilantes were relieved of their duty at around 10:00 P.M. As dusk soon arrived and twilight began to reign, it was time to continue our discussion.

"So are *you* Jewish?" Yael very wittingly proposed the question, "Or are you just an Israelite?"

"Is the Pope Catholic?" I countered, thinking it a clever response, "Or is he just Christian?"

"You would be better suited to ask," Trey now interceded into to conversation, "Is the Pope Christian? Or is he just Polish? That's what she is essentially asking. Seriously guys," he said to us, "I've got to relieve myself. But, don't worry. I won't wander off too far. Not in this place!" He grabbed a small hand-held flashlight from out of the nap-sack which was slung around his shoulder.

"Don't turn it on." Yael alerted him with little more than a slight whisper, barely audible among the sounds of the forest at night. Her training in the army was evident. "It would attract the attention of the guards," she warned us. "Have your eyes not adjusted yet?"

Complete darkness surrounded us. If it wasn't for the sound of their voices, I would have had to strain to make out even the vaguest of shapes that would assure me that my two companions were present. And if the moon had risen even the slightest bit above the eastern skyline, its light had not yet penetrated the thick jungle foliage which covered the treetops above. Yael was cat-like, a regular lioness, attentive and ready to learn. I began to teach her about Hezekiah King of Judah.

> **Hezekiah trusted in the Lord, the God of Israel. There was no one like him among all the kings of Judah, either before him or after him. He held fast to the Lord and did not cease to follow him; he kept the commands the Lord had given Moses. And the Lord was with him**
> **-2 Kings 18:5**

The snap of a twig. Trey was returning with a spring in his step that wasn't witnessed when he first tip-toed off down the path to urinate. "Did you hear that?"

We heard nothing.

"I think it was a warning." Thoughts rushed through my head...guards, machine-guns, *bandidos*, *fantasmas!*

"It sounded like a large feline." Trey tried to describe the noise without actually having to mimic the creature, for fear of being stalked, I assume.

"Did it sound big?" Yael was curious, her eyes searching, trying to pierce the darkness.

"Did it sound mad?" I inquired, placing equal importance on this question.

"Let's just say it wasn't purring," Trey said and left it at that.

We decided now would be a good time to leave our jungle hiding spot and enter into the temple complex. *The guards must have gone home by now.* As we made our way down the tree-tunneled *sendera* and prepared to exit the cover of the forest, a bright shining object was finally visible above the distant tree-line. A wonderfully full moon provided enough light for us to pause for a moment in awe of the entire array of pyramids that stood erect before us.

As we approached the main courtyard of the city, many of the buildings appeared to be in ruins. *How many battles must have been waged here?* I thought, and was reminded of my conversation with Yael. As we set our sights on Temple IV, I began to recant to her in a slightly louder voice; still, however, just a whisper in the stillness of the night.

"Sennacherib king of Assyria came and invaded Judah."

> **In the fourteenth year of King Hezekiah's reign, Sennacherib king of Assyria attacked all the fortified cities of Judah**
>
> **-2 Kings 18:13**

"When Hezekiah saw that Sennacherib intended to make war on Jerusalem, he reinforced the walls and prepared to defend the City of David."

We sat down on the remnants of an old stone barrier formed around the base of the monolithic structure. Moonlight glistened upon our faces.

> **Now Sennacherib received a report that Tirhakah, the Cushite king of Egypt, was marching out to fight against him.**
>
> **-2 Kings 19:9**

"Tirhakah belongs to the legendary 25th Dynasty of Egypt," I said to them, "a royal line of rulers descended from Menelik, son of King

Solomon and Queen Sheba. The Hebrew Cushite kings of Ethiopia of the Solomonic bloodline miraculously gained entire control of Egypt for a short span of time. It happened to be at a very crucial time for Jerusalem and the House of David, the tribes of Judah and Benjamin. Cushite King Piankhi, founder of the XXV dynasty, began the reunification of the Nile Valley at the time when the Assyrians were attacking Samaria and the tribes of Israel were scattered."

"This was quite a rapid rise to power by the Ethiopians, wouldn't you say?"

Yael was very observant. I decided to let her in on a little secret. "They were just a few generations removed from the sons of the Levite priests who left Jerusalem during the time of King Solomon. Now, they were returning. They were returning to Jerusalem with the Ark of the Covenant of the Lord, the Ten Commandments, the manna and Aaron's staff that budded. Remember the prophecy of King David?"

> **Princes and Princesses would soon come out of Egypt. Ethiopia would soon stretch forth her hands unto God.**
> **-Psalm 68:31**

Many rows of steps reached high into the sky, paving the steep ascent towards the highest pinnacle, a platform or room, perhaps an altar, at the top. From the ground below, we admired the impressive pyramid that surely rivaled those of Ancient Egypt.

"About 711 B.C., the Cushite kings of 25th dynasty completed the total reunification of Egypt and became the rulers of a huge empire which extended from the Mediterranean Sea south to the confluence of the Blue and White Nile Rivers, deep in the heart of Africa. Meanwhile, Hezekiah King of Judah was preparing for the return of the Ark of the Covenant to the Temple of the Lord in Jerusalem."

> **In the first month of the first year of his reign, he opened the doors of the temple of the Lord and repaired them. He said, "Listen to me Levites, consecrate yourselves now and consecrate the temple of the Lord, the God of your fathers."**
> **-2 Chronicles 29:3**

(consecrate is from the Latin *con-secretum*, meaning "with secret")

> **So the service of the temple of the Lord was reestablished. Hezekiah and all the people rejoiced at what God had brought about for his people, because it was done so quickly.**
> **-2 Chronicles 29:35**

"Thanks to the Cushites!" Trey announced.

> **There was great joy in Jerusalem, for since the days of Solomon son of David King of Israel there had been nothing like this in Jerusalem.**
> **-2 Chronicles 30:26**

"For first time in over 200 years the Ark of the Covenant had returned to the Temple of the Lord!"

> **The priests and the Levites stood to bless the people and God heard them, for their prayer reached heaven, his holy dwelling place.**
> **-2 Chronicles 30:27**

I felt blessed to be here, now, at this moment, staring in amazement at the old temple as it rose up in glory, a geometrically perfect design constructed with centuries-old, meticulously hand-carved stones of unknown origin. We stumbled up wooden ladders, decades old and rotting. We grasped for securely fastened roots and rocks as we scaled the south face of the four-sided ancient structure, reaching a measured height of 64 meters above the jungle floor. I called out to Yael and Trey, encouraging them in the words of Hezekiah King of Judah...

> **"Be strong and courageous. Do not be afraid or discouraged because of the king of Assyria and the vast army with him, for there is a greater power with us than**

> with him. With him is only the arm of flesh, but with us
> is the Lord our God to help us and to fight our battles."
> -2 Chronicles 32:7

"Do you know the word 'battle' comes from the Hebrew *badal*, meaning to divide or differ?" Yael made a keen observation as we struggled to reach the top level of the pyramid.

Standing on the last rung of the ladder, I balanced myself with my forearms, pulling my body over the edge and onto the flat platform that had been built at this upper level. The others soon followed, shimmying cautiously onto the planar portion of the pyramid where I now stood. Surprised at the magnificence of the architecture, we noticed a mysterious tent-like structure or sanctuary found at the pinnacle of the temple. We entered into it and kneeled down in prayer. We prayed for peace in the world. We prayed for the peace of Israel. As we finished the recitation, I opened up my backpack, took out my Bible and started to read...

> **Hezekiah received the letter from the messengers and read it. Then he went up to the temple and spread it out before the Lord. And Hezekiah prayed to the Lord: "O Lord, God of Israel, enthroned between the cherubim, you alone are God over all the kingdoms of the earth.**
> **-2 Kings 19:14**

"The Assyrian army surrounded Jerusalem and threatened to lay siege to it. What would become of Jerusalem? What fate would befall Judah?"

> **King Hezekiah and the prophet Isaiah cried out in prayer to heaven about this.**
> **-2 Chronicles 32:20**

The Lord declares in Isaiah 37:35 **"I will defend this city and save it, for my sake and for the sake of David my servant."**

The moon hung directly overhead, seemingly almost within reach. With arms outstretched, raised towards the hovering globe as it reflected the bright sunlight of a distant star, I and any other nocturnal beings that dared be active at such an hour were treated to a show of celestial grandeur.

> **That night the angel of the Lord went out and put to death a hundred and eighty-five thousand men in the Assyrian camp.**
>
> **-2 Kings 19:3**

This account is also recorded in Isaiah 37:38 and 2Chronicles 32:21.

[Ten years later, as I write these words concerning the Lord's rescue of Jerusalem and the supernatural powers held by the Ark of the Covenant, my health has begun to degrade. My knee is largely swollen and the infection is spreading quickly. The abscess is filled with pockets of puss and the pressure is mounting. I am losing feeling throughout my appendage and am worried that amputation may be the final result. I continue reading from my Bible, not understanding the sick irony of the situation.

> **In those days Hezekiah became ill and was at the point of death.**
>
> **The prophet Isaiah went to him and said, "This is what the Lord says: You are going to die; you will not recover."**
>
> **-Isaiah 38:1**

Is it merely a coincidence? Why should I suffer the same illness as the King of Judah? I pray for relief, for the pain to subside, to cease, to end. No more anguish can I take. Oh Lord, I cry, save me from an untimely death!

> 'This is what the Lord, the God of your father David, says: I have heard your prayer and seen your tears; I will heal you.
>
> **-2 Kings 20:5**

> **Then Isaiah said, "Prepare a poultice of figs." They did so and applied it to the boil, and he recovered.**
> **-2 Kings 20:7]**

During that night, after hours of enlightened bliss, the moon completed its majestic arch through the heavens and tucked itself behind our temple refuge, the largest native structure in all of Meso-America. Clouds of moist, thick fog rolled in across the miles and miles of impenetrable jungle, blanketing everything in their path. The pre-dawn moments had brought on a damp and hazy dream. Even before the first hint of light cut through the thick primordial soup, the primates had begun to awaken. Grotesque shrieks and ear-piercing screams echoed throughout the ruins. These were the howlers, the Congo monkeys, announcing the beginning of a new day with such deep bellows, unbefitting of their small size.

We could hear voices as well; human voices. The first tourists had arrived and were making their way up the series of ladders and stairs that led to the top of the pyramid. Unbeknownst to them, there we remained, drenched with morning dew and bathed in the moonlit glory of the night before.

"Buenos Días. Hola. Qué tal?"

Trying to be considerate we smiled back and decided to leave them to the morning solitude which they so desired. Soon, waves of people would be arriving; tour-busses by the dozens would carry excited travelers from all over the world to this ancient Mayan city of Tikal. We had accomplished our goal and were content in quietly descending in the same manner in which we came. One by one, we cautiously lowered our tired bodies down the side of the temple.

"The Ark of the Covenant left the temple soon after the death of King Hezekiah." We resumed the conversation. "The very positive reign of Hezekiah was, unfortunately, succeeded by his evil-doing son Manasseh."

> **Manasseh was twelve years old when he became king, and he reigned in Jerusalem fifty-five years. He did evil in the eyes of the Lord**
> **-2 Chronicles 33:1**

> **He rebuilt the high places (each and every bamah) his father Hezekiah had destroyed; he also erected altars to Baal**
>
> -2 Kings 21:3

"We read in the Bible that Manasseh shed so much innocent blood that he filled Jerusalem from end to end- besides the sin that he had caused Judah to commit," I told them.

A very opinionated Trey added, "I really don't think the priesthood would have tolerated the degrading and polluting of the Temple of the Lord containing the Ark of the Covenant."

He was correct.

King Taharka and the Levites, after delivering the Ark to King Hezekiah and rescuing Jerusalem from the Assyrian army, returned by the way in which they came.

Assyria, however, having established control over Palestine, turned its attention to towards Egypt. King Taharka and the Cushites continually fought to protect the Nile Valley from the Assyrians led in force by Esarhaddon, the son and successor of Sennacherib. This occurred as the Ark of the Covenant was in movement from Jerusalem back up the Nile River. In order to divert Esarhaddon and the Assyrians, Taharka stimulated revolts at Sidon and Tyre in Phoenicia.

The Assyrians, however, did not let the matter rest. In 671 B.C., after failing at his first attempt at invasion, Esarhaddon succeeded in capturing the ancient capital of Memphis and plundering it. His successor Assurbanipal marched into Upper Egypt and ransacked the ancient city of Thebes, pushing the Cushites back up the Nile towards Ethiopia.

"Why do you think the Assyrians were so persistent?" I asked. "Was it purely retaliation and revenge against the Hebrew Cushites for having helped protect Jerusalem and Judah against Sennacherib and the Assyrian army?"

"Of course not!" Yael was enlivened. "They were obviously chasing the Ark of the Covenant!"

Yes, indeed, The Ark of the Covenant.

In 664 B.C., Cushite King Taharka, Pharaoh of the 25th Dynasty, died. The ruins of a replicated Jewish Temple have been found on a remote island of the Nile River in Egypt. The structure, built before 650 B.C., precisely matches the dimensions of the Temple of the Lord in Jerusalem. Historical evidence shows that a colony of Jews, including Levitical priests, left Israel and found refuge here. Again in 633 B.C., the Assyrians invaded Egypt and pillaged its ancient cities, massacred its inhabitants and emptied the temples of their treasures. Were they still in search of the Ark?

I believe so.

KINGDOM OF JUDAH		25th DYNASTY (CUSHITES)	ASSYRIA
		Piankhi	
Hezekiah	*701 B.C.	Shabaka	Sennacherib
Manasseh		Taharka	Esarhaddon
		Tantamani	
Amon			Assurbanipal
Josiah			
Jehoiahaz			
Jehoiakim			
Zedekiah	*586 B.C.		

Just a short time after the death of King Manasseh, his grandson Josiah became ruler over the kingdom of Judah and brought great reform to the Jews.

2Chronicles 34:1 Josiah was eight years old when he became king, and he reigned in Jerusalem thirty-one years.

Towards the end of his reign, the Assyrian Empire had fallen from power and a short time of peace was enjoyed in Israel. The Ark of the Covenant was able to, once again, be safely carried down the

Nile and brought to the Passover celebrations in Jerusalem. King Josiah of Judah made a plea for its safe return to the temple…

> **He said to the Levites, who instructed all Israel and who had been consecrated to the Lord: "Put the sacred ark in the temple that Solomon son of David king of Israel built. It is not to be carried about on your shoulders.**
> **-2 Chronicles 35:3**

They had been wandering through the desert carrying the Ark, as prescribed, by the long poles on top of their shoulders.

> **The king stood by the pillar and renewed the covenant in the presence of the Lord**
> **-2 Kings 23:3**

> **The Passover had not been observed like this in Israel since the days of the prophet Samuel; and none of the kings of Israel had ever celebrated such a Passover as did Josiah, with the priests, the Levites and all Judah and Israel who were there with the people of Jerusalem.**
> **-2 Chronicles 35:18**

Why was this Passover so different, you might ask? Well…that's because this year the Ark of the Covenant was in plain sight of all of Israel and Judah, carried by the Levites upon their shoulders, not placed inside the Temple, but in full view of everyone! Never before were things done in such a manner.

Nevertheless, the Lord did not turn away from the heat of his fierce anger, which burned against Judah because of all that Manasseh had done to provoke him to anger. So the Lord said, "I will remove Judah also from my presence as I removed Israel….
-2 Kings 23:26

CHAPTER 11

Cynthia Ann Parker, the nine year old daughter of newly-arrived Anglo settlers, was captured in an 1836 Comanche Indian raid. Stolen away on horseback and carried throughout the night across the Central Texas prairie, she would not be seen again by her family for another twenty-four years. During this time she lived as an Indian princess, was cared for by the tribe and, eventually, became the wife of brave chief Pete Nocona.

Many years later, a bronze-skinned, blonde-haired Indian squaw by the name of Nadua, or "someone found", was recaptured by Texas Rangers during a surprise attack on a Comanche campground. Nadua, known previously as Cynthia Ann Parker, was brought back to "civilization" and reunited with her parents. No longer fluent in English, nor comfortable in Anglo society, she demanded to return to her husband Chief Nocona and the tribe. Never having been permitted to do so, Cynthia Ann Parker starved herself to death, committing suicide.

Quanah Parker, last great chief of the Comanches, was born in southern Oklahoma in 1845, the son of Cynthia Ann Parker and Pete Nocona. In 1875, while suffering from a near-fatal wound, the "half-breed" Indian received treatment from a *curandero,* a native healer who prescribed for him the medicine acquired from a certain cactus plant. *Lophophora williamsii,* also known as Peyote, was used because of its powerful natural antibiotics that cure infection. Used spiritually for thousands of years by Native Americans, this particular species contains strong psychic and hallucinogenic properties. It was during this experience that Quanah Parker claimed he heard the voice of Jesus Christ. The great Comanche chief and warrior would profess that Jesus appeared to him in a vision, sent from the Great Father, and told him to repent, atone for his many killings and misdeeds, forsake a life of violence and conflict and take the Peyote religion to Indian peoples everywhere.

During his lifetime, Quanah Parker integrated into society, made hunting trips with President Theodore Roosevelt and became a wealthy and successful investor. He is also the founder of the Native American Church. Parker taught that Peyote was a sacrament given to Indians by Jesus. He taught about the "Peyote Road", a life consisting of brotherly love, family care, self-support through work and avoidance of alcohol and recreational drug-use. A good life, in his view, was one of kindness, responsibility and, above all else, one that embodies love.

The Peyote cactus is native to the southwestern United States and found throughout central Mexico. Its cultivation is regulated by the United States Drug Enforcement Agency which gives out 225 permits a year to *peyoteros* who legally collect the plant specimens for use by Native Americans, specifically those who are members of the Native Church. These "peyoteros" must also register with the Texas Department of Public Safety. The harvested "buttons", found growing on the top center portion of the cactus, are boiled in water to produce a psychoactive tea of which the effects last 10-12 hours. It is highly recommended that an experienced "guide" be present during a peyote ceremony.

> "The white man goes to his church and talks about Jesus. The Indian goes to his tepee and talks to Jesus."
> -Quanah Parker, last chief of the Comanches

Diego was a shaman, although by his outward appearance he looked like any other Guatemalan selling his wares along the crowded streets of the bustling marketplace. This was Panajachel, sometimes called "Gringotenango" because of the number of tourists that can be found here on any given day. A mile above sea-level, on the banks of Lake Atitlán, vendors line the cobblestone avenues plying their trade. Bargain-hunters and shoppers rub elbows with Mayan Indians clothed in bright, traditionally-embroidered outfits. The smell of roasting corn fills the air, as does the sound of continuous shouts from shoeshine boys offering their services to potential customers.

Twelve small pueblos surround the lake, each one bearing the name of one of Jesus' disciples. I was staying on the opposite side of the lake in the tiny village of San Pedro. A quick ferry ride shuttled me back over to 'Pana' this morning in order to attend the market. The brisk night-time temperatures of the Guatemalan highlands had brought me in search of a hand-knit *pancho,* or jacket, to wear. I browsed the marketplace, passing small shops and kiosks, shaking my head and politely refusing the many items offered to me for purchase.

Diego approached. *"Usted quiere un tambor?"* He wanted to sell me a hand-crafted drum made from native wood and sheep skin.

"No gracias." I turned down the offer.

"Una flauta?" Would I like to buy a flute?

"Tampoco." Neither do I wish to purchase a flute.

"Entonces, que le ofrezco?" Was there anything at all that I desired?

Well...*there was something*. After spending time in the rainforest and being surrounded by such incredible bio-diversity, I had developed a growing interest in studying more about the native *flora* of the region. After all, I had really always been fascinated by Botany.

"Quisiera aprender de las plantas medicinales. I'd like to learn about medicinal plants," I told him. It would be nice to learn more about the healing properties of *Aloe Vera,* or perhaps the many uses of the banana tree.

"Come to San Pablo," Diego accommodatingly replied, "and I will teach you."

That would be great, but I would be leaving Atitlán in just a couple of days.

"Thank you, but there's not enough time." I voiced my concern and regret.

He assured me however, that two days was more than enough time to learn about medicinal plants. We agreed to meet the following morning.

Rule # 1: Never break a date with a medicine-man.

With a little coercing from my friends, I disregarded my scheduled appointment with Diego and decided, instead, to join them on a weekend trip to the local fair in Quetzaltenango, or Xela *(shay-la)* as the locals call it. After an enjoyable two-day excursion, I returned home to the small house we had been renting on the shores of Lake Atitlán where I received twice daily visits from Tzutujilspeaking Mayan girls carrying bowls of fruit on their heads and offering up their bounty. Mangoes, passion fruit, oranges; Relaxation comes easy in this tranquil setting.

I had just reclined peacefully in the swaying hammock, peeled back the pinkish red skin of an apple-banana and prepared to make an entry into my journal when, lo and behold, who comes strolling up the walkway, but Diego. *How on Earth did he find me here? Did he come to confront me on why I'd skipped the lesson?* Embarrassed for not having followed through with our plans, I thought of a million excuses. None was acceptable.

"I'm sorry, I...just didn't..."

"No worries," Diego said as he calmly lifted the thick, heavy necklace, placing it over my head and around my neck. It draped and dangled, hanging down past my ribcage to my lower abdomen. "These stones were found by my grandfather in the fields. He was a shaman. He lived to be 115 years old." Upon closer examination, one of the larger rocks seemed to be a carved Mayan figure of some sort. "The necklace helps one learn about and find the plants," he said.

We quickly rescheduled our appointment. Diego suggested I arrive at his house at 5:00 P.M., where we would start talking around 7, 8, 9 or 10 o'clock. I spent the next half hour contemplating the journey, gathering a few things to take along with me and preparing myself for the two-hour walk to San Pablo.

The heavily-worn footpath leading from the edge of town wasn't difficult to locate and I followed where it led, up rolling hills, gently down again, over rocks, through mud puddles and around the lagoon. You would think this would be a familiar trek for the local townspeople, wouldn't you? No other human shared the path with me that day as solitude and serenity were my only companions. Across slanted hillsides planted in coffee bushes, under the shade of high-reaching hardwoods and into forests of unfamiliar trees and shrubs continued the now lightly-traversed trail until, surprisingly, the outskirts of Diego's *pueblito* were visible up ahead. *Ay, por fin!* Finally.

The unpaved main avenue of San Pablo de la Laguna gradually ascended uphill, flanked on each side by stray dogs and old men. Tired Senoras swept dirt floors with stick-brooms while dust-covered children stirred up what little trouble they could. The impoverished village consisted mostly of shantilly built shacks of the most humble proportions, a few adobe buildings and a handful of sturdier structures made from cinder-blocks and cement. Diego's house was constructed of sun-baked, earthen bricks and mortar, covered by a heavily oxidized tin roof. Hiking past side-streets and alleyways, I happened upon one of his children playing in the street.

"Are you looking for someone?" asked the scraggily dressed, barefoot *niño*.

"Yes. Do you know where I can find Diego?" I wondered as to the likelihood of ever actually locating him in a place like this. *How many Diegos could there be in this town?*

"Of course, he's my father! Come with me." I followed the boy down a skinny corridor, past some gaunt, unhealthy looking chickens and into a tiny hut. By this time, two or three of his brothers had gathered to have a look at the *extranjero,* the strange foreigner who had just arrived at their home. It was 5 o'clock sharp.

"*Dónde está tu papa?*" I inquired of one of the boys. *Was Diego even around today?*

I heard the loud voices of Indian women as they scolded their children, carried on conversations and cooked tortillas over an open fire. The door, slightly cracked open, and a small south-facing window combined to let in a very miniscule amount of natural light.

"He's not here right now. He will come later," one of the boys finally answered.

I yanked on the metal chain of an old brass lamp covered in cobwebs. *Good, it works.* I could see a straw mattress lying on the dirt floor, fit snugly up against the mud walls of the hut. Extra scraps of sheep skin, whole blocks and partial shavings of wood and some old clothes left by travelers littered the corner of the cramped room. One by one, two by two a total of, maybe, eight kids filed into the room. I assumed they were all part of Diego's brood. Some gawked, some stared, and still others asked questions.

"Do you believe in God?" The boy was partially blind. This much I could figure from the way his eyeball rotated downward in its socket, the pupil straining to rise up from below the lower eyelid. Mostly only the cornea was visible with its microscopic red veins and thin capillaries crisscrossing and zigzagging where normally an eye would be seen.

"Yes, I believe in God."

"Good," he said, "Because some people who come here don't believe in God."

They served me a small portion of black beans and scrambled eggs in a plastic bowl and a few lukewarm tortillas wrapped in a napkin. I ate alone. After quizzing me for the better part of an hour about my beliefs and intentions, they had left me to the solitude of the single room. I didn't hesitate in consuming what little food they had brought me. I spooned the entire contents of the bowl into one measly tortilla, wrapped it up, folded it over and called it a *burrito*. A cup of bitter-tasting coffee, still mildly hot, helped to wash down the second dry, plain tortilla. I took a few swigs and emptied the mug, the last few drops of liquid sliding down my esophagus.

Although a relatively small meal, the hunger pangs had now disappeared for good. *The tortillas must have expanded in my belly.* I felt satisfied, content and quite bored honestly, sitting there all alone in such tight quarters. I eagerly awaited a nice sugary desert to quell the bitter taste in my mouth, but none came. There was provided, however, a beat-up, weathered old Bible laying on the wooden *escritorio.* I picked it up and pondered reading a while. No use. Sleep came over me. I tried to fight it, but was overwhelmed, too tired to remain awake for even a moment longer. It must have been shortly after 8:00 P.M. *Strange, I never go to bed this early.* Placing my weary body gently down on the prickly straw mattress, I shut my eyes and quickly drifted off to Dreamland.

Who knows exactly how much time elapsed before Diego arrived? I never saw him enter. We sat down on the dirt floor, legs crossed Indian-style in the middle of the room. I honestly can't remember if there was a small fire burning, but it seems as if there may have been. He began to speak…"I am a shaman. My father was a shaman. And his father, too. The word 'shaman' comes from the Hebrew *Shamayim,* meaning lofty or heavenly, also referring sometimes to an Astrologer. It has come to signify one who guides spiritually, one who helps others on their journey and one who communes with the heavenly realm. I will be your facilitator."

Diego could tell I was nervous. "Just relax and breathe deeply. Remain peaceful and calm. There is nothing to fear." I had a feeling as though we were flying.

He continued, "I am a Hebrew Israelite. A group of my ancestors left Jerusalem around 597 B.C. during the reign of Johoiakim King of Judah. Escaping just before the destruction of Jerusalem by the Babylonians, they came to settle here in this land. They brought with them a record inscribed on brass plates containing Genesis and other books of Moses, as well as scriptures down to Isaiah."

I started to put two and two together. "So you're Mormon?"

"I am many things," Diego replied. "However, yes, this scripture has been handed down within the Church of Latter Day Saints. The prophet Nephi states in the first verse of the Book of Mormon...

'I make a record in the language of my father, which consists of the learning of the Jews and the language of the Egyptians.'"

My mind flashed back to the deserts of Utah and the conversations I had with Paul....*Zarahemla!* I thought.

...And it came to pass that I, being 11 years old, was carried by my father into the land southward, even to the land of Zarahemla; the whole face of the land having become covered with building, and the people were as numerous almost, as it were the sand of the sea...And there began to be much peace in the land; and the people began to be very numerous, and began to scatter abroad upon the face of the earth; yea, on the north and on the south, on the east and on the west, building large cities and villages in all the quarters of the land...And I, Nephi did build a temple; and I did construct it in the manner of the temple of Solomon.

I remembered the expansive grandeur of the city of Tikal, of Chichén-Itzá, and of the ruins at Palenque. I knew the most widely accepted modern theory proposed that the Mayans appeared here in Central America sometime between 1000 B.C. and the Christian era and that their civilization was derived from ancient Egypt. *But, how? Why? I.....*

"You are on a vision quest," said Diego. "However, it is not only what you see that is important, but what you hear on your journey as well. Listen closely. The Lord has searched your heart and found you to be a humble servant. He is aware of your questions and will answer them. You must, then, reveal these things to the children of Noah, strengthen the faith of the faithful, and provide a sign for those who are yet to believe."

A vision quest? Did I ask for this? Questions? What questions could possibly be answered?

I opened my eyes, confused as to what had occurred. My shirt now dampened with cool perspiration, I was not uncomfortable by any means. *But, why was I sweating? Had I been dreaming?* The noises of an Independence Day celebration echoed outside the earthen hut; water boiling, the seething and popping of meat cooking on a grill, the sound of feet running, shuffling, walking. Men and women, young and old, little children, boys and girls, together they enjoyed the happy, festive occasion. It was September 15. *What time is it? Where is Diego?* I looked down at tense fingers and white knuckles, my hands clutching the ancient stone necklace still worn securely around my neck. *Questions?* I remembered the words Buck had uttered a month ago in the airport in Cancún, *"Find the Ark, trace its movements, know its importance, solve the mystery."*

But, I had. At least, I thought I had. I pondered back upon Natty's challenge as he directed me to yet another mystery…the state names. *Find the names of the United States that are Hebrew, Greek and Arabic in origin! That must be it!*

Still another question, a most important one, lingered inside my head and weighed on my mind. *Am I a………?* My head tilted back and rested where it laid, the sheer weight of it becoming too difficult for my neck muscles to support. With heavy eyelids I fought to stay awake, but to no avail. Diego would soon return.

> **Call to me and I will answer you and tell you great and unsearchable things you do not know.**
> **-Jeremiah 33:3**

"Jeremiah was a prophet." Diego began to teach. "The word of the Lord came to him during the reign of Josiah, and through the reign of Jehoiakim, down to the fifth month of the eleventh year of Zedekiah, when the people of Jerusalem went into exile."

The wind began to blow, seemingly through the mud walls of the building. There lay a Bible in front of us on the ground. A gentle breeze stirred inside the hut, the thin pages of the book beginning to turn. I looked at Diego.

"Go ahead," he said. And peering down at the text, I saw certain verses seemed to be highlighted, almost glowing radiantly. I started to read as the pages turned effortlessly with every new gust of wind.

> **This is how Jerusalem was taken: In the ninth year of Zedekiah king of Judah, Nebuchadnezzar king of Babylon marched against Jerusalem with his whole army and laid siege to it.**
>
> **-Jeremiah 39:1**

"Jeremiah was often in danger from political and religious leaders who were angry because of his messages. He had been warning them for years about the coming invasion by the Babylonians. King Zedekiah was furious because of it and had Jeremiah imprisoned within the courtyard of the guard.

> **Now Zedekiah king of Judah had imprisoned him there, saying, "Why do you prophecy the way you do? You say, 'This is what the Lord says: I am about to hand this city over to the king of Babylon, and he will capture it."**
>
> **-Jeremiah 32:3**

"God handed all of them over to Nebuchadnezzar," Diego said in a hushed tone. The wind blew....

> **He carried to Babylon all the articles from the temple of God, both large and small, and the treasures of the Lord's temple and the treasures of the king and his officials. They set fire to God's temple and broke down the wall of Jerusalem; they burned all the palaces and destroyed everything of value.**
>
> **-2 Chronicles 36:18**

Without coal nor wood, nor fuel to even fan them, flames jumped up from the dirt floor and grew in heat and intensity. In an increasingly louder voice, Diego continued…"Nebuchadnezzar set fire to the temple of the Lord, the royal palace and all the houses of Jerusalem. Every important building he burned down."

Diego took a sip of water, swished it around in his mouth then spit on the ground. The fire sizzled and popped and was quickly extinguished. "Zedekiah's sons, the princes of Judah, were killed in front of his very eyes. The king of Judah was, then, blinded and led away to Babylon."

> **There at Riblah the king of Babylon slaughtered the sons of Zedekiah before his eyes; he also killed all the officials of Judah. Then he put out Zedekiah's eyes, bound him with bronze shackles and took him to Babylon, where he put him in prison till the day of his death.**
> **-Jeremiah 52:10**

"Nebuchadnezzar, king of Babylon, ruled the vast Chaldean Empire…."

> **Now I will hand all your countries over to my servant Nebuchadnezzar king of Babylon; I will make even the wild animals subject to him. All nations will serve him and his son and his grandson until the time for his land comes; then many nations and great kings will subjugate him.**
> **-Jeremiah 27:6**

"Jeremiah calls him a servant of God. Nebuchadnezzar writes a letter…**'To the peoples, nations and men of every language, who live in all the world: May you prosper greatly! It is my pleasure to tell you about the miraculous signs and wonders that the Most High God has performed for me.'** It is said that four kings reigned over the entire earth; Solomon, Ahab, Nebuchadnezzar and Cyrus."

I certainly knew about Solomon and Ahab and the global adventures of the Israelites. *But, Nebuchadnezzar, King of Babylon? Did the Babylonians travel the world?*

"They would reach new frontiers in Alaska and Nebraska," Diego informed me. "The state of Nebraska was so named because of its Arabic meaning. The same is true of Alaska. *Nabu* is the personal God of Nebuchadnezzar and can be translated as 'guardian.' The word *aqsa* means 'the furthest frontier.' *Nebraska* is Nebuchadnezzar's furthest frontier."

"And Alaska is simply *Al-aska,* 'the furthest frontier!'" Wow! This is amazing!

"Of course, it carries the same meaning as Al-aqsa, the famous mosque in Jerusalem," Diego added, as if I should already know. "Nebuchadnezzar ruled over North Africa all the way to Spain or *Iberia*. He appears to have rebuilt or restored almost every city or temple in Babylon, Southern Iraq. 9/10ths of all bricks are stamped with his name. And, more than that, the name of the state of California, thought to have come from a historic Spanish novel published in 1510 by Montalvo, is really Arabic in origin."

He paused long enough for me to think for a moment…the word reverberating repeatedly inside my brain. Ca-li-for-ni-a. *California.* Five syllables, three words. Caliph…ore…nia. *That's it! It has to be!*

Shocked at this new revelation, I ran it by Diego seeking acknowledgement and approval. "*Caliph* is the name given to the leader of the global Islamic nation, *ore* is the word for gold or precious metals of any kind, and *nia* is a common suffix meaning 'the land of.' *Caliph, ore, nia*. Caliph's new land of gold and precious metals! California!"

"Very good. Now get some rest," Diego ordered.

"But…I'm not tired! Wait a minute!" *What about Jeremiah? What about the royal bloodline of Judah?* "King Zedekiah's sons are dead! The Lord promised that 'David will never fail to have a man to sit on the throne of the House of Israel.' What has become of Israel?" The more knowledge and insight I gained, the more questions I seemed to have. Diego didn't seem to care. Frozen stiff as a board, with only a slightly comforting stare and a partial smile, he softly whispered, "Go to sleep."

What? Where am I? I sat up in bed. *I'm still here.* The dream seemed so vivid, so clear. I looked around. *Where is Diego?* I heard old men singing, women laughing, the strumming of guitars. It's September 15. *What time is it? I must have been sleeping for hours. Should I go outside, maybe join the celebration?* I looked down noticing that my hands still cradled the ancient stone necklace in their sweaty palms. I attempted to stand. Legs unwilling, I reclined back onto the mattress, too tired to move. There was an open Bible beside me on the bed. *Had I been reading?* Passages of the Scripture stood out, boldly underlined in red.

> Now Nebuchadnezzar king of Babylon had given these orders about Jeremiah … "Take him and look after him; don't harm him but do for him whatever he asks."…So the commander of the guard and all the other officers of the king of Babylon sent and had Jeremiah taken out of the courtyard of the guard….after he had found Jeremiah bound in chains among all the captives from Jerusalem and Judah who were being carried into exile to Babylon…When the commander of the guard found Jeremiah, he said to him…"Today I am freeing you from the chains on your wrists. Come with me to Babylon, if you like, and I will look after you; but if you do not want to, then don't come. Look, the whole country lies before you; go wherever you please." Then the commander gave him provisions and a present and let him go.

A gust of wind. I was awake this time! *Or was I?* The pages flipped and settled open to the first chapter…

> Jeremiah was appointed by the Lord as a prophet to the nations.

A prophet? To the nations?

> "See, today I appoint you over nations and kingdoms to uproot, tear down, to destroy and overthrow, to build and to plant."

>   -Jeremiah 1:10
>
> "...for I am with you and will rescue you," declares the Lord.

I must have closed my eyes. Diego and I were again sitting face to face on the floor of the hut. My shaman guide then reached out his hand and with the tip of an index finger pressed firmly against my forehead, smudged dry ashes onto my skin in the shape of the Star of David. "The small band of survivors, the remnant of Judah, was very few in number," he told me. "Included in the group were Jeremiah, Baruch 'the scribe' and two princesses of Judah. They were the daughters of King Zedekiah who was blinded and taken away to Babylon by Nebuchadnezzar."

The Royal bloodline of Judah, I thought. *Will the line of kings continue? Who will sit on the throne of Israel?*

"Jeremiah had been placed in charge of the daughters of Zedekiah. He was priest and prophet of the small group of Jews that remained; their spiritual advisor."

> **All the people from the least to the greatest approached Jeremiah the prophet and said to him, "Please hear our petition and pray to the Lord your God for this entire remnant. For as you now see, though we were once many, now only a few are left. Pray that the Lord your God will tell us where we should go and what we should do."**
>   **-Jeremiah 42:1**

"Do not go to Egypt," Jeremiah warned them, "It is unsafe. Hear the word of the Lord, O remnant of Judah..."

> **Indeed, all who are determined to go to Egypt to settle there will die**
>   **-Jeremiah 42:17**

Diego looked me squarely in the eyes. "They didn't listen. Instead, they led away all the men, women and children, the king's daughters, Jeremiah the prophet and Baruch 'the scribe.'" The page turned.

> **So they entered into Egypt in disobedience to the Lord and went as far as Tahpanes.**
> **-Jeremiah 43:7**

"To this day," Diego said, "there is a palace there called 'Quasr bint el Jehudi', the palace of the daughter of Judah. The prophet Jeremiah stayed there for a while continuing to warn of the impending doom. He called an assembly for all the Jews living in Lower and Upper Egypt. Still...they refused to listen. **'Go ahead then...'** Jeremiah told them, **'But all Jews living in Egypt will perish. Those who escape will be very few.'** He turned to Baruch his faithful scribe and companion and informed him, **'For I will bring disaster on all people, declares the Lord, but wherever you go I will let you escape with your life.'** Wisely, Baruch decided to leave. He would accompany Jeremiah and the princesses of Judah, together, as they fled the destruction of Egypt. It was said to Zedekiah king of Judah before he was led away to Babylon...**'Take off the turban, remove the crown, It will not be as it was.'"**

But, who will wear the crown? I questioned. *Who will sit on the throne of Israel?*

> **'A great eagle with powerful wings, long feathers and full plumage of varied colors came to Lebanon. Taking hold of the top of a cedar, he broke off its topmost shoot and carried it away to a land of merchants, where he planted it in a city of traders.'**
> **-Ezekiel 17: 3**

Diego took hold of my hands. "Come with me," he said. My body seemed weightless, as if it were gearing up for levitation. Within the blink of an eye I was flying...*like a bird, like an eagle!* I looked down and all around. *Where is my body?* We exited the atmosphere Diego and I, approaching Venus. I could hear his voice, *"Venus, second in order from the sun..."*

As we orbited in elliptical fashion Earth's neighboring planet, a beautiful round sphere loomed in the distance, *100 million miles away, 78 percent water, almost seven billion people and countless different species of life.* Closer and closer we traveled, into the Stratosphere, until breaking through a layer of thick clouds with such speed that I was temporarily blinded. My blurred vision becoming increasingly clearer, I could see a body of water down below. *Atitlán.*

We quickly descended upon the small pueblo of San Pablo. The door to the hut remained open and I saw my body as it rested peacefully on the old straw mattress inside the earthen structure. *My body!*

Before realizing what was happening I re-entered into my bodily form, encapsulated in the still stationary vessel. I opened my eyes in a squint as bright sunlight leaked into the room. *It has to be mid-morning, already.* I sat up in bed, thus causing a ripped and wrinkled piece of paper to fall from my chest. *The handwriting looks familiar....Wait, I wrote this! I must have torn it from out of my journal.* I read the scribbled message...

Job 38:31 Can you bind together the sweet influences the Pleiades? Can you loose the cords of Orion?

I thought for a moment...*the stars...the constellations?* That's it! *Pleiades comes from Greek, meaning 'I navigate.'* I stood up, walked over to the wooden table, grabbed my diary and opened it to the last entry. I had indeed been writing the night before....

September 15

They met while in Egypt. As the daughter of King Zedekiah, Tamar was a Judean princess left in the care of the prophet Jeremiah. Heremon, a Judean prince born in Spain to Milesius of the tribe of Judah and Merian of the tribe of Dan., was to be crowned High King of Ireland. Remember the birth of the twin sons of Judah? And the scarlet cord? The Zerah line of Judean Kings has been ruling across all of Europe. By this time they've established colonies in Spain,

Ireland and Britain. Spain or *Iberia* is 'Hebrew's land' remember? Ireland or *Hibernia* is 'Hebrew's new land.'

In the year 582 B.C. there arrived by boat in Northern Ireland a group of three travelers which included an old man called Ollam Fodhla, his secretary, and a beautiful princess named Tamar. In their possession was a large, strongly-secured chest, a cargo crate which they guarded with utmost care. The aging Ollam Fodhla was known as a teacher and a legislator, his laws sharing a striking similarity to the Ten Commandments. *Ollam* in Hebrew means 'world' and can also be read as 'ancient' or 'secret.' It is the modern Irish word for 'professor.' Fodhla or *fola* can be understood to mean 'wonderful.' All indications point to this person being a Hebrew prophet. The individual mentioned as a secretary is sometimes called Simon Breck, Brach or Berach.

Incidentally, BRK is the origin of the word 'bark' which, in turn, was used as paper (from *papyr*us) by early scribes on which they recorded important events. Tamar is often referred to as Tea Tephi, translated from Hebrew as 'beautiful wanderer.' These three travelers are, you guessed it, Jeremiah the prophet, Baruch the scribe and Tamar, King Zedekiah's daughter, the princess of Judah!

Upon arriving in Ireland, Tamar was married to King Heremon as Jeremiah presided over the wedding ceremony. Together, the royal couple ruled from Tara, the ancient seat of the high kings of Ireland, just to the northwest of present-day Dublin. The name Tara is derived from the Hebrew word *Torah,* meaning 'the law', a fitting name seeing as how Jeremiah or Ollam Fodhla is considered to be 'the lawgiver.' Some even say he was the first to hold the parliament of Tara.

Jeremiah 31:37 This is what the lord says:

Only when the sun no longer shines by day, or the moon and stars by night, **"will the descendents of Israel ever cease to be a nation before me."** With the marriage of Tamar and Heremon, the Zerah line of Judah united with the Pharez line of Judean kings. All the kings of Ireland and Scotland are descended from this royal bloodline of Judah. Contained within the large and heavy cargo chest which they transported, Jeremiah, Baruch and Tamar brought with them a large stone, called in Irish 'Lia Fail', meaning the Stone of Destiny. Upon this stone, Heremon and Tamar were crowned King and Queen of Ireland. This is the famous Bethel stone, the pillar upon which Jacob Israel rested his head while dreaming.

> **When he reached a certain place, he stopped for the night because the sun had set. Taking one of the stones there, he put it under his head and lay down to sleep. He had a dream in which he saw a stairway resting on the earth, with its top reaching to heaven, and the angels of God were ascending and descending on it. There above it stood the Lord, and he said, "I am the Lord, the God of your father Abraham and the God of Isaac. I will give you and your descendants the land on which you are lying. Your descendents will be like the dust of the earth, and you will spread out to the west and to the east, to the north and to the south. All peoples of the earth will be blessed by your offspring.**
> **-Genesis 28:11**

The stone has come to be the symbolic throne of Israel. Weighing over 300 pounds, rectangular in shape, about 26" in length, 16" in width and 10.5" high, it has visible worn grooves due to the constant carrying of it by poles. After all, it was carried by the Israelites for 40 years as they wandered through the desert. Now having been transported from Jerusalem to Ireland by the prophet, the king's daughter and the scribe, it was kept for three centuries at Tara, Ireland where all the descending kings and queens were crowned upon on it. To this day it remains the coronation stone of Great Britain upon which the British monarchs take the famous Oath.

Archeological excavations at Tara have revealed that it was not only the ancient Royal Seat and the capital, but also the main hub or nerve center. Five great roads spread out from Tara to various parts of the country, but no similar rock formations of this type exist in the British Isles. However, sandstone has been found near the Red Sea at Bethel in Palestine which is geologically the same as this Stone of Destiny. Three miles north of Tara is Dowd's Town. *Dowd* is the Irish pronunciation of the Hebrew form of David, or DVD. The prophet Jeremiah brought the teachings of the Torah to Ireland, instituting laws, schools and congresses. In doing so, he laid the foundation of the advanced education system known to have existed in ancient Ireland before the Christian era, consisting of dozens of colleges and universities.

The great Ollam Fodhla and Queen Tea Tephi were both buried at Tara. And, although archeological digs are not permitted into the mounds themselves, it is speculated that inside the casket of Tea Tephi is the harp of King David. Until recently, the Irish flag had the symbol of a harp as its ensign, having long been a national emblem of Ireland. Ancient Tara lies with the confines of the province of Ulster in the present-day county of Meath. The flag of Ulster, incredibly enough, has been represented for many years with a red hand mounted on a Star of David under a royal crown; the red hand being significant because of the scarlet cord tied to the hand of Zerah, twin brother of Pharez, twin son of Judah. The design on the flag shows the union of the two royal bloodlines of Judah and the transfer of the crown. *But, what about the Solomonic bloodline of Ethiopia? What about the descendants of Menelik, son of King Solomon and Queen Sheba? Where is the real throne? Who is the true King of Israel?*

Into the room entered one of Diego's young sons carrying with him what looked and smelled like it might be my breakfast. *Ah, yes! More beans and eggs and a few corn tortillas.* A steaming hot cup of coffee was placed on the desk. I declined the drink and accepted the food.

"Gracias Amigo. Where is your father? Where is Diego?"

"He's still sleeping," said the boy, "But, he taught me everything he knows. I can teach you all about medicinal plants. Okay?"

Hmm, must have been a long night for Diego. Albeit a little skeptical, *'How is this kid going to teach me anything?'* I answered, "Sure, that's fine. Go ahead."

Picking up a book that had been lying on the desk, <u>Medicinal Plants of Central America,</u> the adolescent son of Diego began to read. Having not noticed the book before, *I must have overlooked it,* I instantly began to think…*How long am I going to sit here while this kid lectures straight out of a book? Does he not think I can read?* My mind still a little clouded from the night before and not yet thinking too clearly, I wasn't real attentive, only half-heartedly listening to what he had to say.

"*Citrus Sinensis,* the orange tree," he read. *You've got to be kidding me? I came all the way here to learn about oranges?* "The orange is an important source of vitamin C and is a blood purifier. The rind can be used as a tonic and also helps to cure acne. It is helpful in the treatment of anorexia and can be effective in preventing common coughs and colds."

I must have drifted off, not paying attention to what was being read. There is a blank space in my journal and I'm sorry, but I don't remember the name of the second plant about which he taught. I do, however, remember the third.

"I think you should be taking notes," declared the boy.

I grabbed my ballpoint and prepared to write, suspicious as to why I was subjecting myself to this so-called study which to me was more like Chinese water torture. I contemplated politely excusing myself or just getting up and leaving, but then...

"Peyote..." he began in what was heard by my ears as a time-delayed pronunciation, a warped speech, or something peculiar, like an old phonograph record spinning in slow-motion at only 30 rpm's. Pe-yo-te. Time seemed but to crawl. The word gently rolled off his tongue finding its way into the pages of my diary. **Peyote**, I wrote. A sudden remembrance, a wave of recollection came crashing upon my soul...*What happened last night?* Up until the word was uttered and the point in which the jet black ink of the pen first stained its mark onto the paper, bleeding and coagulating onto the blank page of my journal, the previous night's journey had been completely erased from my memory. *Was it a dream?* How *could* it be?

"...Peyote is a strong natural antibiotic and can be used to treat a variety of different illnesses and ailments. It has resulted in effectively treating Pneumonia, Tuberculosis, Diabetes, Arthritis, Influenza, intestinal disorders; Also, topical wounds, burns, bites and stings." *Okay, okay, alright...I understand.* I think? *Or, maybe...? Had we really sojourned together throughout the universe, the old man and I?*

"That's the lesson for this morning," the boy instructed, closing the book. "My father will awaken soon and will probably want to see you."

"No, no," I said, "I must be going now. I think I've learned enough."

"Yes, of course," said the young fellow, "But, where will you be going?"

I was running low on money and thought of maybe heading to Costa Rica. It would be easier there to find a temporary job before traveling down into South America.

"I've got to go to work," I replied.

"Oh, yes. And what do you do?"

"I'd like to find work, perhaps, as a tour guide."

"Funny," he said. "*Los dos somos guías*. We both are guides."

"When will you be coming back?"

"*Dios sabe,*" I said.

 God only knows.

CHAPTER 12

Three weeks later.

Ezekiel 26:3 therefore this is what the sovereign Lord says: I am against you, O Tyre, and I will bring many nations against you, like the sea casting up its waves.

I stared out at the ocean, the white-capped waves rolling violently towards me as I stood watching, my feet planted firmly in the wet sand. There was a dangerous rip-current directly offshore that could prove to be fatal for any boatman or swimmer foolish enough to try and brave the rough waters. *But, how will I reach the vessel?* The strong *Papagayo* winds blew at full force this time of year. Deemed El Papagayo, 'the parrot', because of the way the cold air mass swoops down in a southerly direction at great speeds through the *cordillera* mountain range, sometimes producing winds in excess of 80 km/h by the time they reach the Pacific coastline of Guatemala, Nicaragua and Costa Rica, today the frequent gusts were quickly approaching hurricane strength.

Ezekiel 26:7 For this is what the Sovereign Lord says: From the north I am going to bring against Tyre Nebuchadnezzar king of Babylon

I readied the fragile, flimsy canoe, not truly believing it was up to the task. It would be a perilous journey as the poorly-constructed wooden dingy carried me out into the confusing darkness. *Which boat was mine?* I struggled to see her, the beautiful 42' catamaran sailboat moored securely out *somewhere* in the blackness of the harbor.

Ezekiel 27:3 Say to Tyre, situated at the gateway to the sea, merchant of peoples on many coasts, 'This what the Sovereign Lord says:

Your domain was on the high seas; your builders brought your beauty to perfection.

Ah, that must be her! Why, yes, I think it is! Or is it? She was one of dozens, maybe fifty or more, glistening ever so vaguely in the pale moonlight, rocking rhythmically back and forth in the far reaches of the bay, seductively hypnotizing sailors and scallywags alike with her deceivingly gentle swish and sway. *Yes, that might be her.*

They made all your timbers of pine trees; they took a cedar from Lebanon to make a mast for you. Of oaks from Bashan they made your oars; of cypress wood from the coasts of Cyprus they made your deck, inlaid with ivory. Fine embroidered linen from Egypt was your sail and served as your banner; your awnings were blue and purple. Men of Sidon were your oarsmen; your skilled men, O Tyre, were aboard as your seamen. Veteran craftsmen of Gebal were on board as shipwrights to caulk your seams. All the ships of the sea and their sailors came alongside to trade for your wares. Tarshish did business with you because of your great wealth of goods; they exchanged silver, iron, tin and lead for your merchandise. Greece traded with you; they exchanged slaves and articles of bronze for your wares. Men exchanged work horses, war horses and mules for your merchandise. Many coastlines were your customers; they paid you with ivory tusks and ebony. Aram did business with you because of your many products; they exchanged turquoise, purple fabric, embroidered work, fine linen, coral and rubies for your merchandise.

I was waist-deep, being tossed around and dragged under by the incoming tide, struggling to launch the canoe while waves pounded my chest and face. One step forward, two steps back. *This is not good. I shall not lose my balance and fall victim to such a raging sea in all its fury and madness, for I surely too must be of half folly and fully crazed to believe this fight would produce anything worthwhile.* I grabbed onto its side, the fragile wooden boat threatening to capsize in the swirling white foam. *Ayúdame Dios!* I rolled over and into the canoe, banging my knees against the hardwood hull, scraping my stomach across a splintered sideboard. Salt quickly entered into every raw scrape and wound with a ruthless and fiery burn.

Judah and Israel traded with you; they exchanged wheat and confections, honey, oil and balm for your wares. Damascus, **because of your many products and great wealth of goods, did business with you in wine and wool. Danites and Greeks exchanged wrought iron, cassia and calamus. Dedan traded in saddle blankets. Arabia and all the princes were your customers; they did business with you in lambs, rams and goats. The merchants of Sheba exchanged the finest of all kinds of spices and precious stones, and gold. The ships of Tarshish serve as carriers for your wares. You are filled will heavy cargo in the heart of the sea.**

The tiny boat was catapulted up onto the crest of a wave, balancing precariously on its upper lip for what seemed like an eternity. I took into my possession a single wooden oar that lay at my feet. Gripping it tightly with both hands, I made a desperate attempt to steady the small craft as it was whisked out to sea. The large wall of water instantaneously released from its grasp the insignificant canoe and, just as quickly, we descended into the deep trough left behind. *Another giant!* Now, being lifted to the top of yet another monster wave, I was in for the roller-coaster ride of my life.

Your oarsmen take you out to the high seas. But the east wind will break you to pieces in the heart of the sea. Your wealth, merchandise and wares, your mariners, seamen and shipwrights, your merchants and all your soldiers, and everyone else on board will sink into the heart of the sea on the day of your shipwreck. The shorelands will quake when your seamen cry out. All who handle the oars will abandon their ships.

Feeling battered and beaten, I closed my eyes to the sea spray as it pelted my face, spewing shame along with insult and guilt at such a poor soul who had been so discouragingly misled. I had come here in search of money, chasing dollar signs, looking to replenish my wallet with local currency.

Wail, O ships of Tarshish! For Tyre is destroyed and left without house or harbor. The harvest of the Nile was the revenue of Tyre, and she became the marketplace of the nations. Who planned this against Tyre, the bestower of crowns, whose merchants are princes, whose traders are renowned in the earth? Who was ever silenced like Tyre, surrounded by the sea? When your merchandise went out on the seas, you satisfied many nations; with your great wealth and your wares you enriched the kings of the earth. Now you are shattered by the sea in the depths of the water. You have come to a horrible end and will be no more.

With the canoe having been smashed to pieces and its novice captain thrown overboard, I awakened only to discover myself floating on the surface of the water, clinging to a decent-sized log and to what little possibilities life had to offer me at this point.

Ezekiel 29:18 "Son of man, Nebuchadnezzar king of Babylon drove his army in a hard campaign against Tyre; every head was rubbed bare and every shoulder made raw.

The remembrance of my many wounds was hard to ignore as the intense pain increased ten-fold from within. The sting of the salt had penetrated every pore of my body and seemed to eat away at the water-saturated, wrinkled flesh that clung to my aching bones.

Yet he and his army got no reward for the campaign he led against Tyre. Therefore this is what the Sovereign Lord says: I am going to give Egypt to Nebuchadnezzar king of Babylon, and he will carry off its wealth.

Dark will be the day at Tahpanhes when I break the yoke of Egypt.

-Ezekiel 30:18

Yet...*I feel so alive!* Had I dreamed this strange sequence of events? I brushed an ant off of my arm as it crawled from the piece of

An Adventure of Biblical Proportions

wood onto which I held. There were more of them, hordes of them, marching towards me in a single file line as if coming out to battle the wicked human stowaway who had uninvitingly welcomed himself aboard their well-defended ship. *There she is! That must be her!* I released hold of the log and swam away from the colony of swashbuckling, water-borne ants, some of them wearing eye-patches and wielding sharpened swords I'm quite sure of it. Strange thoughts invaded my head. *Tahpanhes? Egypt?* Was I no longer drifting out to sea in Playas del Coco, Costa Rica?

The waters, suddenly calm, signaled that the storm had ended. Was this the same harbor as before? Had I been carried off to a far-away place? **'Dark will be the day,'** said the Lord. My mind flashed back to Atitlán, to the earthen hut and my encounter with Diego the shaman. *But Jeremiah and Tamar were already gone. They had escaped disaster.* Egypt may be destroyed, its inhabitants killed by the sword, but the Hebrew prophet and the princess of Judah are alive! They had survived the onslaught, the destructive torrent, the relentlessness of the Babylonian Conquest. Israel had not ceased to exist, but now flourished as a nation in a distant land!

I sliced through the glassy surface of the water, wheeling my arms in freestyle motion, swimming frantically towards what appeared to be my boat. *Thar she floats…hardy, har, har!* I was glad to see her. *Oh, wait!* Deception on the high seas! The writing was now legible. Distinctly visible on her side, painted boldly in dark, black letters was the name of the vessel. She was *Jezebel*. This was clearly not my boat. Although, now I see that see that she has been disabled, her mast obviously broken, her engine lost. Nothing remained but a beleaguered crew of castaway spirits and ghostly deckhands, not a single vestige of her former wealth. The incessant moans and groans, the eerie pleads and squeals of the eternally damned still haunt the ocean fog and mist. I turned from the gruesome sight, hoping to shield my eyes from the ghastly display. **All nations must come to learn from her past mistakes**, Phoenicia has met a horrible end.

Not wanting to ponder too long her sudden downfall, I thrust myself through the water with tired arms, making my way in the general direction of what appeared to be a shinier, new boat; one that seemed unharmed and untouched by the once raging waters of the fiercest of storms. The strongest and most durable vessel of all, it had come through the battle unscathed with no ugly scars to show except for a few small holes where missing nails had once been inserted. Though not fancy nor elaborate, the attractiveness of the white-painted hull, the cleanliness of the rigid canvass sail and the simplicity of the modest décor drew me to her like a discarded iron horseshoe to a strong magnet.

Continuing to tread breaststroke-style through the water, I looked up to notice a name neatly printed in Greek letters on the starboard side of the humble ship. She was called IXOYE. *This is my boat. I found her!* Or had she found me?

Just below her name, I saw this ancient symbol ><, thus producing in me a vivid recollection in which I remembered clearly what Natty had said about the significance of this sign. It was the *Ichthus*, a Greek word meaning, simply, fish. However, its underlying connotations are even more noteworthy. Two intersecting arcs resembling the profile of a fish was used by early Christians as a secret symbol. It is an acronym, formed from the first initial letters of several words in a name. Jesus Christ, God's Son, Savior. In Greek, Iesous Christos Theou Uios Soter. The letters, Iota Chi Theta Upsilon Sigma. IXOYE. Ichthus. Fish. In respect of his West-African Heritage, which Natty believed had roots in the nation of Nigeria, he had changed his name from an adopted English last name of MacIntosh, a slave-owning family, to that of Okoye, a popular Nigerian surname. "I no longer use the name of the former slave master," he told me. "My name is Philip Okoye."

Natty informed me that not many people are aware of the true origin of this name. During an influx of Greek culture into Africa, many Nigerians accepted the new faith and were baptized as Christians. Throughout the centuries, this ancient symbol of the Ichthus proliferated in secret. When the slave trade reached its peak and foreign invaders arrived into West Africa, many Nigerians still revered the ancient symbol and considered themselves Christians. With a smudge of ashes on the forehead, or a rudimentary form of tattoo etched into the skin, these Africans affirmed their faith in Jesus Christ, God's Son, Savior. As a result of the mispronunciation by Latin and, later, Arabic-speaking slave traders, a great number of the people of Nigeria were branded IXOYE, pronounced Okoye. The

African Christians were chained and whipped, humiliated and robbed of their humanity, those strong enough to survive kept in horrific dungeons while awaiting their shipment off to a distant land to live in perpetual bondage.

"Philip was the apostle of Christ who baptized the first African, an Ethiopian eunuch traveling to Jerusalem just a short time after the resurrection of the Messiah," Natty informed me. (Acts 8:26-36) "My name is Philip Okoye in honor of my ancestors, the first Christians of Nigeria."

I climbed aboard using the ladder which hung down from the back of the vessel. Regaining my senses and drying off somewhat in the warm tropical air, I walked to the bow of the boat and took a seat. I thanked the Lord, so very grateful to be alive. God's presence had seemed to always be there during every step of this magical journey, never forsaking me, never abandoning His wayward child who sought adventure and who did seek the face of the Lord. I had come so far and learned so much, but creeping into my conscience once more was that same familiar question to which I had yet to respond... *Am I a Christian?* Seemingly I had been witness to and had experienced enough to have convinced even the most doubtful of naysayers as to the veritable existence of an Omnipotent, Almighty, All-powerful, supernatural Being. But, has it been proven to me that the Messiah did, indeed, come to earth in the form of Jesus Christ, God's Son? *Why am I testing the Lord? It's called faith,* I kept telling myself. *You either have it or you don't.*

Well, what about me? Do I have it? The concern did not dissipate.

I had reclined back onto the fiberglass deck of my boat, the IXOYE, when something suddenly exited the water and took flight. It was an Ichthus, a flying fish, a peculiar-looking species found in all the major oceans, mainly in warm tropical and subtropical waters. Its unusually large pectoral fins enable the fish to leave its normal marine habitat and glide through the air, covering considerably large distances. While moving through the air, the flying fish can top out at speeds of up to 60 km/h. Flights are usually around 30-50 meters in length. However, at times, the fish can be observed soaring for hundreds of meters using the updraft on the leading edges of waves, even stranding themselves on the decks of passing boats. Hence, their Greek name *Exo-coitus,* meaning "lying down outside." *How odd?*

The creature landed right beside me and began to flop around on the deck, looking at me with its relatively large eyes. It did not, however, seem in danger of asphyxiation as its gills had somehow adjusted to enable the fish to breathe the oxygen found outside its normal underwater realm. Instead, the little ichthus wiggled and waggled its way towards the front of the boat in what appeared to be a distinct effort to place itself on a strategically located, new-found launching pad. It paused for a short moment, long enough though for me to approach with curiosity. I bent down for a closer look.

With its eyes still wide open, it maintained its pectoral fins spread out like the wings of a seagull. The pelvic fins were so unusually large it actually looked as if it possessed a total of four capable wings. Its deeply forked caudal fin seemed to double as a rudder slash converted jet engine. The fish began to vibrate producing a slight hum and a noise I swear was the squelch of a motor firing up during ignition. I reached out my hand and the gentlest touch by my extended index and middle fingers resulted as if the launch button had, now, been pressed. With full-powered rocket boosters a go, the flying fish did what it does best…it took to flight. 10 Meters, 30 Meters, 50 Meters, it was just getting started. 100 Meters, 500 Meters, 1500 Meters, a full mile, just a glint of a silvery glow on the distant horizon, then, a brilliant flash! A sudden incredible brightness streaked across the nighttime sky. *Was it a shooting star?* I made a wish for the only desire a lonely sailor boy could have in this, his current solitary state; True love. *Does such a thing exist?* I remembered a blossoming springtime love affair with the sweet and demure Kari. I pondered longingly the walks made to visit an engaging and understanding Kathryn. I thought of a girl whom I had yet to meet.

CHAPTER 13

She peered out the window from her seat next to me aboard Aloha Airlines flight 1084, non-stop from Phoenix to Honolulu.
"Daddy, Daddy…is that Hawaii?"
I leaned over and looked out past the left wing of the Jumbo 747.
"Yes, baby girl, that's the Big Island of Hawaii."
Directly outside the seven layers of protected glass and plastic, we viewed, rising up from the shimmering sea, the tallest mountain in the world at over 33,000 feet. Most of it, however, lay hidden beneath the surface of the ocean. The measured height of the visible portion, which protrudes out of the sea in a fabulous cone-shaped summit, is 13,796 feet, making this peak the highest point in the state of Hawaii. When measured from its base, located on the seafloor some 20,000 feet below the surface of the Pacific Ocean, to its summit, Mauna Kea quickly becomes the second largest shield-volcano in the solar system behind Olympic mons on the planet Mars. The Hawaiian word *mauna,* like the Latin word *mons,* means mountain.
"Its height is slowly decreasing as its massive weight depresses the Pacific seafloor beneath it." Only seven years old, she was a science whiz and loved to hear about the geology of this lovely chain of islands which, in fact, due to plate-tectonics, continues to move 32 miles to the northwest every one million years. Appropriately named Jacinda Kaialani, 'beautiful spirit from the heavenly sea', I was taking her back to where she was born.
"The elevation and location of Mauna Kea make it an important site for astronomical observations," I told her. "The summit is above approximately 40% of Earth's atmosphere and 90% of the water vapor. Additionally, the clarity experienced from the peak is unequaled, allowing for up to 300 cloud-free nights per year." A virtual astronomer's paradise.
The Polynesians, the first people to arrive here to these, the most isolated set of islands on Earth, did so by using the stars as tools of navigation. Setting out in well-designed canoes, they colonized previously unpopulated islands of the sea, bringing with them more

than twenty-one species of plants and domestic animals most necessary and useful for survival in the new lands. Polynesia, today, consists of the Hawaiian Islands, the Marquesas Islands, Tahiti, Tonga, Samoa and New Zealand. It was in Aoteroa, modern-day New Zealand, where the original inhabitants thrived and developed their distinct Polynesian culture. These indigenous people of New Zealand call themselves Maori.

In Hebrew, the word *ma'or* means "light-bearers", or "illuminaries", and in the book of Genesis refers to the creation of the stars. The first Polynesian travelers were, in fact, ancient Hebrew navigators who mastered the art of using the stars and the movement of the constellations to guide themselves during long, trans-oceanic voyages, thus populating new lands and, eventually, colonizing the Hawaiian Islands. The Tahitian island of Moorea owes its name to this Hebrew word *ma'or,* or *ma'ore*. The Moray eel, or electric eel, is also named because of its original Hebrew meaning, "light-bearer."

Another interesting piece of information is that the suffix *ese* means, 'originating in a specified place.' *Poly* is Latin for 'more than one.' The Polynesians, just like the Hebrews (remember *hybrid* and *brew*), are a mix of peoples, originating in different places, who have come together as one, like carpenter bees carrying pollen in the wind, guided innately by the stars to where fertile tropical islands lay waiting, ready to blossom with life and bloom with aloha.

The sun shone brightly and the rainbows dazzled as we landed on Oahu, Hawaiian for "the gathering place." After hurrying to catch the Wikiwiki shuttle which would take us to the inter-island terminal, we boarded an island-hopper (a small airplane) on route to the magnificently beautiful, northwesternmost Hawaiian island of Kauai. The so-called "Garden Isle" because of its lush, green vegetation and natural splendor, is susceptible to enormously large amounts of rainfall. In fact, Mount Waialeale, in the center of the island, is touted as the 'wettest spot on Earth' with an impressive record total of 683 inches of rain in 1982 alone. A merely average year produces a whopping 486 inches of rainfall which cascades down peaks and summits in a plethora of gorgeous waterfalls, eventually replenishing Kauai's miles of rivers and navigable waterways before emptying into the Pacific Ocean.

An Adventure of Biblical Proportions

To the contrary, just 10 miles away on the leeward side of the island, the dry, parched desert-like sand dunes of Barking Sands Pacific Missile Range Facility near Polihale beach (the sand is so dry it barks when you walk on it) receive, on average, a sparse total of 8" of rain annually.

We de-boarded the plane at Lihue airport, jumped in our Avis-rented Chevy HHR (which looked to me like it belonged in a fleet of hearses owned by the local funeral parlor) and started out past the luxury resorts and golf courses that line the 9-mile stretch of highway between here and Kapaa town. Up from Kealia beach, where surfers and bodyboarders enjoy the consistently mid-size sets of predictable waves that roll in on the East Side, we climbed the steep road that backs the coast and headed into the interior part of the island. It was here in peaceful Keapana Valley where Jacinda Kaialani was born in her "little grass shack", underneath the mango tree, amongst the hibiscus flowers and amidst the echoing sounds of Hawaiian chants and the pulsating heartbeat of a native Koa wood drum.

We pulled up in front of the dark green structure, its exterior walls well-camouflaged by the brightness of hue and similar tint of the natural surroundings. The colors here are magnificent. Not much has changed in seven years. The hibiscus plant out front appeared, now, more like a tree. A different group of feral cats scampered around outside. One of them, a familiar looking pink-furred feline male who more than made up for his feminine appearance with a wild inborn aggression, pounced upon the hood of our car as we parked in the red-dirt and gravel driveway fronting the house. Beside us sat a rusted-out 'island-mobile' carrying a banged up and heavily scratched surfboard, a tell-tale sign that the owner was probably home.

"Aloha..." I called out in order to alert whoever lived there that a couple of guests had arrived, "Anyone home?"

A single, middle-aged bachelor named Phil, somewhat surprised to have visitors show up on his doorstep this particular morning, very graciously and hospitably welcomed us inside. We sat down in the tiny living area of the two-room cabin and over a hot cup of tea began to reminisce, or talk-story as the Hawaiians like to call it. Jacinda Kaialani was quite content petting the spunky pink-furred cat while listening to her father recall the events leading up to her birth.

"Strapped for cash one April morning I headed out the door of this very cabin and trod down the steep hill leading to the main road which encircles the island. There I waited with my thumb stuck out, standing beside Prince Kuhio Highway, hoping to catch a ride to the world-famous North Shore, home to both the rich and famous and the down and out. I had read an ad in the Garden Island classifieds seeking locals to be cast as extras in a movie being filmed in the area. With a baby on the way and another hungry mouth to feed, we could sure use the extra dough.

I hadn't done much hitch-hiking before, but within a couple of minutes I had a taker. She claimed it was my warm smile that did the trick. I thanked her for the lift and headed for the check-in line where a lively lady wearing dark-rimmed spectacles and a wide-brimmed hat registered anybody and everybody hopeful of standing around on a production set and collecting a day's wages in the process. She directed me to an adjacent dressing room where I shed my beach clothes and flip-flops in exchange for what looked like something a character out of the Bible would have worn. *What kind of movie is this?* I wondered.

It turns out we were on the property of Director George Lucas of Stars Wars fame. In a field at the base of the some of the most majestic mountains on Kauai, ancient Mayan temples rose up in exotic beauty. An entire mock village had been constructed, the pyramids made of painted Styrofoam and treated bamboo. After some quick direction, I walked into the main plaza of the city, the cameras rolling, recording the recreated historical events believed by Mormons to have taken place somewhere in the Americas around the year 33 A.D. *Have I been here before?* This place looked all too familiar. If I didn't know better, I would have thought I had been teleported back to the ruins at Tikal, Guatemala. No, this was the set of *The Testaments,* a film produced by the Mormon Church of Latter-Day Saints.

A prophet climbed the steps of the temple and addressed the crowd. People began to congregate and, soon, they stood listening to the prophecy of the coming of the Messiah. This was the city of Zarahemla. Half-way around the Earth, 10,000 miles away on a hill outside of Jerusalem, He was being crucified. The baby blue Hawaiian sky became obscured and darkness took its place. The earth began to quake and tremble, opening up huge chasms in the ground. Crowds of people ran frantically for cover. Flashes of lightning, the rumble of thunder, intense shaking. Huge stone pillars cracked and fell. The city was being destroyed. As the last nail was driven through the sweaty palm of the hand of Jesus Christ, God's Son, Savior, the prophecy began to ring true."

From the sixth hour until the ninth hour darkness came over all the land. About the last hour Jesus cried out in a loud voice, *"Eloi, Eloi, lama sabachthani?"*- **which means, "My God, my God, why have you forsaken me?"**
-Matthew 27:45

CHAPTER 14

"Three days later, '*Aloha, hola, hello,*' he greeted me with a smile, grinning from ear to ear."

Phil listened intently as he filled my cup full of Jasmine tea and settled back into his chair. Jacinda Kaialani was content still sitting on the floor tickling the ornery pink cat as it nibbled and nipped at her hands and wrists. We continued to talk-story.

"I left this very cabin having decided to do some exploring on my own. With the island, as you know, being free of snakes and void of scorpions, I felt brave enough to venture out the backdoor and go traipsing through the countryside. Across the hillside, past a grove of aromatic Sandalwood trees, down a steep decline and into a deep ravine, this was the vintage, unspoiled Hawaii of days gone by. I crawled through a tangled mess of hau bushes, seemingly more like a jungle gym uniquely assembled for the most nimble of monkeys. At one point, I became imprisoned among the twisted and distorted roots, trapped within the unbreakable, thick limbs. I was caught on the brink of submission. What a terribly panicked feeling of claustrophobia, suffocation and exhaustion.

I pushed forward, squirming and maneuvering my way through thirty meters of pure hell before finally exiting the terrible maze on the far-side of the gulley. Up another incline and down through more thick vegetation until the soothing sound of flowing water became a delight to my ears. *A trail!* It led beside the river for a short distance to a rope draped down from a ledge above. I grabbed hold of the well-worn cordage and hoisted myself up the embankment. A lightly used pathway continued through the tropical forest. I ran and ran and ran some more, alongside the stream, past a tumbling waterfall and around the bend. That's when I heard the oh-so-sweet sounds of a four-stringed ukulele.

'Somewhere over the rainbow
Way up high…'

A deep, echoing voice bellowed from just up ahead. Around the corner, someone was singing a most melodic tune.

'There's a land that I heard of
Once in a lullaby
Somewhere over the rainbow
Skies are blue
And the dreams that you dare to dream
They really do come true.'

I made my way around the curve. Large stones lay in the shape of what looked to be the remains of an ancient *heiau*, a sacred Hawaiian temple that had been overtaken through the years by creeping vines, lichens and other thick, tropical vegetation. A scattering of fruit trees grew wild. Unattended by any human hands, they flourished in the rich, volcanic soil and welcomed the gentle, life-giving Kauai rains that sustained their growth on this the windward side of the island.

That voice? The singing grew louder…

'Someday I'll wish upon a star
And wake up where the clouds are far behind me…'

Perched upon one of the massive rocks of the heiau and wearing a turquoise blue wrap-around sarong was the largest man I had ever seen in my life, no kidding. Humming a gentle chorus and carefully tickling the tiny chords of his ukulele with fingers as thick as pork sausages sat the big, friendly Hawaiian who in conservative estimates must have tipped the scales at well over 600 lbs.

'Aloha…. What a beautiful day in paradise! How'zit, brah?'
'Uh…fine thanks. And you?' I asked him his name.
'I'm Israel.' He had a long Hawaiian surname that I couldn't really understand. 'Everyone calls me Bruddah Iz.' He continued in a thick pidgin accent, 'I know why yo heah.'
'You know why I'm here?'
'Yes, bruddah. Yo heah to learn about da King.'
The King? I immediately questioned, obscure thoughts running through my head. *Elvis Presley?* The movie Blue Hawaii *was* filmed

here, after all. *Or, perhaps, he's talking about Dr. Martin Luther King?* None of this made much sense to me, so I just listened to the big Hawaiian speak.

'A Hebrew priest, a male descendant of Aaron the brother of Moses, is called a *kohen*, right?'

'That's right,' I agreed. What little knowledge I had of Hebrew vocabulary was sure coming in handy.

'Tru out da yeahs (throughout the years) da name has changed very little,' he said. 'In Hawaii, da word is *kahuna*. I am a priest, a teacha, an advisa.'

Kahuna? A teacher and an advisor? A Hebrew priest? Now, I was beginning to comprehend the significance of it all.

'Take dis,' he said, handing me a neat little package wrapped up loosely in a Ti leaf, Hawaiian-style. 'It's *Kava Kava*. Befo you go to sleep tonight put a little in yo mouth and chew. It helps you to relax. You looking a little uptight bruddah. Yo wife pregnant o what?' he said with a smile. I guess he somehow already knew the answer.

I stuffed the package of Kava down into the pocket of my floral-print swim-shorts. The sun would be setting soon. Down here in the tropics it wastes no time with a long, drawn-out sunset, but merely dips down into the ocean below the western horizon while quickly bidding farewell to the day.

Iz didn't delay in saying his goodbyes, either. 'Dis time, take da short cut bruddah.' He pointed towards the river with a humongously large and flabby arm. There was an obvious dirt road that could be easily accessed by crossing over to the other side of the river. *Must be the road that goes by my house,* I thought. 'Give an 'Aloha' out to my boyz Kane and Lono,' he shouted. 'Dey's gonna come by and pick you up later, brah.'

Who? They're going to pick me up? I waded across the gently moving stream, trying not to lose my balance while carefully stepping on the slippery stones, each one covered with a thin layer of mucous-like green algae that grew in the shallow water. Half way home, I reached deep into my pocket and pulled out the package of Kava. Unfolding the Ti leaves in which the finely ground powder was contained, I grabbed a good sized pinch of it in between my fingers and stuck it in my mouth as if it were a big wad of chewing tobacco. *I hate chewing tobacco.* But, this was an important plant that definitely had its place in Polynesian culture and was held in high regard by Pacific Islanders. It was one of the 21 botanical species originally transported to the islands by the voyaging colonists. My mouth and lips began to tingle and go numb.

It was dusk now and, although already fairly dark, the distant light shed by a few bright early-evening stars was all that was needed to keep me from veering off the road and into the bush. The moon, however, would be up soon enough. Arriving home, I crept in through the front door of our 'little grass shack', rinsed the red dirt and clay from off the bottoms of my feet and joined my soon-to-be wife on the air mattress on the floor. (Admittedly, I do confess, she was six months into the pregnancy when we tied the knot a little tighter, a knot that would eventually come undone.) I laid down close beside her, whispered "goodnight" in her ear and shut my tired eyes. 30-40 minutes had passed since ingesting the *Kava Kava* and, although my thoughts were clear, I felt a considerable amount of sleepiness come over me. I must have quickly dozed off.

Next thing I know, I was rudely awakened from a deep slumber by the bothersome sound of grinding brake pads and a few unnecessary honks on a car horn. I stepped outside the front door blinded and frozen for a split-second as the bright high-beam headlights of an old station-wagon hit me square in the face. I shielded my eyes with the back of my forearm and walked out to where the old jalopy was parked, for I had a good hunch who these midnight visitors might be.

'Dat handle no work. Here you go brah. I got it.' The car door magically popped open from the inside. I quickly slid into the back seat and pulled the squeaky door shut behind me. The loud clanking sound of metal on metal left me wary as to whether the latch had been properly secured.

'Don't worry,' said the driver, 'if you fall out, we come back fo you.' The two Hawaiians snickered and laughed together in the front seat like it was the funniest thing they'd ever heard.

'I'm Kane,' said the big one while using one hand to turn the steering wheel in 360 degree rotations, reversing out of the gravel drive. His large ham hock of a left arm hung out the driver's side window, a strand of barbed-wire tattooed around the massive python-like bicep.

'And this is Lono.' He introduced his skinny, sun-darkened sidekick whose dark, frizzy hair stood puffed up in a natural perm. Lono turned around flashing a snaggle-toothed smile, eyes hidden behind dark sunglasses, totally disregarding the fact that it was the middle of the night.

We sped off into the darkness, me and this uniquely Hawaiian version of Batman and Robin Boy Wonder. I was starting to enjoy the ride and the cool breeze blowing through my hair when Lono popped a cassette into the tape player. On cue, the peculiar pair erupted into verse and began singing along to the music.

'Mystical, marvelous magical Maui
Hero of this land
The one, the only, the ultimate
Hawaiian Sup'pa man.'

The voice on the recording sounded strangely familiar. Was it…?

'Iz told us we was taking you to da end of da road. Lono and me is goin' surfing on da North Shore.'

The end of the road? I knew where the highway abruptly came to an end and was well aware that the only thing that obstructed the road from, in fact, encircling the entire island was the 14-mile stretch of sheer cliffs that made up the Na Pali coastline. We sped on towards my date with fate. *Or was it destiny?*

Passing through Kilauea town, Kane quickly veered the car to the side of the road, pulling over and coming to a halt on the grassy shoulder. In jumped an incredibly beautiful barefoot young Hawaiian girl wearing a bikini top, cut-off shorts and a shark's tooth necklace around her neck, red mud oozing through her toes. In her hand she carried a piece of pumice, a light and porous volcanic rock formed when lava solidifies into glass.

'Dis my daughter, Pele,' Kane announced. 'Careful, she got a mighty hot tempah dis one.' The three of them giggled as if they knew something I didn't.

'Move ovah, *haole*,' the girl immediately commanded.

I meekly obliged, propping myself up against the unsecured door while Pele plopped herself down in the middle of the backseat, leaning forward in between her Dad and Lono. I was biting my fingernails and perspiring when we pulled up to Ke'e Beach.

'Dis is yo stop,' informed the brawny conductor as he practically tossed me from of the vehicle.

'Hang loose, bruddah.' His skinny accomplice added his small tidbit of advice. And just as quickly as they first arrived, they now departed as fast they could down the two-lane highway, leaving me stranded without a soul in sight at the end of the road, standing in a mix of sand and gravel.

Leaving the nicely paved, modern civilization of street signs and dividing lines, I shuffled my feet a few steps forward, or perhaps backwards, into a naturally rough and untamed world of ancient paths and unmarked trails. This one thankfully was well-designated and brightly lit by a burning tiki torch stuck in the sand. Fueled with the oil from a few dozen kukui nuts connected by coconut fronds to the end of a spear, the flame would burn for at least another couple of hours. Luckily, too, for my sake, a boatload of sun bleached, chalk-white seashells placed in the form of an arrow pointed the way uphill, the direction in which I assumed I was supposed to start traveling.

I hesitantly climbed the rocky staircase as it wound its way higher and higher past fern grottoes, bromeliad gardens and mini-waterfalls until reaching a rewarding rest stop and lookout point at the top. I took a deep breath, inhaling the salty, humid air. The trail continued as far as one could see, curving around jagged cliff edges and skirting fearfully close to harrowing, thousand foot drop-offs. I knelt down on one knee, taking in the magnificent view of waves rolling in, splashing against the shore, translucent white spume dancing in the light of the moon. The violent sound of crashing water and pounding surf was almost completely muffled due to the height of this vantage point, hundreds of feet above the churning sea down below.

Paused for a moment on bended knee, I thought to have heard a different sound. With an ear to the ground, I was scarcely able to make out the faint…*Footsteps? Drumbeats?* Whatever it was, it seemed to be getting closer, now clearly discernable. *Loud voices. Chanting.* The stepping of feet. The beating of drums. Quickly approaching, I heard the voices of many men…an army, a war party, climbing, ascending, nearing, closer and closer. *Eloi, Eloi…My God, My God*. Hawaiian warriors all decked out in full-fledged regalia…spears, torches, drums. It was my worst nightmare coming true! *Huaka' i po*. Night marchers!

Hawaiian legend has it that a ghost march such as this one consists of the spirits of ancient warriors and fallen chiefs who roam the islands haunting the sites of old battlegrounds. It is said that if you look one of these night marchers straight in the eye you will disappear, never to be seen again. According to the Law of the Splintered Paddle, instituted by King Kamehameha himself, if one hears an approaching ghost procession, they had best lie face down on their stomach, avoiding eye contact at all costs.

Here they come! I hit the ground in a heartbeat and lay prone beside the trail, remaining as still as possible, my face buried in the moist, red dirt. I didn't dare take a peek at the passing warriors. The drumbeats suddenly ceased and two giant mud-caked, calloused feet stood directly at my side. (In desperate need of a pedicure, I might add.) I held my breath, refusing to exhale. *Don't even flinch*, I told myself, when, out of nowhere, what did I hear but…laughing! Pretty soon the marchers had all joined in the jovial fun, inebriated with a resounding laughter. Then, complete silence.

'Get up boy! What you tink dis is? We no come to divide, we come to unite!' *What year is this?* I rose to my feet in awe. I was instantly face to face with….

"Shhh!" A hush fell over the battle regimen. I noticed the soldiers standing at full attention out of the utmost respect they held for the aged leader. He spoke, 'I, King Kamehameha I, have come to unite these islands and bring them all under my sovereign rule. I now declare this, the island of Kauai, to be part of the United Kingdom of Hawaii!'

Could this be the year 1810? I cautiously followed the others' lead and saluted the great monarch, fell in to rank and file and joined the march at the back of the line.

Together, with the spirited band of ghostly apparitions, I proceeded down the trail, hugging the cliff line while chanting Hawaiian victory songs under the lustrous light of a gibbous moon.

An Adventure of Biblical Proportions

E ho mai ka `ike mai luna mai e	Grant us the wisdom from above
I na mea huna no`eau o na mele e	The hidden secrets of the chants
E ho mai - e ho mai - e ho mai	Grant it to us, give it to us, give it

We reached Hanakapi'ai Beach, the 2-mile mark. Strong rip currents, high surf, dangerous shore breaks and other hazardous ocean conditions make wading even knee-deep into the water extremely dangerous here. A sign with 83 tally marks warns hikers of the number of drownings that have occurred at this very spot. We pressed on in hopes of conquering the remaining nine miles that separated us from Kalalau.

Ka lei aloha i Na Kupuna	In the circle of love of spirit
Noho au i ka manawa	I am in the moment
A me na manawa iki ko'u pono	And all my moments are good and proper
Mahalo nui no pomaika'i nei au	I am so grateful for the blessings that surround me
He inoa no Na Kupuna	Honored is the name of the spirit of our ancestors

I could tell we were getting close after spotting a bonfire burning on a distant beach. Around a few more craggy turns, alongside the menacingly steep precipice, then the final descent down into one of the most magnificent places on the planet, the ancient Kalalau Valley. We crossed through an extensive irrigation system in place to water the many terraced walls lining the spectacular valley. Near-vertical palisades jutted up from the valley floor, covered in a blanket of green and dripping with moisture. We passed through agricultural plots where native taro root, a staple in the Polynesian diet, was grown and cultivated. Banana plants and breadfruit trees were abundant. Sweet potato vines and yams crept down the hillsides. Coconut palms and bamboo were in large supply. I saw many houses and shacks constructed of natural and sustainable materials. The village was buzzing with activity. A group of *wahine* in flower-patterned muumuu dresses and some little *keiki* ran out to meet the returning soldiers, greeting their warriors with hugs and kisses and lots of smiles. Happiness and the Aloha spirit were abound in this place as all the villagers, maybe 1,500 of them, gathered 'round. The festivities tonight would include a huge party, a fiesta, a feast; a real live Hawaiian *luau*!

    I continued walking, exploring the surrounding area, past a babbling brook and alongside another gently-flowing mountain stream where unclothed women bathed and scrubbed in the clear, fresh water. Tall stalks of Awapuhi ginger plants partially shielded from view their brown, naked bodies as they squeezed from the flower heads a cleansing, aromatic, sudsy liquid which they then used as shampoo for washing and conditioning their hair.

    I made my way down to the beach, following the sound made from somebody blowing on a conch shell signaling that the food was ready for consumption. I watched as some of the men shoveled away sand with their hands, uncovering the buried pig and revealing a cooked pork delicacy that had been roasted in the *imu*, an underground oven used by the natives in preparing their meals. A fresh catch of *mahi mahi* and some ahi tuna brought in by local fishermen hung over an open flame, becoming crisp and charred on the outside, soft and tender on the inside. People joked and laughed, *keiki* ran around and played and all who were present gorged themselves with tropical fruits, meats, vegetables and even *kimu*, specially harvested seaweed for dessert.

    After dinner, we were treated to a mesmerizing hula show in which gorgeous barefoot *wahine* dressed in grass-skirts and wearing nothing but empty coconut shells to cover their breasts danced gracefully in sync, telling stories with their choreographed movements. Each woman wore around her neck a fragrant *lei* necklace made from freshly picked plumeria flowers. Their ankles and wrists were adorned with hand-strung beads fashioned from the colorful seeds collected from local flora. When the hula girls finished their performance, it was time for the male fire dancers to have a turn. (I might clarify, here, that some of the men took a turn with a hula girl or two, while a few others tried their hand at dancing.)

    Eventually, the party died down and it was time to leave. A handful of the original marchers remained in the village while Kamehameha, the *ali'i*, the elite royalty, and some of the highest-ranking officers boarded a double-hulled outrigger canoe bound for the Big Island of Hawaii from whence they came. The rest of the warriors paddled out to their respective boats, joining the fleet as we set sail, taking advantage of the light trade winds that were beginning to blow. Though the *luau* was loads of fun and, in spite of the fact that everyone was really very friendly, I wasn't quite ready to permanently join the ghost march and become an eternal member in the King's Royal Army. For my sake, the captain then ordered his crew to steer our ship directly into a brisk headwind, thus causing the vessel to stall, drifting ever so slightly in a southeasterly direction, afloat on the choppy ocean waters.

I noticed a small canoe being launched from shore and heading out towards us. After careful observation, I noted the sharp facial features of one of the occupants and recognized that it was almost certainly Pele. But, there was someone else with her, a muscle-bound young man who guided the boat. The two of them maneuvered alongside us and tied a rope around a metal cleat. This allowed Pele to disembark from her canoe and onto the large outrigger where she pleasured herself in fluttering around flirtatiously like a butterfly amongst the crew, using her allure to try and seduce the easily tempted first mate and all the sailors. The captain, on the other hand, was staunch and strong-willed in having her removed from the ship, knowing too well that, although her beauty seemed irresistible, she could erupt violently at any moment.

How fitting is it that the ghost crew leaves me at Polihale Beach? There exists a common myth that here, on the isolated west side of the island, is where the souls of the dead depart this world and enter into the afterlife.

"*A hui ho!* See you later!" shouted my former shipmates as I watched them sail away and ultimately disappear, fading into the horizon.

Once situated in the canoe, Pele introduced me to her older brother, Kamohoali'i, who resumed his duties as pilot of the small craft, navigating us through deep open waters. To my left! To my right! *Dorsal fins!*

I fretted upon seeing the large school of sharks as they circled ominously around us; tigers, greys, white-tips and hammerheads, some of the most aggressive species found in these Hawaiian waters. However, Pele and her brother insisted they presented no danger whatsoever. The two sibling counterparts didn't in-so-much-as interact by talking to the sharks as they did by communicating non-verbally with them, obviously enjoying their constant companionship while they escorted us to the beach.

As a large swell pushed us forcefully ashore, we landed the canoe in the sand, quickly pulling it to safety away from where giant waves were eating away and eroding this stretch of coastline. My eyes fixated on the glaring headlights of a car parked back behind the rolling white sand dunes. It was Kane and Lono in the old station wagon. Approaching, I was perplexed that, unless I was mistaken, the vehicle had no tail pipe, no exhaust system and hardly made a noise. 'She runs on pure hydrogen,' Kane bragged, 'And a little bit of love.'

We started down a bumpy cane road previously used to truck loads of sugarcane to the mill in Koloa (tall- *loa,* sugarcane- *ko*) until the industry began to falter and the mill was closed down. In the front seat, the guys were passing around a cup-shaped, hollowed out gourd and drinking some kind of foul-smelling refreshment.

'Noni juice!' said Lono as he reached back and offered me a swig of the putrid stuff. 'Lightning in a bottle!' I pinched my nose, held it tightly closed and took several big gulps. With every stinkin' pothole we hit, more liquid spilled down into my lap, the awful stench permeating the inside of the car, my clothes and my entire being.

'Drink samoa!' suggested Pele. 'It helps wit yo stamina.'

Drink samoa? I thought. Oh, yes, yes, drink some more. *My stamina get mo bettah.*

Her pidgin English accent was starting to rub off on me. That wasn't the only thing, either. I could feel Pele's soft hands massaging my tight muscles and sore neck, mashing on my back as if pounding *taro* into *poi.* She was giving me the *Lomi Lomi* and I loved it, so much so that I had soon fallen asleep. Draped around her like the skirt of a volcano, Pele's long hair flowing with its crimson glow became my pillow as I laid down in the backseat. Trouble was imminent as this strikingly beautiful mistress fully developed in all her womanhood gently caressed from the shoulders down to the small of my back in what resembled the foreplay to an intimate encounter. *But, I'm happily married. Or, at least, I will be soon.*

I sat up, stiff as a board, just at the same time the car stopped in front of my house. My sweet Kathryn lay sleeping inside. I quietly entered our bedroom, snuggling down beside her, appreciating the warmth of her body, the curvaceousness of her womanly figure and the plumpness of her voluptuous bosoms, all having been greatly accentuated during the pregnancy. She awoke with a smile as I softly kissed the nape of her neck and slowly....

CHAPTER 15

The cock crowed mid-morning right outside our bedroom window as I embraced her from behind. Simultaneously waking and opening our eyes to the dull light filtering in through the blinds, she turned to face me and, with a deep-seeded look of love and contentment, placed a tender kiss upon my cheek. "Good morning. And thank you for last night," she softly whispered. "We hadn't slept like that in a long time."

"Like what?" I asked.

"You holding me in your arms, so intimately, so lovingly, all through the night, David. I really loved it."

All through the night? But did we? Did I? "You mean I never left the house?"

"No, silly! You came home late from your walk and lay down in bed with me. You must have been really tired, you slept so soundly. At one point you were snoring as loud as a pig, but I didn't mind. You were so cuddly!"

I got up, sliced in half a fresh papaya, sprinkled on a little lime juice, spread some guava jelly onto two pieces of toasted bread and, over breakfast, told Kathryn about my dream.

"Sounds like you were about to cheat on me with that slut" was the first thing she had to say. Go figure. A woman will get mad if you're unfaithful to her even in your dreams.

"Pele's not a slut," I said in her defense. "She's just overly affectionate, that's all."

"Seriously, David, if you feel like you need to go back there, to the heiau, you should go. That's fine with me. Just don't stay too long, o.k.?"

I took her up on the offer, desperately needing to talk to Iz.

I took the shortcut this time, out the front door of the cabin, down the road, across the, across the....

In the river I saw him. He was floating buoyantly, suspended weightlessly on his back, singing with such a sweet, soothing voice that it was certain to pacify all of heaven and angels.

An Adventure of Biblical Proportions

I see skies of blue and clouds of white
The bright blessed day, the dark sacred night
And I think to myself, what a wonderful world

The colors of the rainbow, so pretty in the sky
Are also on the faces of people passing by
I see friends shakin' hands, sayin' "How do you do?"
They're really saying "I love you."

I hear babies cryin', I watch them grow
They'll learn much more than we'll know

And I think to myself, what a wonderful world

He rose up out of the water to greet me. "Hey Bruddah! How you sleep?"

"Good, Iz. I slept good. And you'll be happy to know that I did meet the king!"

"You met da king! And what he say? Whatchu learn?"

"Well, for starters, I learned all about ancient Hawaii. But, Iz, you didn't warn me about a ghost march."

"Ghost march? Where you go? Who you meet? Kamehameha? Oh, bruddah, you no *kanaka maole*. You a Native Hawaiian? Some ting messed up. You was supposed to meet a different king. We gonna haf to try dis again, brah." He reached into his pocket and pulled out another package wrapped in Ti leaves.

"Dis my prized kava from Kona on da Big Island. Mr. Don Ho gave me dis hea kava as a gif. Oh, bruddah, let me tell you, we had a big ol' kava drinking ceremony some of da newcomers an me. Let's see, there was Frank Sinatra, 'ol' blue eyes' dey call him, an King Hussein of Jordan, nice guy, Stanley Kubrick, a filmmaker was wit us and, oh, Joe Dimaggio was dea, too. We had some laughs wit dat crew, let me tell you bruddah."

He continued, "My firs yea (my first year), my induction yea in '97, was great. You shoulda been dea, brah, let's see...dey was Jacques Cousteau, James Michener, Gianni Versace, John Denver, we sang a duet he and I, 'Country Roads Take Me Home.' I also got to meet Princess Di, what a beauty, and had a talk wit Mother Teresa, too. Good times, bruddah."

Iz handed me the folded package containing his favorite Kava. "Now mek yo self a tea right befo bedtime. Jus boil it in some water and drink two, three, maybe fo cups if you like. You'll be fine."

I awoke inside a musty, damp, dungeon-like basement that served as a jail cell or a holding block of sorts. The gentleman here with me, a General, or maybe even a Commander-in-chief all decked out in fully-decorated military garb, his impeccably clean suit emblazoned with numerous awards and medals, was obviously under house-arrest. A dank, dungy odor invaded my nasal passages as little droplets of rust-colored water dripped down from the ceiling, creating puddles on the cement floor. The seemingly frail elder statesman/old war veteran sat at an antique escritoire looking almost gaunt and feeble; this, however, could merely be attributed to his advanced age and, perhaps, his diminutive build and stature. This man, in my estimates, measured no more than 5'4" tall. The old codger was making an entry into his journal when I undisturbingly walked over and stood behind him. Peering over his shoulder, I noticed the date he had logged at the top of the page. *My God!* July 23, 1975. *The day I was born!*

There was loud rapping on the bolted, iron door. The old man quickly responded to the pounding knocks, "Come in."

A key momentarily rattled around inside the lock, the door slowly swung open, and in walked a uniformed guard carrying what was a nondescript, simply-decorated chocolate cake.

"I did not order this," voiced the General from his desk. "We do not wish to have cake. Please take it away."

"But, sir, you have had no food or drink for forty days, now," said the sincerely concerned guard, to which the old vet replied…**"One cannot live by bread alone, but by every word that comes from the mouth of God."**

He refused the cake.

"But, Your Majesty, it's your 83rd birthday." The guard continued to plead.

"Leave it there if you must. Thank you for your well-intentions."

The young guard exited with a respectful bow and I remained there alone with…

An Adventure of Biblical Proportions

Your Majesty? Who is this man? Where am I? Could this miniature, little figure be the King?

He had opened up a Bible and, while seated at his desk, was reading page after page of Scripture. After a couple of hours passed, I felt the need to interrupt, to say *something* in order to break the silent monotony. Therefore I casually asked, "You like to read from the Bible a lot, don't you?" To which he replied,

"We in Ethiopia have one of the oldest versions of the Bible, but however old the version may be, in whatever language it might be written, the Word remains one and the same. It transcends all boundaries of empires and all conceptions of race. It is eternal. And I might say for myself that from early childhood I was taught to appreciate the Bible and my love for it increases with the passage of time. All through my troubles I have found it a cause of infinite comfort. "Come to me, all ye that labor and are heavy laden, and I will give you rest." Who can resist an invitation so full of compassion? Because of this personal experience in the goodness of the Bible, I was resolved that all my countrymen should also share its great blessing and that by reading the Bible they should find truth for themselves. Today man sees all his hopes and aspirations crumbling before him. He is perplexed and knows not wither he is drifting. But he must realize that the Bible is his refuge, and the rallying point for all humanity. In it man will find the solution of his present difficulties and guidance for his future action, and unless he accepts with clear conscience the Bible and its great message, he cannot hope for salvation. For my part I glory in the Bible."

What eloquent speech, such beautiful language. This man must be an orator of some kind. "Who are you, sir, if you don't mind my asking?"

Obviously more accustomed to being introduced as opposed to this kind of self-introduction, he answered, "I am the Emperor, of course. Haile Selassie I of Ethiopia. I....Nevermind, it's not important." He finished abruptly.

Haile Selassie of Ethiopia? "Are we in Ethiopia?"

"We are," responded the Emperor.

But, I thought...? I immediately reflected back on Menelik and the Ark of the Covenant. *Is Ethiopia a Hebrew nation, a nation of Jews?* I thought of the surrounding countries and kingdoms. *Is it a Muslim nation?*

"Ethiopia, an island of Christianity, is recorded in history as having received first the Old Testament, and then the New Testament, earlier than most of the countries of the world. It is centuries past since Our country, Ethiopia, accepted the Gospel of Christ. We learn from the Holy Scriptures that the first Ethiopian who confessed faith in Jesus Christ was baptized only a few months after the death and resurrection of Our Lord. From then on Christianity spread steadily among the Ethiopian people and became the religion of the Ethiopians in the Fourth Century. Christianity has flourished in Our country, keeping its original features and character through the centuries. At the time when several Christian peoples in the North became subservient to non-Christian powers, our country gladly provided asylum to thousands of Christian refugees. It had equally given asylum from religious persecution at an earlier date to the followers of the founder of Islam. Ethiopia, an island of Christianity, has made her own distinctive contribution to the Christian faith; for, ever since her conversion to Christianity, she has remained faithful, her age-old ties with the Apostolic church uninterrupted."

The Emperor reached into his patent leather attaché case and retrieved some old photos which, upon my delight, he offered to show me; the stone-carved churches of Lalibela, St. Mary's of Zion church where the Ark of the Covenant is kept, pictures of himself alongside Presidents John F. Kennedy, Eisenhower, Nixon and Johnson. There was another photo of him with Queen Elizabeth among other notable royalty. I intended to interview the aged monarch by asking him more questions when what occurred, in fact, was that he ended up quizzing me.

"Perhaps we should share some cake?" suggested the Emperor. **"Man does not live by bread alone. The spiritual life, however, does not deny the need for bread.** It *is* your birthday, isn't it?" *Not only that*, I thought. *Today is the day I was born!*

He asked me about my writing. "How is your book going, David?" And he shared with me some advice.

"It is our conviction that all the activities of the children of men which are not guided by the Spirit and counsel of God will bear no lasting fruit. They will not be acceptable in the sight of the Lord and will therefore come to nought as the Tower of Babel came to naught."

"But, I *do* feel this is what I'm supposed to do, what God is *calling* me to do, to write this book."

"Once a person has decided upon his life work and is assured that in doing the work for which he is best endowed and equipped, he is filling a vital need, what he then needs, is faith and integrity, compiled with courageous spirit so that no longer preferring himself to the fulfillment of his task, he may address himself to the problems he must solve in order to be effective. Whatever the task may be, man may begin it but he cannot complete it, unless God sustains and supports him."

That's easier said than done, I thought. "Sometimes I feel like there's just not enough time. I get so busy and occupied with other things. There are just not enough hours in the day. I just wish that I could muster up more willpower and find the strength to finish…"

"Spiritual power is the eternal guide, in this life and the life after, for man ranks supreme among all creatures. Led forward by spiritual power, man can reach the summit destined for him by the Great Creator. It is our firm belief that if you forego self-love and self-indulgence and break away from worldly desires you will be able to make great contributions to your family, community and country."

I wondered…*What great contributions could I make? What could I really accomplish?* "What if I do publish a best-selling novel and become filthy rich? What then?"

"If the wealth of a person is not for the general welfare, what will he gain for himself and his offspring but grudging and hatred? The fruits of one's sweat and mental labor are always rewarding, not only to oneself but also to succeeding generations. Be resolute in your work and attempt to complete whatever you undertake; if you face failure, try again and persist in your determination to attain your aim.

"But, what could *I* possibly do to help others, to serve my community, to make the world a better place? I want to help, but sometimes I just don't know how."

"A qualified man with vision, unmoved by daily selfish interests, will be led to right decisions by his conscience. Wise men have always known the deep and pervading truth that it is better to give than to receive, for even as it conflicts with selfish and ambitious desires, it moderates and controls them. Giving always demands sacrifice. There is nothing more worthwhile and rewarding in life than to work for the benefit of others. Man, who is selfish by nature, must learn that only in serving others can he reach the full stature or attain the noble destinies for which God created him. You are from the United States of America, are you not?" questioned the Emperor.

"Yes sir, the land of the free and the home of the brave!"

"Freedom, liberty, the rights of man- these mean little to the ignorant, the hungry, the ill-clothed, the badly housed. It is both the duty and responsibility of the world's fortunate few to help fulfill the legitimate aspirations of the unfortunate many. Let us not deny our ideals or sacrifice our right to stand as champions of the poor, the ignorant and the oppressed everywhere. We must become members of a new race, overcoming petty prejudice, owing our ultimate allegiance not to nations but to our fellow men within the human community.

"So are you saying we shouldn't cherish, preserve and protect our nation and our freedom?

"The preservation of peace and the guaranteeing of man's basic freedoms and rights require courage and eternal vigilance: courage to speak to speak and act, and if necessary, to suffer and die, for truth and justice; eternal vigilance, that the least transgression of international morality shall not go undetected and unremedied. It is our hope that efforts for peace would not confine themselves to verbal statements, but would work out in the actual relations between the nations of the world."

"How then is it suggested that we promote peace, might I ask?"

"We must speak out on major world issues, courageously, openly and honestly, and in blunt terms of right and wrong. Disarmament has become the urgent imperative of our time. I do not say this because I equate the absence of arms to peace, or because I believe that bringing an end to the nuclear arms race automatically guarantees the peace, or because the elimination of nuclear warheads from the arsenals of the world will bring in its wake that change in attitude requisite to the peaceful settlement of disputes between nations. Disarmament is vital today, quite simply, because of the immense destructive capacity of which men dispose. Conflicts between nations will continue to arise. The real issue is whether they are to be resolved by force, or by resort to peaceful methods and procedures, administered by impartial institutions. Were a real and effective disarmament achieved and the funds now spent in the arms race devoted to the amelioration of man's state; were we to concentrate only on the peaceful uses of nuclear knowledge, how vastly and in how short a time might we change the conditions of mankind. This should be our goal. We demand an end to nuclear testing and the arms race because these activities, which pose dreadful threats to man's existence and waste and squander humanity's material heritage, are wrong. A program of progressive disarmament must be agreed upon."

The Emperor suggested that we now go to the Lord in prayer, **"How can we pay our gratitude to God but by thanking him,"** and requested that he be allowed to pray for my personal well-being. I was grateful for this, for I needed all the prayers and encouragement I could get.

He quietly stood, motioning that I kneel down in front of him and, upon my doing so, placed his hands gently upon my head, **"May God our Creator, the Helper and guiding light of us all, grant you His wisdom."** The Emperor continued, **"No matter what may befall a human being, he can always succeed in overcoming it in a time if he had the strength of faith and praise to God, for inevitably He comes to the assistance of those that believe in Him and those that through their work live an exemplary life. This goes not only for Christians in my view, but for all men. I think God commiserates with those that find themselves in misfortune."**

Not only for.........? Was he referring to me? The question he inquisitively posed next stunned and shocked me more than anything. I wasn't ready for it. Here I was, standing before...*His Majesty,* The Emperor Haile Selassie I of Ethiopia, and he wanted to know, he wanted me to answer...*What would be my response?*

"Are you a Christian?" he calmly asked.

What on earth should I say? The moment has come. *You either are or you aren't,* I told myself.

Well...am I? Am I a Christian? Could I not be permitted just a little more time to weigh the evidence, to make a well-informed, rational decision? Must I decide now?

"But, sir, if I may ask, how can a person be certain, entirely convinced, without a doubt, that Jesus is the Son of God? That He is the Messiah?"

"I would tell a person that is considering the claim of Christ for the first time that it is necessary to have faith in the Almighty, that it is necessary to have love, and that its necessary to conduct oneself in a manner that we have been taught to do in the Bible. I would also advise him to read and study the Bible. I would also advise him to seek the secular knowledge, for the more one knows, the more he realizes the need for a prime mover, the need for a Creator, a Creator who is good and the need for salvation

and also for peaceful life upon earth. I will also tell him to learn and to think for himself the ways he would serve the Lord. In this thought and in this undertaking of his, he will inevitably find the way of serving his fellowmen. For this faith would then be manifested in his conduct."

But, I'm not considering this for the first time. "Your Majesty, I *have* studied the Bible and I have sought secular knowledge. I do believe in God. But, how can I be assured that Jesus really was born of a virgin? That He did miracles? That He came back from the dead? That He came to…

He quickly finished my thought, "That He came to save the world? That He came to save you and me?" It wasn't necessary that he respond to the question. *Faith. How can you prove faith?* I already knew the answer.

"The mystery of Bethlehem reveals itself in our spirits, more fascinating the more we advance on the path of life, and the more we realize the magnitude of the mission each one of us has to accomplish in this world, be it humble or noble, arduous of thankless. An unheard of event, expected for more than forty centuries has at last been accomplished: The Son of God is born. He has only a stable for a palace and a manger for a cradle. The hearts of the wise are thrilled by this majestic humility, and the kings of the Earth bend their knees before Him and worship Him. When Jesus Christ was born from Virgin Mary, from that time on He lived an exemplary life, a life which men everywhere must emulate. This life and the faith that He taught us assures us of salvation, assures us also of harmony and a good life upon Earth. Because of the exemplary character of the life of Jesus Christ it is necessary that all men do their maximum in their human efforts to see to it that they approximate as much as they can the good example that has been set by Him. It is quite true that there is no perfection in humanity. From time to time we make mistakes, we do commit sins but even as we do that, deep in our hearts as Christians we know we have forgiveness from the Almighty. He taught us that all who seek Him shall find Him. To live in this healthy life, a Christian life, is what makes me follow Jesus

Christ. After Our blameless Creator was sent to this world by His Father, then the hearts of all believers become the Temple of God. The love of God cannot be fathomed by a series of questions and answers, and man's soul cannot experience deeper enrichment as a result."

A knock on the door. The sound of a key. The iron hinges squeaked. It was the same spirited, young guard who had earlier attended The Emperor. This time he carried with him a tray on which was balanced a ceramic vessel, a container. "Your Majesty sir, I have brought you your daily water, sir. Please, consider accepting a drink today. It has been too long. Allow me to pour you a cup, please, sir." The young fellow bowed his head in respect as permission was granted him.

"**Thank you, for your genuinely kind service to us,**" the Emperor spoke, "**Without love all of our human efforts in the sight of God can be useless. He loved us and on our behalf He was given as a ransom, and it was because of love and His love for us that He accomplished the act of love. May Almighty God who proposes and disposes of everything bless you and keep you.**"

The guard was excused and, as we sat there alone, the Emperor's gaze turned to me. He took from the tray the cup of water, gave thanks, and offered it to me saying, "Drink from it," that it was, "necessary for the journey." After that, he poured water from the vessel into a basin and began to wash my feet, drying them with a handkerchief that had been tucked into the pocket of his coat. *Was he making me a disciple? But how could I...?*

I must have fallen asleep. *What is this? A dream within a dream?* I was awakened suddenly by the young guard and two others who escorted me from where I was still seated in the wooden chair. The Emperor was back at his desk; his Bible, unsurprisingly, lay open as he sat, flipping through pages, reading the Holy Scripture. He looked up momentarily from the text as I was being led from the room and offered these last words of advice...

"**However wise or however mighty a person may be, he is like a ship without a rudder if he is without God. A rudderless ship is at the mercy of the waves and the wind, drifts wherever they take it,** and if there arises a whirlwind it is smashed against the rocks and becomes as if it has never existed. It is our firm belief that a soul without Christ is bound to meet with no better fate. The love shown by our God to mankind should constrain all of us who are followers and disciples of Christ, to do all in our power to see to it that the message of salvation is carried to those of our fellows who have not had the benefit of hearing the good news...... Save no effort in working and making others work for the propagation of the Christian faith. A brother cannot be of more valuable service to his brother than in this."

But, did I ever answer the question? Did I even answer it? Did I tell him, yes, that I am a Christian? How could...? How do I...?

The guards led me through a series of hallways, up a couple flights of stairs and out the back door of the palace to where a long, black, stretch limousine was parked, engine running. I was whisked away from the palace grounds and taken to a nearby airstrip where a plane sat, awaiting my arrival. It would be a quick departure. The Emperor had apparently summoned the aircraft and had planned the entire escape. *It was the year 1975.* The communist party had succeeded in their overthrow and had gained control of the government. *It's 1975!* Millions of boat people in Vietnam were fleeing the VietCong militia and the fall of Saigon.

I boarded the Boeing-made 747 aircraft painted red, gold and green, the colors of the Ethiopian flag. On the sides of the plane were printed the words 'Lion of Judah'. The jet screamed as we took off and were soon passing over the Red Sea, over Arabia, India, Asia, the Pacific. I slept soundly through the night, waking only at dawn and peering out the window at the first rays of morning sunlight. I had a very good seat, me being the only passenger on the plane.

"Please remain seated, your seatbelt fastened," the pilot announced over the intercom. "We are starting our final descent." *Hey, wait, I know this place! I know where we are!*

Flying high above, it was unmistakably easy to recognize the beautiful island of Kauai down below. The captain gently steered the iron bird as we glided on air currents down into the Lihue airport, landing and coming to a stop on the runway. I deboarded the aircraft by exiting down the ramp and, wearing only boxer shorts and a nightshirt, stood barefoot on the warm pavement of the tarmac. A speeding car came whizzing up to me, screeching to a halt.

"You need a taxi, bruddah?" It was Kane and Lono. They had come to pick me up and take me back home.

CHAPTER 16

The rooster crowed three times before I accepted the fact it was morning and could no longer reject the idea of getting out of bed. I forced myself to get up, walked over to the sink, turned on the faucet and splashed some cold water on my face. It seemed I had slept for ages. *Am I suffering from some acute form of jetlag syndrome? What an intense dream. Where is...?*

"Here's your smoothie." Kathryn handed me a pureed mango, pineapple, and banana tropical fruit concoction. "Why were you so distant last night?" *Probably because I traveled half way 'round the world.* "You didn't even so much as touch me. No goodnight kiss, no sweet dreams..."

"I'm sorry. You know, I drank the tea and next thing I know..."

"Are you sure you've been meeting with that big, ukulele-playing Hawaiian guy? What'd you say his so-called name is? Bruddah Iz? That seems a little far-fetched. I don't know? You're not meeting with....?" She accused me of a having sexual escapade with old what's-her-name down the street.

"No, of course not," I said, trying to assuage her unmanageable suspicions and allegations of infidelity. I chalked it up to her bouts with the uncontrollably haywire hormonal changes suffered during pregnancy but, in spite of that, I didn't want to stay and argue anymore.

Within an hour I was crossing the valley stream, soon to be arriving at the *heiau* where I would meet with Iz for our third encounter. I rounded the final bend, following the low-pitched crooning and the soft, soothing voice of Bruddah Iz which had a remarkably tranquilizing effect on my soul.

Where trouble melts like lemon drops
High above the chimney tops that's where you'll find me
Oh, somewhere over the rainbow way up high
And the dream you dare to, why, oh why, can't I....?

"Hey, bruddah."

"Aloha, Bruddah!"

"How'zit, bruddah?"

"Good, Bruddah."

"So you meet da King?" he asked.
"Yeah Iz, I think so. If the tiny little, pint-sized Emperor, Haile Selassie, who spoke with such eloquence is the King, then, yes, I did meet him."
"Fo sho?"
"For sure Iz, I was in Ethiopia."
"Yeah, bruddah, dat's him alright. Dat's da King."
The King of what? An Emperor rules his empire, but...a king sits on his throne!
"Many people consider him to be the modern-day King of Israel," acknowledged Bruddah Iz. "Some think he was God, the representation of Jesus Christ in his kingly character, fulfilling the Biblical prophecy found in the Book of Revelation. Still others believe him to be a prophet or a saint. You telling me you never heard of Ras Tafari?"
"I've heard the name mentioned, you know, in Reggae music and stuff. So, you're saying that Ras Tafari is really Haile Selassie, Emperor of Ethiopia? And the Rastafarian movement? It's not all just about happy, feel good Caribbean music and positive vibrations, using marijuana and all that?"
"No, bruddah, Ras Tafari was thought to be a direct descendant of King Solomon and Queen Sheba. Prophets and Astrologers had for yeas foretold of his birth. During his early childhood it was rumahd that wild animals, lions and leopards became docile in his presence. He astounded priests and scholars wit his ability to quote freely from all important religious texts. Some even say dat on the palms of his hands were stigmata or scars from being nailed to da cross and dat his lifeline circled back in da sign of infiniti."

An Adventure of Biblical Proportions

Iz continued, "In an excerpt from <u>Catch a Fire, the Life of Bob Marley</u> it is stated, 'He (Ras Tafari) recounted to these scholars and holy men the story of Solomon and Sheba as vividly as if he had witnessed the events himself. After his explanation of how the Ark of the Covenant was taken from Israel to Ethiopia, they demanded to know the source of his detailed information. Instead of replying, Ras Tafari addressed a monk who had served in the St. Mary's of Zion church where the Ark is kept. He described to him the Kodesh Hakodashim, the Holy of Holies or inner sanctuary where the Ark is kept, and recited various inscriptions written upon it."

I was amazed. Still, I had my doubts, "But, he was imprisoned, incarcerated, overthrown and disrespected." It was hard to imagine that the small, elderly, shadow of a man I saw in Ethiopia would be the King of anything, let alone the King of Israel. *But, alas! His words, so eloquent, so well spoken and so true!*

"Is it not enough to see Jesus suffering on the cross," asked Bruddah Iz, "chastised and rebuked, mocked and beaten, weak and dying, the King of the Jews?"

[The inscription etched on the wooden cross was written in Latin, Greek and Hebrew, 'Jesus the Nazorean, King of the Jews', which in Latin reads: *IsvsNazarenvsRexIvdæorvm*. When the primary language of the church was Latin, people were very familiar with the phrase and it became customary to abbreviate the lengthy wording to the initial letters: INRI. From the pronunciation of INRI we find the origin of the name Henry, given to the King of England by his father William the Conqueror who led the Normans, an invading group of Christian Israelites, into Britain in the year 1066 A.D.]

Iz continued, "What you want? You wanna see da King in all His glory? Only, den, will you believe what I'm tellin' you is true? Whatevah, brah, dis time forget da kava an jus go meditate fo a while. Den you will see."

Meditate? "But, how do I meditate when I've never done it before? And isn't meditation for Hindus? But, I'm a...... I'm a....."

Iz responded, "It was His Majesty Haile Selassie, himself, who said…'**We must stop confusing religion and spirituality. Religion is a set of rules, regulations and rituals created by humans which** were supposed to help people grow spiritually. Due to human imperfection religion has become corrupt, political, divisive, and a tool for power struggle. Spirituality is not theology or ideology. It is a simple way of life, pure and original as was given by the most high. Spirituality is a network linking us to the most high, the universe and each other. As the essence of our existence it embodies our culture, true identity, nationhood and destiny.' You see, it's not only for Hindus," Iz reassured me. "You can practice meditation and still be a Christian. You are a Christian, aren't you?"

I think so.

"Den, go now to da Temple over on Kaholale Road, along the upper Wailua River. Dat's a real good place fo you to go an meditate."

Three hours later I arrived at the front gate, nervous and somewhat apprehensive about entering into a traditional Hindu monastery-temple complex. *What am I doing here? Am I welcome?* The sign posted at the entrance read, **'Dedicated to the divine within everyone and everything.'** I took a deep breath and entered the premises.

Wandering along the trails, admiring the well manicured gardens amid such a peaceful setting, not twenty minutes had passed when I heard a voice call out to me from behind. "Welcome, David." *What? Who? How does he know my....?* "Glad you could make it. We were expecting you. I am Satguru Sivaya Subramuniyaswami. Many people refer to me simply as Gurudeva."

I turned to face the tall, pale-faced, seemingly gentle soul in his early-seventies who donned a hand-woven, saffron-colored cotton robe commonly worn by swamis and Hindi holy men, his long white beard flowing down the front of the outfit, his silky white hair tied in a knot atop his head.

"Relax into the peace; absorb the sanctity," he said to me. "Let it pass through you like a purifying wave. This monastery spreads out over 458 acres of gardens, groves, glens, paths, ponds and waterways and is a secluded home and theological seminary to two dozen monks from six different nations who live and serve here full time, striving to fulfill the dual goals of selfless service and self-transformation through yoga, which begins with good character and piety and leads to deep meditation and ultimate enlightenment."

"But sir, Mister Swami, sir, *I mean* Gurudeva, sir....your philosophy is beautiful, your faith commendable and one would be wise to adhere to the principles of your religion, but I must admit, your holiness, that I myself have chosen a different path. I am not a Hindu, I am a...."

"Relax, David. Be at one with the universe. According to the ageless, timeless words of Haile Selassie..."

What? "Wait a second." *Did he say...?*

"Yes, David, like I said...we knew you would be coming."

He gave me a little wink and a smile before continuing, "His Majesty taught us that...'**In the mystic traditions of the different religions we have a remarkable unity of the spirit. Whatever religions they may profess they are spiritual kinsmen. While the different religions in their historical forms bind us to limited groups and militate against the development of loyalty to the world community, the mystics have always stood for the fellowship of humanity. Were the thoughts of Plato and Socrates, the beliefs of Christianity and Judaism not harmonized with Hindu philosophy; were Yoga and its various stages not exposed to Western thought; had Western religion and philosophy not been exposed to the philosophy and religion of the East, how much the poorer would human thought have been! Since nobody can interfere in the realm of God we should tolerate and live side by side with those of other faiths.**"

"Now let me describe the similarities," voiced the Swami, "between Krishna of the Hindu faith and the Christ of the Christian religion. To begin with, both were the sons of God who had their God-designed missions foretold. They were both born in lowly places, Christ in a manger in a stable and Krishna in a prison cell. Another likeness of the two is that Christ is depicted as a shepherd of sheep and Krishna, he is a cow herder. Also, take into consideration the similarity of their teachings, both emphasizing love and peace."

Very interesting. "I never thought of...*I mean*...I never realized..."

"What is the meaning of the word Christ?" asked Gurudeva. Then, answering his own question, he stated, "Christ comes from the Greek word *Christos*, which means 'the anointed one'. Krishna is the Hindi version of the word *Christos*. To further prove this point, the father of the Krishna Consciousness Movement, AC Bhaktivedanta Swami Prabhupada, once remarked: 'When an Indian person calls on Krishna, he often says Krsta. Krsta is a Sanskrit word meaning attraction. So when we address God as Christ, Krsta, or Krishna we indicate the same all-attractive Supreme Personality of Godhead. When Jesus said, 'Our Father who art in heaven hallowed be Thy name', the name of God was Krsta or Krishna. 'Christ' is another way of saying Krsta and Krsta is another way of pronouncing Krishna, the name of God. Therefore whether you call God 'Christ', 'Krsta', or 'Krishna', ultimately you are addressing the same Supreme Personality of Godhead."

The sagacious, old yogi continued his discourse, "The problem is that the Christians do not follow the commandments of God. Do you agree?"

"Yes, to a large extent I do."

"Then what is the meaning of the Christians' love for God? If you do not follow the orders of God, then where is your love? Therefore we have come to teach what it means to love God. If you love Him you cannot be disobedient to His orders. And if you are disobedient your love is not real. All over the world people don't love God. The Krishna consciousness movement is therefore necessary to teach people how to revive their forgotten love for God. Not only the Christians, but also the Hindus, the Mohammedans and all others are guilty. They have rubber-stamped themselves as Christian, Hindu or Mohammedan, but they do not obey God. This is the problem. By chanting Hare Krishna we are saying, 'O energy of God, O God, please engage me in Your service.' It is our nature to render service. Somehow or other we have come to the service of material things, but when this service is transformed into the service of the spiritual energy, then our life is perfect. To practice yoga means to become free from designations and simply to serve God."

He led me down a narrow pathway to a small, grassy knoll which sat a little higher than the surrounding, mostly flat area alongside the banks of the river. The water gurgled past, flowing peacefully downstream, providing a relaxing backdrop to such a tranquil setting. Another branch of the Wailua, a side stream, gently tumbled down the rocky hillside creating a series of cascades which then connected into the main water flow and meandered through the temple complex.

"This will be a good place for you to practice your yoga meditation!" exclaimed the swami as he went teetering up the steps that had been carved into the hill, all the while blessing me and chanting, "May you be bathed with Divine Love in the presence of Lord Krishna. May you be washed clean with the love of Christ."

The misting spray coming off the falls dampened and cooled my face and arms while the shade from a towering banyan tree provided shelter from the burning tropical rays of the sun. As I stared hypnotically into the clear, transparent pool of water a suddenly surfacing fish caused a few ripples to appear and I watched as the reflection of myself faded away into oblivion. A school of koi swam by, continuing over to the base of the waterfall where churning water added infused oxygen into the river causing an abundance of algae to grow there in the shallows.

Sitting cross-legged on the ground, I closed my eyes and let my mind wander, drifting out into the universe. I thought of the *Ichthus*, the shooting star in flight. I thought of Christos and the light of Jesus Christ.

A dull white glow, a brilliant flash, then....

At first a vague image did appear, then more vivid, then so clear. I saw the imperial crown, fashioned out of gold and jewels, bearing the seal of Solomon and the Lion of Judah crest. I was there! There in the cathedral of St. George in Addis Ababa, Ethiopia! I watched with the wide-eyed interest of a small child at Christmas as dignitaries and guests from around the world began arriving one by one, bearing with them gifts of the greatest variety in honor of the momentous occasion. A one-ton cake was delivered from Great Britain. Five hundred bottles of fine Rhine wine were sent from German President von Hindenburg. The French government dispatched a private airplane.

A special envoy appointed to represent the United States was entrusted with a great largess, including an autographed and handsomely framed photograph of President Hoover and an inventory of unofficial, privately purchased presents; an electric refrigerator, a red typewriter emblazoned with the royal coat of arms, a radio-phonograph console, one hundred records of "distinctly American music," five hundred rosebushes, a new strain of *ofamaryllis* developed by the U.S. Department of Agriculture, a bound set of the *National Geographic* magazine, a bound report of the Chicago Field Museum's expedition to Abyssinia and prints of three motion pictures: *Ben Hur, King of Kings* and *With Byrd at the South Pole.*

"Here they come!" shouted voices from the crowd.

Riding in a stage coach, said to be that of Kaiser Wilhelm, the emperor and empress were transported by a team of snow-white Hapsburg stallions. They had just completed a night of prayer and devotion at the altar within the church. It was Sunday, November 2, 1930. All of Addis Ababa had prepared for the impressive event of the morning. The chanting of praises continued to rise and reverberate off the lofty ceiling of the cathedral, accompanied by the dancing of priests with great pulsating drums, all suggestive of the ancient Jewish rites in use at the time when King David danced before the Ark of the Covenant.

Prince Tafari Makonnen, taking the name given to him at birth, becomes Haile Selassie I, the 225th King of Ethiopia in a lineage descending from the dynasty of Menelik I, born of the union of King Solomon of Israel and the Queen of Sheba. His Imperial Majesty is given the titles King of Kings, Lord of Lords, The Conquering Lion of the Tribe of Judah, Defender of the Faith, Light of the World and Emperor of Ethiopia.

Haile Selassie I, whose name is translated as Power to the Holy Trinity, gives his sacred pledge to uphold the religion of the Church, to support and administer the laws of the country for the betterment of the people, to maintain the integrity of Ethiopia and to found schools for the development of the Spiritual and Material welfare of her subjects. One by one with the solemn rites and blessings of the clergy, he received the gold-embroidered scarlet robes, the jeweled sword, the gold scepter and the orb and the diamond encrusted ring.

Following the ancient custom, as when Samuel anointed King David, and Zadok and Nathan anointed Solomon, so His Majesty's head is anointed with oil. Seven differently scented ointments of ancient prescription are received on the Imperial head, brow and shoulders. The bishop then concludes with the words: "That God make this crown a crown of glory. That by the grace and the blessing which we have given, you may have an unshaken faith and a pure heart in order that you may inherit the crown eternal. So be it."

Applause erupted inside the cathedral. The band struck up a tune. Outside, cannons roared a 101 gun salute as cheering could be heard from the throngs of spectators that had amassed in the vicinity of the cathedral in order to witness this monumental event. *Was I actually witnessing the historical Coronation of His Majesty Haile Selassie I of Ethiopia? I'm a witness!* I thought. *I'm a witness!*

Then, it was time for the final ceremony, a grand tour of the cathedral by His Imperial Majesty escorted by bishops and priests, princes and high dignitaries, assistants and others, myself included! I was selected to carry one of the many palm branches as everyone joined together, chanting in mighty volume, "Blessed be the King of Israel." I was there! I was there! *I was there! I was... I...*

Now, I'm here? Where am I? Oh, yes, the amazing wonders of meditation! I sat cross-legged, eyes closed, the moist condensation from the waterfall mist dripping down my face and brow, soaking my light cotton t-shirt. My ears, meanwhile, remained attentive to the sweet musical sounds of a Hawaiian ukulele, its melodic strum slowly bringing me out of a trance-like state back into the here and now. A voice echoed over the rushing sound of falling water.

There's a place I recall
Not too big, in fact its kinda small
The people there know they got it all
The simple life for me

Hele a to Kauai
Hanalei by the bay
Wailua river valley is where I used to play
The canyons of Waimea standing all aglow
The magic of the garden isle is calling me back home

I opened my eyes to see Bruddah Iz, his massive frame straddling a giant boulder which sat in the river, diverting the water's steady flow and current. Flashes of red, orange and yellow shot from his fingertips each time he tenderly plucked a chord on his four-stringed wooden instrument. Green, blue, indigo, violet, all the colors of the rainbow danced and darted, weaving about in a splendorous electrical display, tethering together the music and the air with imaginary cords of supersonic light. Was I running a high risk of shock and electrocution? Should I dare wade out into the electromagnetic stream where Iz was compelling me to join him? I felt forcibly pulled into an oscillating field of transmitted radio waves in which Bruddah Iz was the illustrious conductor of the symphony.

"It hasn't always been dis peaceful hea in Hawaii," Iz said. "You heard of Pearl Harbor, haven't you?"

"Sure Iz, my grandfather was stationed there during the attack."

"And you know da history of World War II, about Italy's invasion of Ethiopia. You evah heard Haile Selassie's famous speech before da League of Nations, actively pursuing help from Europe and da Allied powers, warning them of their impending doom if they refused to act?"

"No, I'm not familiar with that."

"Lemme tell you, bruddah, Selassie addressed the assembly about da use of mustard gas by Mussolini and da Italians, even though it was outlawed at da Geneva Convention. He informed dem dat, **'Special sprayers were installed on board aircraft so that they could vaporize, over vast areas of territory, a fine, death-dealing rain. Groups of nine, fifteen, eighteen aircraft followed on another so that the fog issuing from them formed a continuous sheet. It was thus that, as from the end of January, 1936, soldiers, women, children, cattle, rivers, lakes and pastures were drenched continually with this deadly rain. In order to kill off systematically all living creatures, in order to more surely poison waters and pastures, the Italian command made its aircraft pass over and over again. That was its chief method of warfare. That is why I decided to come myself to bear witness against the crime perpetrated against my people and give Europe a warning of doom that awaits it, if it should bow before the accomplished fact, defending the cause of all small peoples who are threatened with aggression. Apart from the Kingdom of the Lord there is not on this earth any nation that is superior to any other. Should it** happen that a strong Government finds it may with impunity destroy a weak people, then the hour strikes for that weak people to appeal to the League of Nations to give its judgment in all freedom. God and history will remember your judgment.'"

Iz continued, "After his speech, Haile Selassie went to England in exile. In fact, during World War II, London played an integral role by hosting nearly a dozen European royal families. Upon da arrival of His Imperial Majesty in London, Chinese, Hindus, Arabs and Africans, side by side wit English of every class, simultaneously waved British and Ethiopian flags as dey greeted him with a host of cheers and applause. Unlike da majority of his fellow exiled kings, da Emperor did not stay in the English capital. Instead he settled into a quiet, country life in da town of Bath."

"I've heard of Bath, England," I commented, interrupting Iz for a moment. "Bath was a major Celtic spiritual center and place of worship. I believe it is home to the only natural hot springs in Great Britain and was named after the baths that were put into use there by the Romans. Right, Iz?"

Iz chuckled and laughed, the rolls of his belly shaking like a bowl full of jelly. "Dat's where you wrong, bruddah!" he said with a big grin. "Dis da good part! Listen up. In Hebrew *BT* is *bayit* and is da word for 'house or seat', remembah no vowels, bruddah. Most of da time, *BT* is pronounced Beth. Fo example, Bethlehem is 'the House of Lehem', Beth David is da 'House of David' and Beth Israel..."

"The House of Israel!" I answered. "And the name Elizabeth?"

"Dat's da House of Elisha. You pretty smart, bruddah!"

I thought for a second. *So BT is the word 'bayit' and can be pronounced Beth or even Bath. Could it be that...?* "Bath is Beth!" I exclaimed to Bruddah Iz in utter amazement. "So, what you're saying is that His Majesty Haile Selassie I, King of Kings, Conquering Lion of the Tribe of Judah went to live in exile in Bath, England and to, perhaps, maybe..."

"Fulfill his duty and sit on da throne as da King of Israel? Preside over Beth David and Beth Israel, da Twelve Tribes of Jacob? Yes, bruddah, I'm da one sayin' it, but you da one thinking it! Am I right?"

"I.... I really don't know?" I stuttered. "Maybe he *was* the King of Israel or, perhaps, a prophet or a saint." *But, is it even remotely possible, even in the slightest, that he was…? No way, not plausible! Not a chance. Or, maybe…?*

Iz interjected, "Towards da end of da war, upon leaving Great Britain and, with help from the British Army, returning to his palace in Addis Ababa, nice place by da way, dis is what he said…

'Four years ago I declared: If there is justice in this world, and I know there is, then I shall some day, in God's own good time and when He considers it suitable and fitting, sit on the throne of Solomon. God's time is now at hand. In order that the work of evil may not triumph again over this redeemed humanity, all peace-loving people must rally together for the definite re-establishment of right and peace. It is not only war that can stop war. Men of goodwill, conscious of their mission, and strengthened by the support of free peoples, can yet save this precious treasure, peace, and stop war.'

Da famous Winston Churchill, Prime Minister of England at dis time, you know what he say? He spoke before da United States Congress an said, "He must indeed have a blind soul who cannot see that some great purpose and design is being worked out here below, of which we have the honor to be faithful servants." Iz finished the sentence, such a profound and meaningful statement; then, right before my eyes, I swear…he disappeared.

As I would come to find out later (while watching a newscast commemorating 'The Man and his Music') the legendary, native-born Hawaiian, Israel Kamakawiwo'ole (who struck such an uncanny and inexplicable resemblance to my friend Bruddah Iz) had in fact died of heart failure two years prior, his body cremated and his ashes scattered into the Pacific Ocean. It would be hard to deny that I had been in the presence of a true angel. *That voice!*

Upon the arrival of Haile Selassie, returning to England for a visit in 1954, British Naval ships flew the Ethiopian flag and cannons fired royal salutes. The Royal Air Force staged a fly-by.

"We greet you as the Sovereign of an ancient Christian State which has many links with our own church and as the Sovereign of the country which was first to regain its freedom during the last war."

-Queen Elizabeth II

We left da house. *I mean*...We left the house where Jacinda Kaialani was born and drove our rental car up Kuamoo Road., taking a sharp left on Kaholale. Seven years later, I was entering for a third time through the gates and into the traditional Hindu monastery-temple complex. As a baby, Jacinda had been baptized, if you will, sprinkled on the head with Holy Water bottled up and brought from the Ganges River by the old swami, Gurudeva, whose cremated ashes now lay encased inside the new temple currently being constructed on the property with hand-carved stones, chiseled and shaped by master stone-cutters in India and shipped to this peaceful 458 acre sight on the beautiful garden island of Kauai.

Hand in hand we wandered around for a short while admiring the well-manicured grounds, the lotus gardens and the ponds. A gentle voice called out to us from behind and we were slowly approached by a bearded gentleman wearing a saffron-colored, long-flowing, cotton robe. It was the newly appointed swami, Satguru Bodhinatha Veylanswami, the successor to Subramuniyaswami, or Gurudeva as we like to call him.

"Welcome to the monastery," he said. "I see you've had a chance to tour the grounds. Can you tell me, what was your favorite part?"

Jacinda Kaialani was quick to respond. "The fish," she said.

The fish, I thought, *good answer,* and with the loving smile of a proud father, gave her a kiss on the cheek, softly whispering in her ear...

"IXOYE"

"Oh, Daddy, you might as well be speaking Greek!" she said.

I turned and addressed the swami, "I've been here previously and distinctly remember a gorgeous waterfall. Isn't there...?

"Yes," he answered, his eyes widening in a surprised look, "But, we don't usually....I mean visitors don't normally....It's kind of hard to find. I'll show you where it is." He explained to us that we continue down the path, cross a tiny footbridge, go down a sloping hill and…"There's a nice grassy knoll where you can sit and view the waterfall," he said. "It's a wonderful place to practice meditation!"

CHAPTER 17

I never dreamed I would end up a single dad, raising two young girls alone, by myself. Divorce was a word I had tried to erase from my vocabulary ever since my parents had bitterly broken off their nuptial vows and sadly terminated their marriage. For me, that wasn't a possibility. Family values, the matrimonial bond and the true sanctity of marriage are to be held in high esteem, protected, nurtured and strengthened. Divorce is to be avoided at all costs, like an ugly stain on a pure white bridal gown on an otherwise picture-perfect wedding day. Such an epidemic in our society, something so hurtful, so final, the mere idea or consideration of it should be rejected and vanquished, never to be discussed again. *No, it could never happen to me.*

I was aware of the Scripture and the words of Jesus Christ...

> **But at the beginning of creation God 'made them male and female.' 'For this reason a man will leave his father and mother and be united to his wife, and the two will become one flesh.' So they are no longer two, but one. Therefore, what God has joined together, let man not separate.**
> **-Mark 10:6-9**

> **I tell you that anyone who divorces his wife, except for marital unfaithfulness, and marries another woman commits adultery.**
> **-Matthew 19:9**

Unfortunately, when infidelity is merely a suspicion, a glint in the eye of the accuser, it can be a tough pill to swallow and the cause of innumerous arguments and many sleepless nights.

It's hard to say, but I'd have to wager that nobody in their right mind would probably ever want to move from the unparalleled natural beauty of the Hawaiian Islands to the sprawling concrete streets and suburbs of H-town, the Bayou City, Houston, Texas, the petrochemical capital of the world. But, we did and had, in fact, carved out a little niche, a small enclave in the heart of the big city, our own personal Garden of Eden. A modest 1950's built two-bedroom one and a half bath cottage in about as quaint and quiet a neighborhood as could be found in this booming metropolis became our new home.

On the exterior, our marriage, like our house, looked fresh, well-kept, tidy and unblemished, but upon crossing the threshold one could see that on the inside, within its sturdy, hardiplank walls, it needed some fixing up, some remodeling, an entire makeover, really. Buried deep down below the surface, underneath the framework, invisible to the naked eye, the foundation was cracked and breaking and in dire need of repair. With further inspection, it became obvious that the entire structure was poised to collapse. The house could be saved. The marriage, however, would be lost.

I guess everyone tries to justify their reasons for wanting to get out. A failing marriage can be like the nightmarish hell of a prison cell for a wrongly accused inmate, shut up in solitary confinement because of poor behavior, fighting and constant complaining to the warden about the uncomfortable living conditions. There is such a fine line drawn between distrust and mistrust and either/or can have a lasting effect on one's psyche.

Whatever the reasons, she wanted out. Although, I was actively employed in the Recreation Ministry at a local church, we somehow always failed to attend Sunday morning services. God was not the foundation of our marriage. If you had asked me, I would have told you, however, that I had put my faith in God, that I was fully committed to Him, that I had already begun writing this book and that my intentions were good; I would publish a best-selling novel in order to bring others to a closer knowledge of the Lord, etcetera, etcetera. And, if you had asked me at the time, I would have told you that Kathryn was my true love, my *alma gemela,* my twin soul, that I was completely faithful in our marriage and that the thought of me being with another woman had never crossed my mind. That was until....

> **But I tell you that anyone who looks at a woman lustfully has already committed adultery with her in his heart.**
>
> -Matthew 5:28

July 22. The eve of my 28th birthday. Tomorrow will be the anniversary of the birth of His Majesty Haile Selassie and the first day of the astrological sign of Leo the Lion, the symbol of the twelve signs of the Zodiac most commonly attributed to the Tribe of Judah. The stars were aligning! It was all coming together; my research, the book. My dream of penning a manuscript, authoring an award-winning novel, writing an internationally acclaimed best-seller seemed, finally, after an exhausting effort, to be so very attainable. I could see the finish line up ahead in the distance! I sprinted towards it. If only! If only I could receive one last burst of speed, a fresh gust of wind in my sails, one last mind-boggling revelation, something to impress, to make the head spin, to convince my future lectors that, yes, God is real, that the Lord is alive and willing to listen, to hear, respond to and answer the sincere pleas and prayers of the very least of us, the genuinely meek, the humble, the young at heart! *GIVE ME A SIGN, OH LORD!!!*

    I awoke startled, drenched in sweat and perspiration, shocked I had asked for a revelation and confused by what I had received. *A dream... so intense, so erotic, so sensual and so real!* I...had dreamt...of another woman. *It was Kari.* But...seven years had passed since we last spoke.
    Before my travels in Central America, before Hawaii, before my marriage to Kathryn, I had beckoned....and she had come. She drove down from St. Louis and had come to my aid, to console me in my time of need, no doubt expecting to pick up where we had left off and proceed with an amorous encounter; a hot, steamy night spent in ecstasy as two young lovers reunited after a hiatus of more than a year would be expected to do. I, on the other hand, needed her to listen, to be a friend, to reassure me that I was alive and not deceased, not stuck in some unknown mystical realm where poor, sorry souls await their eternal judgment, an ascendance into the glories of heaven or an

abominable descent into the fiery infernos of hell. The visions were too intense to handle for me, a confused adolescent slowly embarking on the journey of manhood.

I related to her all the recent happenings, perhaps hoping for an explanation, a gentle hug, a warm embrace, *something*. "And the bumper sticker read, 'I BELIEVE IN ANGELS,'" I told her, "And they pointed at me proclaiming, 'He's a witness. He's a witness.' The verse on the screen, Kari...it read Job 3:14. And I had asked for a sign!"

"But, what does it mean? What should I make of it?" I asked, taking her in my arms, holding her close to me as we collapsed onto the silky sheets of the Queen-size bed, she wanting nothing more than for this Prince Charming to kiss her passionately, unlock the secrets of her body and take her into his clutches, ravaging with no restraints her entire being.

I wanted to. Believe me, I tried. I even smoked a cigarette and drank some tequila earlier that week. I wanted to feel human again, to put a stop to these visions, to return to some sort of normalcy and regain the lost innocence of a boy who had no other care in the world than that of satisfying the virgin desires of the girl he supposedly loved. I guess that was the moment in which I decided, not without regret, that she was not my true love. *No, ella no era mi verdadero amor.* She was not the girl of my dreams.

But, now....

I stripped myself of my sopping wet t-shirt, rose out of bed and jumped into the shower. It's here where a person can do some of their best thinking, relaxed and uninhibited, with the feel of warm, flowing water massaging, caressing and running down the back of the neck. All lathered up with soap from head to toe, I began to rinse myself clean, trying to rationalize in my mind the entire situation while excusing myself from any wrongdoing. *What would be the consequences of writing her? Just a brief note, a friendly greeting, a short 'hello', certainly nothing bad could possibly come of it, right?*

That's where I was wrong. Dead wrong. Whatever matrimonial bliss that was being sustained up until that point, in all realities, died that day, never able to be revived or even function artificially for a short time while hooked up to a life support system. The truth of the situation was that I had no intentions of rekindling some silly, meaningless childhood romance. I was happily married, a young father of two and, as far as I was concerned, that was all a man could ever really want...two healthy kids, a beautiful wife; a family to call his own. I sent the first letter, a harmless little message, in hopes of making initial contact.

Kari,

It has been so long. Are you still alive? I recently had a dream about you. I hardly have any recollection of it, you know, after waking, but I do remember we were someplace really green and vibrant, maybe a jungle, a rainforest or somewhere like that. I hope this letter finds you in good spirits!

I told her a little about my life, of my past experiences over the last seven years, not at all neglecting to inform her that I was happily married with children and working for the church. Shortly thereafter, I received a reply.

David,

Wow! You have this really great timing when contacting me! I hadn't thought about you in a long time and, then, just yesterday a friend asked me to name someone who had been a major influence in my life, someone who had made an impact on me. I said you, David! It's incredible that you've written to me! And what's more unbelievable...about your dream...I *did* just return from a Spanish immersion program in Guatemala, studying in the Peten region of the Mayan Biosphere. It was so beautiful there, so lush and so green!

Too ironic, I thought. *Guatemala!* Had she visited Tikal? Maybe even staying at El Mirador del Duende? Perhaps, she had met my friend Pedro the Congo monkey and had shared a banana with him? And how had I influenced her life? It must have been those long, philosophical talks on theology and religion. *I'll tell her about the book!* Or maybe it was that I had been the one to convince her to study abroad and experience other cultures? She was now attending the University of Missouri in Columbia, getting her Master of Arts in Teaching Foreign Languages. *Gonna be a Spanish teacher,* I thought. We had a lot in common and, thus, began our correspondence.

Kari,

You'll be glad to know that the book is coming along great! I honestly think I can actually prove that Jesus is the Messiah of the Jewish faith.

I told her about some of my research and awaited her response.

David,

What about the feminine aspect of God? I have recently done some reading on the subject and tend to question whether or not God is just a man. I mean, why is God always portrayed as a male? What about the sacred feminine? What are your thoughts on that?

I would gladly answer the questions, but in the meantime, I had done a little investigating into the origin and etymology of her last name.

Kari,

I imagine you'll find it interesting to know that your last name is of ancient origin, having its roots in the archaic written language of Sanskrit, *san* meaning 'holy' and *skrit* meaning 'script' or 'writing.' Your surname name, Daus, can be originally traced to Dyaus, the Sky God of the Indo-European Vedic religion of which modern Hinduism is based. It is from this root, Dyaus, which we get the Latin word for God, "Deus", the Spanish "Dios" and the Greek "Theos." And to answer your question, yes, in my opinion, God is as much female as male. According to the Bible.....

Genesis 1:27 God created man in his own image, in the image of God he created him; male and female he created them.

So, I would then conclude that when a man, who is made in the image of God and in whom lives the Holy Spirit, which is of God, unites with a woman, who is made in the image of God and in whom lives the Holy Spirit, which is of God, it becomes as if the female representation of the characteristics of God has combined with the male representation of the characteristics of God to form a holy and sacred Divine Union of one flesh.

We continued our exchange of letters as I shared even more with her about my research and ideas. She responded with more questions.

David,

So Rastafari is Haile Selassie? That's interesting. I'd like to know more. But, let me ask, what does the ex-leader of Ethiopia who died in 1975, albeit even if he is an Emperor, or perhaps even the King of Israel, have anything at all to do with the innumerable problems that are plaguing the world today? And, oh, by the way, that's neat what you told me about Dyaus. What's more amazing is that I received your letter the morning after a big Halloween party at my cousin's house. How coincidental that her costume was that of a Hindu Goddess? Her last name is Daus as well!

Kari,

His Majesty Haile Selassie devoted himself to interpreting Biblical teachings and prescribing them to the modern world. These lessons are just as relevant today as they were fifty years ago. Just like those of the Bible, the divine teachings of His Majesty are timeless and eternal. I know you are very much concerned with environmental issues, global warming and the like, are you not? Read, for example, the following words spoken by Selassie about the importance of being good stewards of the Earth:

We are greatly grieved to observe the many thousands of acres of rich forest land being destroyed every year by reckless timber-cutting, thoughtless forest burning, unregulated forest grazing and other misuses of our forest wealth, due to popular ignorance and desire for temporary advantage. The increasing pace of deforestation caused by unregulated tree-cutting, and the failure to replace these by new plantings give us occasion for anxiety. It is essential that steps be taken here and now to stop this wastage and check this destruction. It is our wish and desire that each and every citizen follows the example we set on this Arbor Day in planting this tree, and himself plants as many trees as he can, for his own benefit as well as for the benefit of future generations.

It is equally important in this day and age for us to be aware of the lessons and advice given by His Majesty about the internal affairs of other countries. How incredible is it that these same words are even more relevant today than they were when first uttered by the modern-day King of Israel?

Regarding the recent appointments in the Iraq government, We would consider this an internal matter of that government, and would not like to express any opinion, since We believe in the principle of non-interference in the internal affairs of other nations. In matters of foreign policy we have been ever guided by three basic principles. First is our deep conviction that, where there is no lack of goodwill, all international disputes can be resolved through negotiations, without recourse to violence. An inevitable corollary of this belief is our firm conviction that all nations, whatever their political persuasions, can live together in peace.

After swapping a few more letters back and forth for the duration of about another month, I received in the mail this response...

David,

First of all I want to thank you! For a long time, even though I received a religious education and, as you are well aware, attended a Catholic parochial school for many years, I admittedly have struggled quite a lot with my faith. If forced to proclaim my belief in God, I would have had trouble saying for certain that Jesus Christ was my Lord and Savior...that I was really, truly a Christian. I am so grateful that by our reconnection, and through our exchange of letters and information, you have helped me to regain something that I had previously lost and that, only now, am I really beginning to truly understand. Thank you for giving me the most precious gift imaginable. Thank you for giving me back my faith in God! I dreamed of you last night.

It should be noted that Kari and I had been corresponding the entire time in Spanish which, of course, is considered a romance language, the loving tongue, *la lengua del amor*. Nothing more really needs to be said here, except for the fact that I ended my next letter with these two or three words...*Te amo!* I love you!

I don't wish to spend too much time discussing it, but will briefly touch on the subject. Sadly enough, I suddenly became depressed. One morning not so different from all the rest, after casually opening up the Bible to whichever page and chapter it happened upon and hoping to come across something inspirational and encouraging, instead I found that the sorrowful, yet poignant, printed words of King Solomon had leaped off the leaves of paper and into my consciousness.

> **For with much wisdom comes**
> **much sorrow;**
> **the more knowledge, the**
> **more grief.**
> **-Ecclesiastes 1:18**

Was this my latest and greatest revelation? That I had mistakenly married the wrong woman?

> **Enjoy life with your wife, whom you love, all the days of**
> **this meaningless life that God has given you under the**

sun- all your meaningless days. For this is your lot in life and in your toilsome labor under the sun.
                                                   -Ecclesiastes 9:9

But, what if my wife does not reciprocate? What if she is not happy? What if she does not love me? What if I possibly married the wrong woman?

To make a long story short, Kathryn discovered the letters and read them, thus having to come to grips with the harsh realization that maybe she wasn't my twin soul, my true love and the only girl for me. I had to learn to cope with it as well. After a few more cold, chilling months of marriage, in which I endured ample punishment, the silent treatment, the cold shoulder, piercing stares, no form whatsoever of affection, a complete lack of love, caring and understanding, the withdrawal of sex, hugs, kisses, a warm touch and, eventually, a friend and a partner, she finally asked for a divorce. My sobbing and crying didn't work and neither were the kicking and screaming cause for reconsideration.

"You can't force somebody to love you," she told me.

Now, I'd like to think I'm a believer that all issues and disagreements can be resolved peacefully between a husband and a wife so that the marriage union becomes more complete, more tested, stronger and more durable with the passage of time, that through sickness and in health, whether that infirmity be alcoholism, drug-addiction, heartache or depression, a couple can overcome, together, their struggles and persevere through the hard times that life sometimes throws at us. *Are these not the vows we pledge to uphold?*

I exhausted each and every method in trying to salvage the marriage and reconcile our differences, but to no avail. She rejected the entire notion. Decimated and distraught, though still yearning to be united with my soul mate, to have a significant other, to love and to be loved, I had to keep on searching, scanning the horizon for the announcement of her arrival, my one true love, *mi verdadero amor*. I desperately wanted so much for it to be Kathryn, but was quickly gaining acceptance of the fact that it must be....

An Adventure of Biblical Proportions

Six months later.

Kari,

 I can't believe it! Who would have ever guessed the name of your home state of Missouri is really Hebrew, Phoenician and Arabic in origin? In all three languages, *Misr* is the name for Egypt. *Misri* is the Arabic word used to refer to native Egyptians. In Hebrew, *Mizrahi* means 'eastern' and is used to describe people descended from the Jews of the Middle East and North Africa. The word *misr* is derived from an ancient Egyptian word meaning 'fortress', usually referring to Egypt as a land with naturally protected borders. It is common for Egyptians to refer to Egypt as Misr if they are residents of Cairo, the capital. Outside of the city, they will usually refer to Cairo as Misr. *Mizrahim* are Jews indigenous to the Middle East and Egypt! And, Kari, all this ties into how the modern-day state of Missouri got its name! You've heard of the mounds at Cahokia, right? They are pyramid shaped, earthen structures built many centuries ago by a mysterious civilization about which archeologists are continuing to study and discover new information. And guess what? The civilization of Cahokia was located at the confluence of the Missouri and Mississippi Rivers, directly across from the present-day metropolis of St. Louis, Missouri, your hometown! Can you believe it?
 Meet me there, Kari! I'm serious! In two weeks there is a gigantic celebration planned in the city of St. Louis. It's called Riverfest and is in commemoration of the 100-year Anniversary of the World's Fair and the bi-centennial Anniversary of the expedition of Lewis & Clark. Right there on the steps of the famous Gateway Arch in downtown St. Louie there will be fireworks, music and a huge waterwall specifically designed for use as a movie screen on which historical images of the city will be projected. What a grand event! I have also acquired tickets to the Cardinals-Giants baseball game on Saturday afternoon. (Did you know the Cardinals mascot has as much to do with the history of the Catholic church in St. Louis as it does the pretty, little redbirds?) And that same night my favorite band will be doing the

honors of playing in front of the Arch during the Riverfest celebrations. All this takes place on July 23rd, Kari. My birthday! I have reserved a very nice hotel room which possesses a magnificent view of the Arch and overlooks the Mississippi River where all the festivities will be taking place. I'll see you there! I can't wait!

Almost two weeks later and I still hadn't heard from Kari. No confirmation, no regretful decline, no excited reply, nothing. However, I wouldn't let that deter me from enjoying this momentous occasion. *It's my birthday, dammit, and I'm going to have a good time.* This event was too large, too monumental, too perfect, and I absolutely refused to stand aside and let the chance of experiencing it pass me by as if I were a miserable miser living in complete misery. *No, siree, not me, I'm headed to Missouri.*

'Twas nothing but smooth sailing on the Interstate highway as I, no longer able to contain the increasing excitement, pulled into the fast lane, put the pedal to the metal and made a mad dash towards the state line driving like a bat outta hell, reminiscent of Kane and Lono in the old clunker on Kauai. *What I wouldn't give for a little Noni juice right now,* for it was five o'clock in the morning and my energy was rapidly dissipating.

A Home Depot parking lot on the wrong side of Texarkana became the site of my first pit stop. *A two-hour catnap will definitely do me some good.* Still, my preference would have rather been to locate a train depot where I could, then, take the fast track to....Zion, Arkansas. I turned off the blacktop and onto a seldom-used dirt road, choosing to take an intentional detour with the sole purpose of passing through this out-of-the-way Ozark Mountain town with such a catchy name. I had already passed through the tiny populace of Hope, birthplace and boyhood home of Bill Clinton, 42nd President of the United States.

Hope...Zion....The Hope of Zion, my thoughts were focused on the things above which proved better than a power-packed, nutri-grain energy bar to keep me going, traveling on, bouncing up and down in the driver's seat like the Energizer bunny after a few fully caffeinated cups of Folger's Select. *Maybe she's just waiting to surprise me,* I thought. *She'll be there for sure!* Who wouldn't jump at the chance to be united with their One True Love? For these events have, without a doubt, been divinely inspired, all part of an intricately designed and foolproof master plan developed by the Grand Matchmaker, Himself!

Shortly after I arrived in St. Louis, it became increasingly clear that Kari was nowhere to be found and would not be showing up, ever. It was midnight in the garden of good and evil, and I wasn't about to allow myself to get discouraged and start feeling low, neither would I permit any negative thoughts or energy to perforate my soul and ruin what promised to be a positively fun-filled weekend. *But, it's getting so late....* Why waste good money paying for hotel accommodations when I'd only be forced, after a few short hours, to adhere to the policy of an always strictly enforced early check-out time? *11:00 A.M.? It's already three in the morning.* I had managed to let three or four precious hours of sleep time slip silently away while wandering aimlessly through these unfamiliar streets, in this unfamiliar town, dazzled by the bright city-lights, flashing neon signs, tall buildings and prospective possibilities of what lay ahead in the not-so-distant future.

I'll just crawl into the backseat and get a little shuteye, I told myself. *This is really quite a piece of cake.* After having bedded down in many a moldy Central American hammock deep in the heart of mosquito-infested jungles and swamps, the back of my Corolla was more like the Grand Suite at the Hilton. And I was pretty convinced there weren't any scorpions in downtown St. Louis. Maybe a brown recluse or two, but what's another bite from an arachnid when you've already been captured in the tightly spun web and stung by the penetrating fangs of a black widow? I guess in some species of spiders, as in some cases of divorce, the smell of blood triggers the instincts to take over, thus, causing one to go straight for the jugular, in turn debilitating their defenseless prey, wrapping them up and saving them for a rainy day, a savory snack. Did I ever mention that hourglass-shaped birthmark I spotted on her...*Oh, never mind.* This was no time to start feeling sorry for myself. But, I couldn't help to think of that damn Bible quote on the T.V. screen. Job 3:14. *Why did I ever have to ask for a sign?*

Well...it seems things have finally come full circle. *I mean, the Book of Job, come on?* Job happened to be chosen as the unlucky participant in a gentleman's bet between God and Satan. The stakes, you ask? His wife and family and every last thing he owned in this sometimes cruel and unforgiving world. God rolled the dice with Job's fortune and won. Unfortunately, that meant Job losing everything he had. *It could be worse,* I thought. I lost my wife, but with a large attorney and a decent sum of money I was able to retain joint-custody of my children. Jacinda Kaialani and her little sister, Eden, will be waiting for me at home. And Job? He was cursed with some kind of leprosy or skin disease. *So what?* I, on the other hand, have been suffering from what in Hawaii they would call 'haole rot', Latin name *tinea versicular,* an unwanted fungus that causes unsightly white spots and splotches to appear all over the body. *Big deal, who cares?* It's nothing a little Selsun Blue or a good dermatologist can't cure with a small price tag. And, believe me, I've paid the price. *But, you know what?* I'm familiar with the story and I know how it ends.

> **After Job prayed for his friends, the Lord made him prosperous again and gave him twice as much as before. The Lord blessed the latter part of Job's life more than the first.**
> **-Job 42:10, 12**

What was it Selassie said? **I think God commiserates with those that find themselves in misfortune.** *You see?* I've got plenty of reasons to hold my head up high, to stay in the saddle, to keep pushing on. *Don't give up!* God blessed Job and He'll bless me. I was almost certain of it. I prayed for my friends, Paul and Trey, Buck, Natty, Diego and Iz. I prayed for my enemies, too. *This could be the start of something big.*

It's 7:00 A.M.? Already? 'Twas the dawning of a new day as I zigzagged around a few right-angle city blocks, working my way down towards the riverfront in what felt like a ninety-degree humid heat. I parallel parked the car in order to capture a better view of the July morning sunrise and the bright, rose-colored sphere burning pink on the eastern horizon. Slow-moving barges carried coal and other supplies up and down the mighty Mississippi, using the massive

An Adventure of Biblical Proportions

waterway to transport loads of goods from Minneapolis-St. Paul down to New Orleans, Louisiana and anywhere in between. On top of the levee on the west bank of the river, stagehands and early arriving crew members worked diligently to get things prepared for what would transpire here this evening.

Two hundred years ago, in this exact spot, Meriwether Lewis and William Clark attended the signing of the Louisiana Purchase in which the U.S. acquired a large portion of territory previously belonging to France. The two explorers had been commissioned by President Thomas Jefferson to set off in search of an overland route leading west to the Pacific Ocean and back again in what was deemed, 'The United States Westward Expansion.' A hundred years later, to commemorate the success and achievement of the Lewis & Clark Expedition, the city of St. Louis hosted the 1904 World's Fair, the largest ever held.

Years later, a nationwide competition was held to try and find a symbol that would best represent this location and reflect its role as 'the Gateway to the West.' The winner? A huge 630 foot stainless steel monument in the shape of an inverted catenary (from the Latin *cadena,* meaning chain), an ancient Egyptian design in the shape of a hanging flexible chain or cable when supported at its ends and acted upon by a uniform gravitational force. The Gateway Arch, designed by architect Eero Saarinen and erected in 1963, seemed to me like a huge doorway, an opening, a gateway into another dimension. I admired the impressive structure, only imagining what was to take place there that night. For now, getting a little rest was absolutely imperative and mission number one would be finding a decent place to take a snooze.

I drove the car across a wobbly suspension bridge to the Illinois side of the river where at a cheap motel I would sleep away the rest of the afternoon. Noon to 4 P.M. was plenty of time for a perfect little *siesta* to recuperate my strength and make up for a lack of rest the night before. On the way back into the city limits, while still on the outskirts of St. Louis, I took a roundabout route through the suburban countryside, past a few small subdivisions mixed with cornfields and agricultural plots.

Oh, my Lord! Totally oblivious due to the absence of a sign, or maybe because I wasn't really paying much attention at all, now suddenly surrounding me were dozens of very large piles of dirt on each side of the highway. But, let me expound on this a little bit and make it clear that these were not just your normal, average piles of dirt, but huge flat-topped mounds of sculpted earth, *bamah* or, heck, maybe they could even warrant the recognition of being dubbed as pyramids.

This is it! I thought. This was the site of the Lost Civilization of Cahokia! In Pre-Colombian America, it was the largest native settlement and urban center North of Mexico. *And here!* Cruising down the two-lane road, trying not weave across the yellow line and into oncoming traffic, I cautiously turned my head and caught a glimpse of Monk's Mound. A massive structure with four terraced levels, it is the largest manmade, earthen mound in North America, standing about 100 feet high with a base 1,037 feet long and 790 feet wide. For the record, it has been referred to as "the world's largest pyramid." *May the Good Lord help me if I don't climb to the top of that thing*, I said to myself, thinking it would have to be tomorrow before I'd have a chance to do it. *What a view must be had from up there!* Surely a large portion of the flat American Bottomland for miles and miles around would be visible from the summit.

But, right now there are other things on the agenda. There was a concert to attend. This particular artist headlining tonight's show has been billed as the world's most popular deejay and not without good reason.

I walked out of the public parking garage on ground level, somewhere in close proximity to the Jefferson National Expansion Memorial where the Riverfest events were taking place. Almost instantaneously, the amplified sound of a pulsating, thumping electronic beat resonated throughout the city streets, the parks and the alleyways. I followed a crowd of people as the majority of them moseyed down the sidewalk at a pace that, as I gradually approached closer and closer to the music, became too slow for my liking. The closer I got, the louder the volume, and the louder the volume, the faster I walked, until, finally, I started running. My legs were picking up steam as the beats grew louder, more intense. I broke into an all out sprint, ecstatically encircling at full speed the metal base of the Arch as it towered with its fluid curve high overhead.

An Adventure of Biblical Proportions

I burst onto the scene and witnessed the electrified crowd bouncing and jumping, gyrating and spinning, young and old, elderly and adolescent, every last one of them mesmerized and entranced by the euphoric rhythm and intensified sound that came blaring out from the wall of speakers, a virtual fountain of youth. Babies and young mothers, grandmas in bifocal spectacles, handicapped men in wheelchairs, everyone dancing and grooving so excitedly as if they had all swallowed a handful of methamphetamines causing their heart rates to shoot through the roof. It was as if, instead of fruit and fiber, protein and iron to sustain them, their bodies thrived off of the highly-charged electrical current and the megawatts of energy that were being conducted through the air waves.

An ominous storm loomed, brewing on the distant horizon. Flashes of heat lighting bolted across the sky, fingering down and filling in the empty creases left over by burned up electrons. *What a fascinating show of pyrotechnical wonder!* And just as quickly as we had all converted our high-voltage adapters over to the alternate current, inserting our power cords into the live, exposed and unprotected electrical outlet, the fire marshal decided because of safety concerns to pull the plug on the entire evening. The circuit breaker had become overloaded and the risk explosion was just too great.

The crowd quickly dispersed shocked the event had been cancelled, the main energy source zapped, their rapidly draining batteries now running off the residual juices left over from the initial power boost. Where was I to go? What was I to do? *That's easy. Of course!* I thought. The spirits of Cahokia were calling my name from across the river, for I was still buzzing with emotion, having already switched over to my back-up power generator and energy supply pack. I said a little prayer and decided....*Now is the perfect time to climb Monk's Mound!*

With the car parked as inconspicuously as possible in the tall grass off the opposite shoulder of the highway about a quarter mile from the huge, earthen mound, I now stood directly across from the massive structure, waiting for a pause in the traffic before darting across the road at full speed as to avoid being captured in the headlights of a passing car or truck. I bounded up the steps reaching the first of four flat, leveled-off terraces, then the second. *Here comes*

THE TRUE LOVE MESSIAH:

a car! I hit the cement and lay prone and motionless as to where even the faintest of shadows produced by my body would not be visible to the driver of the vehicle as it went speeding past.

I stood up, brushed the dust and dirt from off my t-shirt and jeans and continued the ascent to the top. *Ahhh, yes!* After reaching the upper terrace, which was once an active religious center and the location of a ceremonial temple, I relaxed a bit while feeling a sense of accomplishment. Sitting Indian-style on the hallowed ground and gazing out over the flatland below, I watched as continual lighting strikes illuminated the sky to the south, the bright city lights of St. Louis shone like a beacon to the west and hundreds of stars twinkled above as the hot summer night was lit aglow in a wondrous fashion.

Sitting all alone by oneself on top of a pyramid like this one, a person's mind starts to wander and they begin to wonder…and think. Some of the thoughts are obviously theirs; still, others seem to just appear, having surfaced from God knows where, owing their origin to some uncharted, undiscovered place, maybe deep within the cerebrum, perhaps deep within the confines of outer space…because, you know, who in their right mind could possibly know what just may exist exactly outside that boundary, or even further? *That boundary….that territory…..the Missouri Territory!*

Early settlers use to call this area 'Little Egypt.' *Hmm, wonder why?* Some of the little towns down south of here even have names referencing Egypt. *Let's see, there's Cairo, Thebes…and one called Mounds.* But, Misr means Egypt and Misrahi are the Egyptian Jews, right? What then is Illinois? After all, it's on this side of the river where Cahokia is located, and most of the mounds, too. *Illinois…..Illinois…?* What's the name of Greece, again? I mean the name the Greeks have always used to refer to their own country? Hellen? And the people of Greece? Hellenes?

Using a small stick to scratch into the surface of the hard ground, I wrote the name Hellenes as it would be written in Greek.

Ελληνες

I took a closer look and instantly realized that this was, almost undoubtedly, Illinois. *My God!* In Latin, *nova* or *novus* means 'new.'

An Adventure of Biblical Proportions

Hellen nova or Hellen novus is Ελληνες *That's it!* Illinois is New Hellen...New Greece! *Hellen nahua, 'the people of Greece.' Incredible!*

The word 'new' is directly related to the Indo-European *nau*, the Sanskrit *naua* and the root *noua* of the Romance languages, all being handed down linguistically from the famous Noah of the Bible. Noah or *nau* not only means 'new', but 'boat' as well. I thought of the many words that stem from this ancient root: *nautical, nausea, cosmonaut.* Throughout the years, the 'u' has been sometimes confused and pronounced as a 'v'. We have *navy, navigate, novel, novice, naval* and *navel*, the root of the word *renovate,* among many others.

The name Illinois was previously thought to have come from the Illinois Confederacy made up of six different and separate Native American tribes. They were called the Illiniwek. *Wait just a second here. Illiniwek? That's Hellenic!* Hellenic was used to describe anything from or relating to Greece, or any land that Greece had conquered! *Illinois was chock full of Ancient Greeks!* (Interestingly enough, the Illinois Confederacy was a part of the Algonquian Nation which was, in turn, at war with a union of tribes across the river in Missouri.) *Hellenes vs. Mizrahi.* The Greeks were at war with the Egyptians! Incredible!

I looked down below from the top of Monks Mound in the ancient city of Cahokia. The Mississippi River was down there somewhere in the darkness, snaking its way through the heartland, the Midwestern United States, providing much needed water for crops and irrigation, a via of transportation for loads and supplies, feeding, supporting, sustaining an entire civilization, just like in the olden days when there were no dams to restrict and control the flow of water and the citizens of Cahokia and the inhabitants of the land were at the whim of the river, not at all different from the lives of the Egyptians living along the Nile. I knew that in the past, before the Army Corps of Engineers got their hands on her and built a never ending series of dams and unnatural lakes, the river was freely navigable. From Minneapolis to New Orleans, the Mississippi flowed unobstructed. And travel on the Missouri was possible from just a few kilometers north of St. Louis, *hell*, all the way to Montana and the Missouri Headwaters State Park, right outside the town of, *you guessed it,*

Helena, Montana, near the Helena National Forest and Lewis & Clark State Park.

One particular scenic and winding stretch of the river forms the 385 mile eastern and northern borders of the state of Nebraska. Remember Nebraska? Nebuchadnezzar's furthest frontier? The Mississippi River also forms the 361 mile eastern border of the state of Iowa. The state of Iowa, you should know, derives its name from the mere pronunciation of YHWH, the written name for God, Yaweh. IOWA is YHWH. The letter 'y' is even called in Spanish 'I Griega', the 'Greek I'. Another way of saying YHWH, as we know, is Jehovah. *Amazing!* This must be coming from the mouth of God. *Surely these aren't my thoughts.* My thoughts...and by mine I mean the ones I actually conjure up that have something to do with my current status, my wellbeing or my future...my thoughts, at that moment, returned to the present situation; me sitting alone, by myself, somewhat bored and a little disappointed that I never did hear from Kari and that neither she nor anyone else was here to experience this wonderful evening with me....s*omeone......anyone. Aw, damn, who needs love anyway?* A flicker of light, a flicker of hope, another and another, tiny little lights flashing on and off signaled that fireflies were looking for a mate, *maybe searching for their soul mate? Oh, who am I fooling?* We all need love.

> **"A new command I give you: Love one another. As I have loved you, so you must love one another."**
> **-John 15:12**

Then, out of nowhere, guess who shows up on the scene? Surprise! It was a well-orchestrated stealth attack by a couple of rabid ghost dogs, two miniature hounds of hell in the form of ferocious little Yorkie terrier mixes, biting and nipping at my heels, anxiously pursuing me with the intentions of each sinking a set of sharp and pointy little canine incisors into my soft and juicy backside.

Most everywhere you go, if you're aware his many disguises, you'll notice that the Devil will make an appearance in some way, shape or form. I usually try and do my best to ignore him and not pay him much attention. However, these rude, little pups were looking for a confrontation. I turned around to face them, fixing my most intimidating gaze into their glowing red eyes.

"Down you miserable beasts of Satan! Heal!" I yelled, making a lot more noise than I probably should have. They didn't back down an inch. *Oops, that didn't work!*

A porch light switched on at an old farmhouse across the way, followed by the sound of screen door flinging open. "Hey. What's all that racket up there? You best be gone!"

I felt like Jesus being taken up to the top of the temple in Jerusalem and told by Satan he could jump, "Don't worry, angels will catch you!" To tell the truth, if tempted to fly in this instance, I probably would have done it.

Nevertheless, I descended down the steep incline faster than a mountain goat fleeing a cougar and, once on level ground, did my best impersonation of a cheetah in fifth gear, hauling butt across the road, not stopping 'til I reached the car. I managed to elude the evil Hell Hounds hot on my tail and make a clean getaway, the only thing successfully nabbed in the heist being the heavily guarded and previously unknown secrets of Cahokia. Back towards the Gateway, back to Saint Louis, back to Misr, back to Egypt.

As I came down from the altar, the bamah, the pinnacle, I felt I was returning from a meeting with JAH, Jehovah, The Lord Almighty, and re-entering the world....a world that desperately needs my help...and yours.

> **You are the light of the world. A city on a hill that cannot be hidden. Neither do people light a lamp and put it under a bowl. Instead they put it on its stand, and it gives light to everyone in the house. In the same way, let your light shine before men, that they may see your good deeds and praise your Father in heaven.**
> **-Matthew 5:14**

Thoughts long since buried resurfaced inside my head and the words hit me like a ton of bricks.

THE TRUE LOVE MESSIAH:

"Man must learn that only in serving others can he reach the full stature or attain the noble destinies for which God created him."

What was I doing? What had I done to serve humanity, to help others? *Absolutely nothing.* Had I even admitted to anyone that I was a Christian? And the number of times I'd been to church in the last ten years was definitely in the single digits and could probably be counted on one hand. But, I could honestly say that, now, I was ready for service. I wanted to do good, really wanted to serve the Lord and lend a hand to my fellow man.

"There is nothing more worthwhile and rewarding in life than to work for the benefit of others."

The following night at the Arch, the scene wasn't quite as electric as during the previous evening but was very spiritual nonetheless. I secured a good spot right next to the stage, eagerly awaiting one of the world's greatest Reggae bands as they prepared to perform live in front of a multitude of diehard fans and thousands of other curious onlookers.

Wearing brightly colored, eccentric attire and sporting wildly untamed, Medusa-like waist-length dreadlocks, the lead singer of the group stepped to the forefront, guitar in hand, and proceeded to belt out the intro to the uplifting musical anthem so adored by anyone with a pulse, and not just the faint murmur of a weak, barely audible heartbeat, either. No, this was Steel Pulse, live and in concert, July 23, on the levee in front of the Gateway Arch, on my birthday, Selassie's birthday, a bicentennial Anniversary event, Fair St. Louis, Riverfest, a celebration of life, past and present, and hope for a better future, together. The words of the well-composed lyrical masterpiece, a fan favorite, echoed out into the night for all to hear…

Rejoice, rejoice
Good tidings I bring you
Hear ye a message to you my friend
Voices cry invoke your angels…

To the righteous revealed
The secret of the scriptures
The wicked dem portion is vanity
Disciples of Lucifer

In your hands lie your destination
The book of true life you hold the key
Mystical powers to you unfold
Seek ye the half that has never been told
Get behind me Satan
I've got to chant

Chant a psalm a day

Attract these angels in dreams and your prayers
Remember the three holy children
Remember the visions of Daniel
Remember the magic of Moses so

I got to chant

Chant a psalm a day

Moses he did chant chant
Samson he did chant chant
Elijah he did chant chant
I want the whole a we fe chant chant
Solomon he did chant chant
His father King David chant chant
John the Baptist chant chant
I want the whole a we fe chant chant.

    I chose Psalm 23 for sentimental reasons, obviously, and for the fact that it's a good one. Well, The Lord didn't lead me to green pastures beside still waters, but I did just come in from the verdant, grassy park area alongside the slow-moving Mississippi River. And my soul did feel restored! And as I looked out the window of my comfortable 18th floor hotel room admiring a gorgeous view of the Arch, the river, and the last few pedestrians in the street down below strolling home after the show, I felt like a king in his palace, sitting on his throne, although for me there was no Bathsheba, no Queen of Sheba nor a Tea Tephi. *No, senorita*, for me there wasn't even a Jezebel or an Athalia. *Oh well*, I'll keep on searching, *maybe tomorrow I'll find my special lady.* Little did I know she'd be the most well-known virgin around.

Our first meeting was immaculate, couldn't have been better. She was everything you'd think a woman should be: faithful, trustworthy, patient, motherly. Her name, she told me, was Miriam, but most people call her Mary. I had gone to the National Shrine of Our Lady of the Snows, just ten short miles southeast of St. Louis as the crow flies and not more than a leisurely bike ride from Monk's Mound and Cahokia, merely looking for a place to spend a peaceful afternoon in contemplative solitude. On these 200 beautifully landscaped acres, guests and pilgrims of all faiths are invited to deepen their relationship with God and one another and, as the mission statement reads, "to be inspired to share the healing and hope they find here so they are refreshed on their journey" and, like Mary, "courageously bring Christ's hope to a world in need."

"That's exactly what I wish to do!" I excitedly told her upon our initial introduction. "But, sometimes I simply lose faith. Can you help me to become more devoted?"

With a loving smile and a few small teardrops streaming down her face, she responded, "I thought you'd never ask."

From that point on, it was a match made in heaven.

She took me gently by the hand and softly whispered, "Follow me."

Holy Mary, Mother of God! This was the woman I had been looking for!

She led me quietly down a pathway through the woods to the first of what they call the Stations of the Cross, also called in Latin 'The Via Dolorosa' or the Way of Sorrows, referring to the depiction of the final hours of the life of Jesus. The object is to make a spiritual pilgrimage of prayer to the chief scenes of Christ's sufferings and death.

Mary and I watched from a distance as He was accused of blasphemy and were overcome with sadness as they fit him with the cross. We painfully looked on as Roman soldiers spit on him, called him names, lashed him with their whips and led him to his death on Mount Calvary. Crucified in an excruciatingly cruel display of the evil and hatred mankind is capable of committing, he hung there bloody and limp, his last breath exasperated in an attempt to pardon

An Adventure of Biblical Proportions

the very ones who tormented him, "Forgive them, for they know not what they do."

Mary wept sorrowfully, as did I, as we kept on walking silently through the trees. Then, suddenly, up ahead there appeared on the path in front of us a figure, a man all dressed in white, his arms open wide.

"Greetings," he said. "Do not be afraid. It is I."

He walked slowly over to Mary and embraced her saying, "Mother, weep no more," and with the snow white cloth of his tunic wiped her face clean of the tears.

"Go," he commanded me, "and make disciples, baptizing them in the name of the Father and of the Son and of the Holy Spirit, and teaching them to obey everything I have commanded you. And surely I am with you always, to the very end of the age."

Early the next morning I drove the thirteen hours straight back to Houston (okay, I admit the speedometer probably flirted with touching 90 mph at one time or another, but I was really excited) and immediately became enthusiastic about getting as much involved in the church as possible. I couldn't be stopped, completely gung ho about being a part of every activity, every service project, every Bible Study group and each and every calling to which I thought I was being led. As part of a Global Missions team, we traveled to impoverished countries, built dental clinics, medical clinics, led relief efforts after hurricanes and natural disasters, repaired churches in need of fixing up, helped construct new homes for AIDS orphans in Africa and carried supplies and necessities to far away lands, all the while sharing the love of Christ with those in need.

Closer to home, at the gymnasium where I worked, a group of young men from the inner-city would meet for pick-up basketball games twice a week. At some point during the evenings, we would stop play and pause for a devotional, a short Bible Study or prayer time and reflection. Sometimes we would read excerpts from the sermons of Dr. Martin Luther King. Other times we heard motivational stories about famous Christian athletes, sports figures or positive role models who are making a difference in the world.

Soon, however, I was told by those in charge to quickly stop what I was doing. "Don't get burnt out," they said. But, this didn't make much sense to me.

But, I have a dream! Believe you me. I have a dream of starting a Mission Training Center where people from all walks of life can come together to learn the skills necessary to, then, go out into the world and serve. A place where kids of all socio-economic classes and backgrounds could come and learn, not only about the Bible, but about gardening, perhaps growing food to be donated to a food pantry or a homeless shelter. I dream of a place where people could come to learn about nature and the environment, about building with their hands, possibly constructing a church or a chapel using mud bricks and adobe. At the same time while learning and having fun, they would also be gaining an overall respect for life and an increased love of God.

"Sounds more like a mini-Woodstock or a hippie commune," I was told. But, that didn't discourage me. It's true that many churches around here do a heck of a lot of good, but in some cases a large percentage of money is earmarked for massive building campaigns, bigger sanctuaries, larger fountains and prettier landscaping, which, don't get me wrong, is really great and all, but I'd like to donate more than the standard 10% mini-tithe towards helping the poor, the needy, the hungry and the lost.

Why not fix up some of these overgrown and neglected parks and youth sports facilities in the inner-city? The weed-infested baseball diamonds, the ugly soccer fields and the forgotten basketball courts on the *other* side of the tracks, in the ghetto? Let's give *these* kids a safe place to play. A place where families can come together and parents can learn to become active participants and positive role models in their children's lives. *But, how could I hope to raise enough capital to do this, to make even the slightest difference?*

And, then, it came to me in a flash...*Aha! The book!* That's it! *I'll publish a book and with the proceeds start a non-profit organization dedicated to the funding of community service projects!* Okay, great. *But, where do I start?* I guess the first step would be to find an editor, and maybe an agent?

CHAPTER 18

*"There is nothing concealed that will
not be disclosed, or hidden that will
not be made known.*
-Matthew 10:26

In Celtic spiritual tradition, the term Anam Cara, or "soul friend", is applied to the special bond created when you are very open, appreciative and trusting with another person and your two souls flow together. This is not an erotic love as experienced between two partners, but an ever-lasting friendship that awakens the fullness and mystery of your life and your own passionate sense of the Divine. Your Anam Cara provides support, direction and guidance to help you grow spiritually, always beholding your light and beauty and accepting you for who you truly are. It is believed that forming an Anam Cara friendship will help you to foster an awareness of your own nature and inner light and to experience the joys of others. You are joined in an ancient and eternal union with humanity that cuts across all barriers of time, convention, philosophy and definition. When you are blessed with an Anam Cara, it is believed that you have arrived at a most sacred place, home. I have been lucky enough to have developed two or three of these special friendships during this lifetime. In Spanish, the slang term *"carnal"* may be used to refer to one of these lifelong friends. In English, one might call him a "blood brother."

    I met my good friend Benny Gardner as a young, pubescent, twelve-year-old seventh-grader at the local junior high school we attended, both part of the same circle of friends, good buddies who enjoyed many an afternoon hanging out together, playing football at the nearby athletic field, tennis at the courts down the street, or basketball on the goal outside Benny's house. Ping pong, Indian baseball, sand volleyball, Monopoly... you name it, we played it.

Despite his slight build, "Beege" as we affectionately call him, had a pretty deadly jump shot and was a better athlete than most.

Benny's real name, the one written on his birth certificate, is Benyamin which in Hebrew means "the right hand son" and is one of the sons of Jacob and one of the twelve tribes of Israel. The only Jewish kid in our ragtag group of friends, he grew up in a bilingual household speaking Hebrew and English, went to the synagogue on Saturdays and was an active member of the congregation at Beth Israel temple in Houston. That didn't matter much to us. Most young people in our generation have learned to be accepting of all races, colors and creeds and, besides, Benny didn't look or act much different than we did. More importantly to us, he played good defense and could throw a pretty tight spiral to boot. Fast forward almost twenty years later and Benny and I remain pretty tight, close friends. I casually mentioned to him one day that I had recently begun writing a book.

"That's cool. Do you need an editor?" That was the first thing out of his mouth.

I thought for a minute. *But…It's actually…How? Oh, well…*

"As a matter of fact, I do," I said to him. And the more I thought about it, the more perfect it seemed…two lifelong friends, a Jew and a Christian, studying intensely the word of the Lord, working together to publish a book that might make a difference, that just might change the world. *Who would have thought?*

To tell you the truth, Benny had suffered a sort of a falling out with Judaism, as I had done with Christianity, and he didn't quite consider himself to be a common practitioner of the faith. At one point a few years ago, he even made the comment that he was pagan.
I think many young people go through this stage when they realize that most of those who proclaim to be members of their religion do not embrace the same environmental concerns they hold so dear. There are a large number of people in my generation and younger who, because of the fact they are environmentally aware, have turned their back on religion and have struggled with their faith merely because most mainstream churches and synagogues do not want to be a part of the "Green Revolution." Thankfully, this is beginning to change. Every day you read of more and more churches that are putting up solar panels, starting community gardens, implementing

recycling programs, and about pastors who are preaching the importance of being good stewards of the Earth, about caring for God's creation.

Maybe Benny was *already* a Christian? I didn't ever really ask. And, as we've seen, just because someone may have been born into a Christian home doesn't mean they don't have a Jewish heritage, does it? By the mere act of someone fourteen generations ago in my family tree deciding to become or forced into becoming a Christian, should I automatically accept the tenants of the faith as complete truth, no questions asked? Of course not! How many of us, as we've proven, are children of Abraham? Are we all descended from Noah and the survivors of the Great Flood? What *has* been proven in this book? That a large majority of us are descended from the Twelve Tribes of Israel? Why, then, would it mean that just because Benny was born a Jew that he shouldn't accept the Messiah and be a follower of the Way? After all, Jesus was King of the Jews. It's a Jewish belief, a Jewish prophecy. The Virgin Mary was a Jew. Jesus' father, Joseph, was a carpenter and a Jew. John the Baptist was Jewish. Matthew was a Jewish tax collector. Mark was a Jew as well. As for Peter, he was a Jewish follower of the Messiah. And Paul, he most certainly was born a Jew.

All the disciples were, in fact, Jews, as were most of the apostles. Yet, they saw in Yeshua Ha Meshiach the fulfillment of the prophecy, convinced that he was the long-awaited savior of the world, the Son of God whose coming and appearance had been talked about for over four thousand years.

"Messianic Jew," said Benny after reading through a rough copy and editing the first draft of the fully typed-out manuscript, "I like that term." And so began our study, quickly becoming the basic subject matter for the final chapter of our newly titled novel, <u>True Love and the Messiah</u>.

By the year 40 B.C., Jerusalem had been conquered by the Roman Empire and was under direct Roman rule. Rome appointed Herod as 'King of Judah' and he would reign for the next 44 years over Judea and the Jews. The Romans didn't stop there, however, also invading Cush and Britain, knowing very well the importance of controlling the global trade in tin and accessing the vast supplies of it found in Britain. Around this time, a Roman city was founded in Ancient China, named Li-jien. This is also the Chinese name for the Roman Empire and is derived from the word legion, as in the Roman Legion or Army. By 15 BC, King Herod had begun to rebuild the temple in Jerusalem; Southwest England being the primary source of tin for the Roman Empire.

"So, why don't you tell me about the New Testament," Benny requested, "I've never read it."

"It would be my honor," I replied. Of all the friends and acquaintances I've known in my lifetime, Benny might be the most intelligent. Highly analytical, able to comprehend the most difficult of concepts, a mathematical wizard blessed with incredible intellectual capabilities and an extremely high IQ on par with, it would suffice to say, an Albert Einstein, he would be more than qualified as a candidate to give his opinionated judgment as to just how reasonable and effective my research and studies have proven to be.

"So," he asked, "the New Testament was written by Jews in order to convince other Jews that Jesus was the Messiah for whom they had been waiting?"

"That's right," I answered.

"Then how come so many failed to believe?" he wondered, which upon hearing I felt the need to explain...

"Many failed to believe, it's true. But, an ever-increasing number did believe, proclaiming that the Messiah had in fact come and, professing their faith in Jesus Christ, they began to spread the Word.

> **Therefore many of the Jews who had come to visit Mary, and had seen what Jesus did, put their faith in him.**
> **-John 11:45**

However, persecution by the Roman Empire of what was viewed as a dangerous sect within Judaism made things very difficult for believers...

> **If we let him go on like this, everyone will believe in him, and then the Romans will come and take away both our place and our nation."**
> **-John 11:48**

Any recognized followers of the Messiah were crucified and killed because of their faith. Because of this, they routinely met in secret, in private houses and underground caves, unbeknownst to the ruling authority. As the number of followers continued to grow, the Roman state became very concerned to say least. They had already conquered Judea and Jerusalem and required of its citizens full allegiance to the Roman Empire, only permitting the practice of 'legal' religions allowed by Rome. The belief in this Jewish Messiah presented a major problem to the stability of the Roman government and its autocratic rule and control over the region. They wanted the Jewish followers of 'The Way' to be humiliated, intimidated, obliterated and deceased in order to quash the rebellion before it took root, although they would not succeed in their attempt, as it proliferated, growing like wildfire. Without the thousands upon thousands of these strong-willed and faithful Jewish believers in the Messiah, there would be no early Messianic Movement and Christianity today would not exist." This is how it all began...

> **And, behold, thou shalt conceive in thy womb, and bring forth a son, and shalt call his name Jesus. He shall be great, and shall be called the Son of the Highest: and the Lord God shall give unto him the throne of his father David. He will reign over the house of Jacob forever.**
> **-Luke 1:32**

"Notice how it says He will reign over the house of Jacob. This means he will rule over, both, the House of Israel AND the House of David."

> **All this took place to fulfill what the Lord said through the prophet: The virgin will be with child and will give birth to a son and they will call him Immanuel- which means, "God is with us."**
> **-Matthew 1:22**

"Who is the prophet to whom Matthew is referring?" questioned Benny. "Was it not Isaiah who gave this prophecy?" And he was correct in that it was Isaiah the Prophet who foretold of the birth of the Divine Child seven hundred years prior to its occurrence.

THE TRUE LOVE MESSIAH:

Therefore the Lord himself will give you a sign: The virgin will be with child and will give birth to a son and will call him Immanuel.
-Isaiah 7:14

A record of the genealogy of Jesus Christ the son of David, the son of Abraham:
  Abraham was the father of Isaac,
    Isaac the father of Jacob,
    Jacob the father of Judah and his brothers,
    Judah the father of Perez and Zerah, whose mother was Tamar,
    Perez the father of Hezron,
    Hezron the father of Ram,
    Ram the father of Amminadab,
    Amminadab the father of Nahshon,
    Nahshon the father of Salmon,
    Salmon the father of Boaz, whose mother was Rahab,
    Boaz the father of Obed, whose mother was Ruth,
    Obed the father of Jesse,
    and Jesse the father of King David.
  David was the father of Solomon, whose mother had been Uriah's wife,
  Solomon the father of Rehoboam,
    Rehoboam the father of Abijah,
    Abijah the father of Asa,
    Asa the father of Jehoshaphat,
    Jehoshaphat the father of Jehoram,
    Jehoram the father of Uzziah,
    Uzziah the father of Jotham,
    Jotham the father of Ahaz,
    Ahaz the father of Hezekiah,
    Hezekiah the father of Manasseh,
    Manasseh the father of Amon,
    Amon the father of Josiah,
    and Josiah the father of Jeconiah and his brothers at the time of the exile to Babylon.
  After the exile to Babylon:
    Jeconiah was the father of Shealtiel,
    Shealtiel the father of Zerubbabel,
    Zerubbabel the father of Abiud,
    Abiud the father of Eliakim,
    Eliakim the father of Azor,
    Azor the father of Zadok,
    Zadok the father of Akim,
    Akim the father of Eliud,
    Eliud the father of Eleazar,
    Eleazar the father of Matthan,
    Matthan the father of Jacob,

> *and Jacob the father of Joseph, the husband of Mary, of whom was born Jesus, who is called Christ.*
> *Thus there were fourteen generations in all from Abraham to David, fourteen from David to the exile to Babylon, and fourteen from the exile to the Christ.*

> **In those days Caesar Augustus issued a decree that a census should be taken of the entire Roman world. And everyone went to his own town to register. So Joseph also went up from the town of Nazareth in Galilee to Judea, to Bethlehem the town of David, because he belonged to the house and line of David. He went there with Mary, who was pledged to be married to him and was expecting a child.**
>
> -Luke 2:1-5

"So *that's* why Mary and Joseph were in Bethlehem," said Benny, who, always full of wit, stunned me with the revelation of the following information. "You do know that *Beth* means house, but are you aware that *lehem* means bread?" he asked. "Bethlehem is 'the place or house of bread.' Is it just a coincidence that Yeshua was born there? After all, he persistently claims in the Scripture that he is 'the bread of life.' And when one partakes of Holy Communion and consumes the bread, it is given as a representation of the body of Christ."

Wow! I never cease to be amazed. How great it is to have a native Hebrew speaker for an Anam Cara! But, how did he know this? *How much does he already know?* As we continued studying the New Testament, every now and again Benny would simply nod his head very assuredly. What was he doing? What might he be thinking? *Am I just preaching to the choir here?* I had to wonder.

> **And there were shepherds living out in the fields nearby, keeping watch over their flocks at night. An angel of the Lord appeared to them, and the glory of the Lord shone around them, and they were terrified. But the angel said to them, "Do not be afraid. I bring you good news of great joy that will be for all the people. Today in the town of David a Savior has been born to you. He is Christ the Lord.**
>
> -Luke 2:8-11

> **After Jesus was born in Bethlehem in Judea, during the time of King Herod, Magi, or wise men from the east, came to Jerusalem and asked, "Where is the one who has been born king of the Jews? We saw his star in the east and have come to worship him."**
>
> -Matthew 2:1-2

"Christ is sometimes called the Bright Morningstar," I mentioned to Benny, not placing too much emphasis on it.

"Well, of course," he said. "You've read the ancient prophecy given by Moses in the Torah, have you not?"

I had not. "No, I am not aware of it. Please divulge this precious information my dear friend," I said with a smile, at which he kindly turned back the thin pages of the Good Book and pointed me to the following verse.

> **"I see him, but not now; I behold him, but not near. A star will come out of Jacob; a scepter will rise out of Israel...**
>
> -Numbers 24:17

"The scepter was given to the line of Judah to rule forever in perpetuity over Israel!"

> **When King Herod heard this he was disturbed. When he had called together all the chief priests and teachers of the law, he asked them where the Christ was to be born. "In Bethlehem in Judea," they replied, "for this is what the prophet has written: 'But you, Bethlehem, in the land of Judah, are by no means least among the rulers of Judah; for out of you will come a ruler who will be the shepherd of my people Israel.'"**
>
> -Matthew 2:3-6

"Yeshua is, also, sometimes referred to as the Good Shepherd," I said to Benny. "Some say He came to gather the people of Israel under one banner, under one law, from the islands of the sea, from the

Americas, from Europe, from Africa, from the Orient, saying to the lost sheep of Israel...

'My command is this: Love each other as I have loved you.'

King Herod was so convinced that the "King of Kings", the Jewish Messiah, had been born and that his position of leadership was in jeopardy that he quickly plotted to kill the infant son of Joseph and Mary."

> **Then Herod called the Magi secretly and found out from them the exact time the star had appeared. He sent them to Bethlehem and said, "Go and make a careful search for the child. As soon as you find him, report to me, so that I too may go and worship him." After they had heard the king, they went on their way, and the star they had seen in the east went ahead of them until it stopped over the place where the child was. When they saw the star, they were overjoyed. On coming to the house, they saw the child with his mother Mary, and they bowed down and worshiped him. Then they opened their treasures and presented him with gifts of gold and of incense and of myrrh. And having been warned in a dream not to go back to Herod, they returned to their country by another route.**
> **-Matthew 2:7-12**

"I imagine this must have ticked off Herod just a little bit, don't you think?"

> **When Herod realized that he had been outwitted by the Magi, he was furious, and he gave orders to kill all the boys in Bethlehem and its vicinity who were two years old and under, in accordance with the time he had learned from the Magi.**
> **-Matthew 2:16**

"But, Mary and Joseph had already taken the young, diaper-wearing Jesus and fled from Israel, leaving right after a visit from the Magi, correct?"

"That's right. The wise men had come to worship the Christ Child."

> When they had gone, an angel of the Lord appeared to Joseph in a dream. "Get up," he said, "take the child and his mother and escape to Egypt. Stay there until I tell you, for Herod is going to search for the child to kill him." So he got up, took the child and his mother during the night and left for Egypt, where he stayed until the death of Herod. And so was fulfilled what the Lord had said through the prophet: "Out of Egypt I called my son."
>
> -Matthew 2:13-16

> After Herod died, an angel of the Lord appeared in a dream to Joseph in Egypt and said, "Get up, take the child and his mother and go to the land of Israel, for those who were trying to take the child's life are dead."
>
> -Matthew 2:19-20

"After returning to Israel, an adolescent Jesus grew up learning Jewish customs and traditions, observing all of the Holy Days and festivals."

> Every year his parents went to Jerusalem for the Feast of the Passover. When he was twelve years old, they went up to the Feast, according to the custom. After the Feast was over, while his parents were returning home, the boy Jesus stayed behind in Jerusalem, but they were unaware of it. Thinking he was in their company, they traveled on for a day. Then they began looking for him among their relatives and friends. When they did not find him, they went back to Jerusalem to look for him. After three days they found him in the temple courts, sitting among the teachers, listening to them and asking them questions. Everyone who heard him was amazed at his understanding and his answers.
>
> -Luke 2:41-47

"Twelve years old?" I felt the need to stop here and pose a few questions to my comrade. "Isn't this the traditional age at which a young Jewish boy would usually have his Bar Mitzvah? What exactly does this mean, *Bar Mitzvah*?"

"Well, according to Jewish law," began my good friend Benny, "when Jewish children reach the age of maturity they become responsible for their actions. A boy is said to become a Bar Mitzvah, or 'one to whom the commandments apply.' After reaching this point, they are privileged to participate in all areas of Jewish life and are, now, personally responsible for observing Jewish ritual law, tradition and ethics."

> **Then he went down to Nazareth with them and was obedient to them. But his mother treasured all these things in her heart. And Jesus grew in wisdom and stature and in favor with God and men.**
> **-Luke 2:51-52**

Messianic Jew? Maybe. But, I don't think Benny was quite ready yet to call himself a Christian, which I totally understand, as I was still a little hesitant calling myself a Jew.

However, that would soon change.

"Do you think I'm too old to have a Bar Mitzvah?" I almost jokingly asked Benny, "I mean, you've read the first 17 chapters of the book and are aware of my Jewish heritage." I giggled a bit. But, when he told me I was, in fact, not too old, and even slightly encouraged me to have one, I started to seriously consider it. I mean, *why not?*

And so, just like that, began my early adulthood training in Jewish laws and customs, in hopes of preparing myself for my big coming out party, the Bar Mitzvah which had been put on hold, delayed for the last eighteen years. And, as one might have it, I was being groomed by the one of the best. Benny's mom, Shifra, named after one of the midwives who rescued the life of baby Moses, hiding him in a basket and placing it amongst the reeds along the bank of the Nile, is probably *the* top Hebrew language teacher in the entire city. For the next twelve months or so, I would be involved in an intense foreign language course study, receiving private tutoring lessons and gradually becoming more and more fluent in the Hebrew tongue, the ancient language of the Holy Bible. I spent many a night over at the Gardner household enjoying home-cooked Middle-Eastern meals, learning rituals, laws, customs and traditions, celebrating Jewish holy days and festivals, and practicing my speech and grammar while seated around the dinner table. They accepted me with open arms as part of their family and, for that, I will be forever grateful.

We started off in September by celebrating Rosh Hashanah, the Jewish New Year, dining on knishes and blintzes, dumplings and potato pancakes as the average *goyim,* or non-Jew, might call them. We consumed Challah and experienced the traditional breaking of the bread, round-shaped and circular, representing the cycle of life. Soon after came Yom Kippur, during which we observed a Day of Atonement set aside for fasting, depriving oneself of pleasures and repenting of sins committed the during the previous year. As Christmastime approached, so also began the Hanukkah season with me filling my belly with all sorts of kosher foods: matzah-ball soup, bagels and lox, and gefilte fish. By the time Passover rolled around, a week before Easter Sunday, I had developed a good grasp of the Hebrew language as we celebrated this important Jewish holiday commemorating the Exodus out of Egypt by Moses and the Hebrew Israelites.

As the Jewish calendar year came winding to a close I had to wonder, *who's converting whom here?* But no one was converting anyone and that's the beauty of it all. I was simply adhering to the traditional laws and customs found in Judaism. If I was to be a Jewish believer in the Messiah, I would, after all, only be following in the footsteps of the original apostles, the first Disciples of Christ. I *can* be Jewish and also remain a faithful Christian. And the thought was a comforting one, one that brought much peace.

"I'm a Messianic Jew!" I declared to Benny, wondering deep down if he considered himself to be the same.

"What you're getting, David, is a crash course in Judaism," Benny told me, "Because at your age, you're as old as Yeshua upon returning to Israel to begin his ministry."

What? How was he aware of Jesus' eighteen year absence in which the Bible mentions NOTHING about his life? And what makes him think Yeshua was not present in Israel during this time? We would address these questions later, but it sure does make you wonder.

"But, I'm not Jesus," I objected, "I'm just a man." A lonely, single, divorced father of two, who despite the rejection and failure of a first marriage, perhaps, naively still intended to seek out and find his one true love; that hard to find, but so very attainable, *amor verdadero,* my soul mate. *But, alas, where might I find this beautiful damsel?*

Benny and I may have been studying intensely the Word of the Lord, but like David and Solomon and so many others, we did not abandon our social lives altogether. In our eyes we were two of the most eligible bachelors in town, neither one of us was cloistered, nor was there any sworn celibacy or oath undertaken on either's part. We discussed profoundly our interest in the opposite sex and, for me, after just getting out of a long committed relationship and finally getting over the pain of the whole ordeal, I was like a kid in a candy shop or, better yet, an old dog who after years of being tied up and chained to a post in the backyard was set free to roam the neighborhood. It was love at first sight, at least three times a day.

First, it was the exotic hostess at a local Tex-Mex restaurant, Fatima Al-Zahara, a pretty Muslim girl from Morocco. *Ah, Fatima, and the three little children who witnessed the miraculous appearance of the Virgin Mary in Portugal! She would convert in due time* (after reading this book, of course) *and become a faithful Christian! Together, we would foster a dialogue and understanding between the two religions, Islam and Christianity!*

"Do you know the U.S. state names which are Arabic in origin?" I asked, trying to impress and woo the Moorish beauty from Marrakech. Impressed, she was not. However, I pressed on, continuing the search, seeking out my true love, my soul mate, my twin soul.

Now, exiting the public library, I came face to face with a fine, young maiden; a born-again Christian named Laura Cross. It just so happened that as we crossed paths for the first time, I coincidentally was wearing my Crosstrainers t-shirt supporting a local Christian running organization. *Laura Cross! How perfect! And she loves to jog!* It was very ironic and all, but in the end it failed to produce more than a second date. I mean, how many twenty year old girls consider a thirty-something father of two to be an ideal catch. *Oh well, there are plenty more fish in the sea!* I kept reminding myself.

A strikingly gorgeous single mother of one, a fellow alumni having graduated from the same high school as I, we certainly had something in common. Her last name... Teran. *Teran? Aha, Phoenician in origin!* A modern-day princess from Tyre, just like Jezebel, but without the mean streak. Her ancestors must have ridden the waves, sailed the high seas, having hailed from the Tyrrhenian Sea coast of Lebanon, embarking on worldwide journeys! *How wonderful it will be,* two Phoenicians from the House of Israel, reunited! *I'll surely dazzle her with such a profound knowledge of history and information!* But, sorry to say, again there would be no alliance, no formal union. Her ship would enter into international waters, docking in foreign ports of call, anchoring in distant, unknown harbors. But this high-ranking sailor, as perhaps only I truly considered myself, would keep on navigating the channels and the straits, trying to locate that special someone...that sturdy, unfailing life raft with which to tie up my wandering, ever-drifting vessel, always at the mercy of the elements, the wind, the rain and the rough seas.

And then along came Angelica, a single mother of two, a Mexican beauty. *My, oh my,* she was so very angelic, angel-like! That is, until I heard her speak. She cussed like a seasoned sailor just relegated to deck-mopping duty on a return trip bound from Hanoi. What a dirty mouth on that senorita! I was forced to raise the mast, unfurl the sails, move on to nearby cays and capes, inlets and bays, although completely abandoning ship had at more than one time crossed my mind.

At times, I felt more like a bantam-weight boxer than a boatman, and a piss-poor one at that. It seemed I'd been dealt a combination of hard blows to the kisser by a relentless flurry of stinging jabs and was just awaiting that final knockout punch, a roundhouse right hook that would surely connect with such fury as to floor me, send my mouthpiece flying, and me collapsing down to the canvass in utter defeat as I flailed away at an imaginary opponent that didn't even exist. I was beating myself up mentally between rounds and was now prepared to raise the white flag, throw in the towel and tell the referee the bout was over, "Stop the ten-count, I'm done."

Fortunately, for my sake, I had one of the best cornermen/medics in the business and quickly to the rescue came my Anam Cara, doctoring my cuts and bruises, giving me strategic words of advice, encouragement and some mighty powerful ether, too. Benny shoved the bottle of "smellum sauce" underneath my nose and held it there long enough for me to get a big whiff of it.

"David. If you're looking for an unfailing life raft to hitch onto, shouldn't you give yourself up to God? Isn't that what your book is about?"

Wow. A slap in the face from my own head trainer. Though, I've got to admit, he certainly did have a point.

"But, it's normal to try and find a partner, to want a soul mate, to have a wife, to yearn for a lifelong love," I answered.

"Yes, that's true. Some say that even Jesus was married. I saw the Da Vinci Code, you know." Benny smiled and awaited my reaction.

"Yeah, I'm aware of it, the whole Mary Magdalene controversy and whatnot. But, that's just a rumor. Who knows if it's really true? And, besides, who cares? What would that change anyway? If God came to live on Earth in the form of a man, why *wouldn't* He get married?"

I was surprised by Benny's response. "You're right," he said, "Jewish rabbis are expected to marry, almost to the point of obligation. How else would they be able to counsel and teach their congregation if they did not live as a normal layman? Jesus was a rabbi, was he not?"

"I suppose He was. And I suppose he may have been married as well. But, for me, a more exciting question would be, 'To where in the world did the Son of God disappear during his eighteen year absence from Israel? Where did He go? Where did He preach?"

"You really want to know?" asked my good friend, seemingly having all the answers. "Haven't you read the advice of Timothy found in the New Testament?" *What? I thought he hadn't...He had asked me to teach...How?* Who was this guy I thought I knew so well, some kind of *shamayim,* a Jewish shaman come down from Heaven?

"No, what did Timothy say? Please do tell." I pleaded with him.

This is what he said, "He commanded **'certain men not to teach false doctrines any longer, nor to devote themselves to myths and** endless genealogies. These promote controversies rather than God's work—which is by faith. The goal of this command is love, which comes from a pure heart and a good conscience and a sincere faith."

I was flabbergasted. *Has this all been for nothing, what I considered to be a work of art, my masterpiece?* I was on the brink of rendering the whole thing useless. To tell you the truth, if it wasn't for those little fortune cookies they kept giving me at Hunan Café, the local Chinese food place down the street, I may have given up a long time ago. But each time I cracked open one of those little fellas it was like a warm cup of ginseng tea to my system, the little pep-me-up I sorely needed.

**Bide your time, for success
    is near.**

**All the effort you are making will
    ultimately pay off.**

Rest not from duty, but find rest in it.

Okay, okay, myths and genealogies maybe, but false doctrines they are not. No way. The Messiah was Jesus. The guidebook is The Bible. And the doctrine is love. That much I knew. And what I didn't know, I wanted to find out.

"Call them myths, call them genealogies, call them endless, what I desire to know is the truth. What happened during the life of Yeshua the Christ? What was it that occurred during those eighteen years, the 'lost years' of Jesus? Where was He? Where did He preach?"

"That's easy," answered Benny. "According to religious teachers in India, Jesus visited the Himalayan kingdom of Nepal while still a young man. Some of the Lost Tribes of Israel had traveled along this same Silk Road and into the countries of the East in times past. Their descendants can be found in Afghanistan, Pakistan, Burma, China, Japan, Korea and elsewhere. An ancient manuscript mentions King Shalivahana meeting in Kashmir with Issa Mashiha, Son of God, born of a virgin. They state that from there he went on to the sacred isles of the West, called Britashtan."

"That would be Britain, right?" *It must be.*

"I would assume so, wouldn't you?" he responded. "There is plenty of evidence to support the belief that, as a young man, Jesus Christ spent time in England. Have you ever heard of Joseph of Arimathea? Do you know who he is?"

"Well, yes, of course," I answered. "He's the one who recovers the body of Christ after the crucifixion. He is mentioned in the New Testament in all four books of the Gospel, Matthew, Mark, Luke and John."

> **Going to Pilate, he asked for Jesus' body. Then he took it down, wrapped it in linen cloth and placed it in a tomb cut in the rock, one in which no one had yet been laid.**
> **-Luke 23:52**

"He took out the nails one by one, then, after lowering the body down from where it had been hanging for the previous ten or twelve hours, arms outstretched to the side, legs dangling down below, Joseph carried away the corpse."

[The cruel practice of crucifixion almost always began in the early morning hours so as to more successfully torture the victim, who hung facing due east, with the gradually increasing daytime temperatures and the heat and intensity of a rising sun. The crucified person would literally be cooked, baking in the mid-afternoon sunlight with absolutely no shade and no water, struggling for every breath, every last gasp of air, having to try with all their strength and might to raise up ever so slightly in order to relieve, if only for a second or two, the intolerable mounting pressure on the ribcage and spine, eventually expiring due to asphyxiation, dehydration, exhaustion or all three. It is from the Latin root *crux* where we get the word 'crucible', a container used to melt substances at extremely high temperatures, and also the term 'croc pot', which is used primarily for slow cooking over a steady heat, in the same way a condemned human being or in this case God was cooked and baked, crucified on a cross.]

> **Joseph took the body, wrapped it in a clean linen cloth, and placed it in his own new tomb that he had cut out of the rock.**
>
> **-Matthew 27:53**

"Joseph of Arimathea cut, dug and excavated a tomb and then as evening approached, boldly asked Pontius Pilate for permission to retrieve Jesus' dead body from where it hung on the cross. Why do you think he would do this? What else do you know about him?" asked Benny, all the while the drama seeming to build more and more.

I thought for a moment, then answered, "Joseph was a rich man and a member of the Council, but fought against their decision to condemn Jesus. He was a disciple of Christ, but kept it a secret due to his high position in the government." *That much I've read in The Bible.*

> **Now there was a man named Joseph, a member of the Council, a good and upright man, who had not consented to their decision and action. He came from the Judean town of Arimathea and he was waiting for the kingdom of God.**
>
> **-Luke 23:50**

"You're right! He held a high government office and was a member of the Jewish Sanhedrin. Joseph was also given the Roman title 'Nobilis Decurio' which commonly designated an official under Roman authority in charge of mining. He was reputed to be one of the wealthiest men in the world at the time, a major controller of the tin industry and owner of a private merchant fleet which traversed the seas in transportation of the precious metal. But, why would this Joseph of Arimathea retrieve the body of Jesus from off of the cross? Or, better yet, why would Mary and the disciples even let him have the body of Our Lord and Savior? Why would *he* be in charge of the burial? It was a long-standing Jewish custom, as it is in most cultures, that the relatives are to care for the deceased and plan the funeral. In fact, by law, only a relative could claim the body. How, then, was Joseph able to retrieve and bury Yeshua Meshiach in his own tomb?

"I don't know? Is it possible that he was related to Christ?"

"As a matter of fact…"

I stopped him before he could finish. "You're kidding, aren't you?"

"No. Not in the least. According to the Talmud, Joseph was the Virgin Mary's uncle. As the brother of Ann, Virgin Mary's mother, he was also the great uncle of Jesus Christ. He even acted as the coroner for his dead nephew, preparing the body as required for burial."

> **He was accompanied by Nicodemus, the man who earlier had visited Jesus at night. Nicodemus brought a mixture of myrrh and aloes, about seventy-five pounds. Taking Jesus' body, the two of them wrapped it, with the spices, in strips of linen. This was in accordance with Jewish burial customs.**
> **-John 19:38-40**

"Now that you know a little about the relationship between Joseph and his great-nephew, you will understand more about where Jesus spent his so-called 'lost years' between the age of thirteen and thirty, during which the Bible reveals absolutely nothing about his life."

"Go for it!" I was ready to hear the rest of what he had say. "I suppose you're gonna tell me that Jesus went to England with his uncle, right?"

"Joseph, as we've established, was a wealthy tin merchant. Where else would he sail to in the Roman world, but the farthest outreaches of the Empire, the hub of the tin trade and the location of its plentiful supply? Britain was known as the Cassiterides or the 'tin islands.' Like cast metal, you know?"

"Okay, I follow you so far, but I'd like to know more," I said.

And this is what he told me.

"Gildas the Wise, an early Celtic Christian historian, recorded that 'the light of Christ shone in Britain during the last year of Tiberius Caesar in 27A.D.' Thomas Aquinas in his letter to Pope Gregory wrote that 'there is a land surrounded by water that has a church built by the Lord himself and was visited by most of the apostles.' St. Augustine, the famous Roman Catholic Evangelist, supported this belief, stating that here lies a church 'constructed by no human art, but divinely built.' Indeed, the famous Glastonbury Abbey in England has become the focus of a very sacred Christian pilgrimage. It is here where the ancient island of Avalon, surrounded by mist and water, was called in Latin 'Secretum Domini', the Secret of Our Lord, and sometimes 'Domus Dei' or the house of God. On the outskirts of town rises a distinct and impressive landmark, the unmistakable Glastonbury Tor. Its name originating from the Hebrew word *Torah*, this is the famous 'hill of the law.'"

Consequently, both Glastonbury Abbey and the Tor are located within just a few kilometers of the town of Bath, or *BT,* meaning 'house or place.' He continued, "It is here where as a young man Jesus Christ humbly lived while becoming well versed in the Torah and Jewish law, thus preparing Himself for his upcoming earthly ministry in Israel." The poet laureate, William Blake, in his 'Summertime in England', asks…

And did those feet in Ancient time
Walk upon England's mountains green?
And was the Holy Lamb of God
On England's pleasant pastures seen?

> **He came to His hometown and began teaching them in their synagogue, so that they were astonished, and said, "Where did this man get this wisdom and these miraculous powers? Is not this the carpenter's son? Is not His mother called Mary, and His brothers, James and Joseph and Simon and Judas? And His sisters, are they not all with us? Where then did this man get all these things?"**
>
> **-Matthew 13:54-56**

> **And all were speaking well of Him, and wondering at the gracious words which were falling from His lips; and they were saying, "Is this not Joseph's son?"**
> **-Luke 4:22**

Wherever it was that Yeshua Meshiach had been during those eighteen years, it was obvious that upon his return to Israel he was recognized by some and by others he was not.

> **The beginning of the gospel of Jesus Christ, the Son of God.**
> **-Mark 1:1**

> **When he began His ministry, Jesus Himself was about thirty years of age**
> **-Luke 3:23**

Benny and I would continue our study and at this point I was nearly fluent in Hebrew. I donned a yamakah for the first time and visited Temple Emanu El in Houston. We also traveled around together to different churches of every denomination imaginable, listening, learning, praising and praying. We entered the sanctuaries and graced the pews of some the largest, most grandiose megachurches in the city, some with congregations in the tens of thousands. Benny and I were quite attentive, paying close attention to the words of each and every priest, preacher, pastor and clergyman. Sermons, prayers, songs and hymns, homilies, recitations and readings, we opened our hearts and souls, minds and ears to what was being said.

> **Andrew, Simon Peter's brother, was one of the two who heard what John had said and who had followed Jesus. The first thing Andrew did was to find his brother Simon and tell him, "We have found the Messiah" (that is, the Christ).**
> **-John 1:40-41**

We attended Sunday morning services at small Southern Baptist chapels, sang along with lively "Down Home" Gospel choirs, took road trips to evangelical events, festivals and revivals, all the while witness to the teachings of Yeshua the Christ.

> **Philip found Nathanael and told him, "We have found the one Moses wrote about in the Law, and about whom the prophets also wrote- Jesus of Nazareth, the son of Joseph."**
>
> **When Jesus saw Nathanael approaching, he said of him, "Here is a true Israelite, in whom there is nothing false."**
>
> **Then Nathanael declared, "Rabbi, You are the Son of God; You are the King of Israel."**
>
> John 1:45, 47, 49

At one point, Benny and I decided to take a jaunt into the Appalachian Mountains of the Western Carolinas, maybe round up some action and discover something totally different and new, a drastically foreign culture tucked away in them thar hills and hollers. Soon, we found ourselves worshiping with snake handlers and snake charmers, some of the most exotic (or perhaps strange would be a more fitting description) Christians in the world. These people had somehow become immune to the bite of the venomous serpents which they carried around in their hands, dancing, whirling, twirling, enlivened, so they claimed, by the Holy Spirit.

Christians or not, neither Benny nor I would dare touch one of those damned forked-tongue vipers, not even with a ten-foot pole, let alone grope a hissing rattler with our bare hands. After refusing a swig from the jug of poison being passed around (maybe arsenic, maybe formaldehyde, perhaps cyanide, who knows?) we loaded up the car and headed back home, if not strengthened in our faith, a little less naïve to the peculiar ways of the world, or at least to the backwoods country lifestyle of some of the most staunchly convinced Christian believers I had ever seen.

> **Many of the Samaritans in that town believed in him...They said, "We know that this man is really the Savior of the world."**
>
> -John 4:39, 42

An Adventure of Biblical Proportions

Arriving back in Houston, home of heavyweight champion, Olympic gold-medalist and first class preacher, Evander Holyfield, this time we hopped in Benny's van, popped in a tape of Martha & the Vandellas and went to visit some of the top evangelists and televangelists around, a few of them true 'vanguards of the faith', some of them just vain. I'll relate to you about the good ones; la crème de la crème, the cream of the crop.

Starting with one of the best, we trucked on over to Lakewood Church to hear Pastor Joel Osteen. Having been recently converted into a gargantuan-sized sanctuary and house of worship, services now take place in what used to be known as the Compaq Center, the old home-court arena for the Houston Rockets basketball team where during the 1994 and '95 seasons, sixteen-thousand and some-odd lucky fans underwent a religious experience of their own, watching as devout Muslim and Hall-of-Fame player, Hakeem "The Dream" Olajuwon, helped win back-to-back NBA championships in front of the hometown crowd.

It was in this same building where, as a rookie, modern-day Goliath, 7'6" giant Yao Ming took to center court, a place that's now reserved for the old veteran, Rock of Ages, Jesus Christ. Take who you want, be it in a three-point shootout or a dunk contest, you *know* who I'm bettin' all the marbles on. I will, unequivocally, have it *all* riding on Yeshua Ha Meshiach. *So that's why Jesus' middle initial is H?* Jesus H. Christ! Who would have thought? Down there on center stage, in the same spot where Clutch the Bear used to trampoline through the air doing kamakazi style flips with 360 degree twists, now the word of the Lord is fervently preached with the same intention of exciting all of those in attendance to "get up, get out of your seats and make some noise!"

I heard Joel mention in his very uplifting and empowering 'gospel of prosperity' that we should, "Think big. Think increase. Think abundance. Think more than enough."

But, after reading the Scripture…

You cannot serve both God and Money.
-Matthew 6:24

...still, I wrestled with what to do. What if I *do* happen to make millions of dollars off this book? What if it *does* sell five, ten, fifty million copies? What if the checks *do* start rolling in? *What then?*

> **From everyone who has been given much, much will be demanded; and from the one who has been entrusted with much, much more will be asked.**
> **-Luke 12:48**

*Well, I'll be damned...*Is this not what 'old King Selassie' told me while down in that dark, musty dungeon beneath the palace? Should it sink in even more now that the words have come straight from the Bible and the mouth of Jesus Christ? As we left the church, outside on the streets of the city, people were begging.

The following Sunday, Benny and I put on our least offensive scruffy suits, mine a K-Mart special and Benny's like something picked up at a Thrift Store or, perhaps, salvaged from a rummage sale, and we parked the old van in front of Second Baptist, intent on listening to the preaching of the highly revered minister, Dr. Ed Young. It is a grand and impressive church, crowned with a huge golden dome, spires and a bell tower. The beautiful sanctuary rivals the size of large airplane hangar and is adorned with thousands of panes of bright stained-glass, a state-of-the-art sound system, entire walls covered with video screens, control decks, swinging, rotating cameras on swivels, high-tech recording equipment and an organ that could wake the living dead. This is the technologically advanced, 21st century, modern way to worship.

Outside, we filtered through the expansive parking lot, dodging expensive foreign cars, fully customized luxury models with plush leather seats and convertible tops all decked out with every optional accessory and gadget known to the automotive industry. But inside, as we quietly slid into the pew, grabbed the provided hardcover edition of the Holy Bible and opened up to the Gospel of Jesus Christ, the message remained the same. The words, believe it or not, had not changed in almost two thousand years. Outside the church, people begged, hungry and hopeless.

An Adventure of Biblical Proportions

> **Then Jesus said to his disciples, "I tell you the truth, it is hard for a rich man to enter the kingdom of heaven. Again I tell you, it is easier for a camel to go through the eye of a needle than for a rich man to enter the kingdom of God.**
> **-Matthew 19:23**

We headed 'cross town, over across the tracks to Windsor Village Methodist, home church of Reverend Kirbyjon Caldwell, chosen spiritual advisor to President George Bush and the man hand-chosen and selected to give the benediction at the 2001 Presidential Inauguration.

The location was not in the most desirous part of town to say the least and most of the members were by no means affluent. This place seemed very unpretentious as dozens of used Honda Civics and Nissan Sentras overflowed from the lot and lined the surrounding streets, replacing the high-end Caddie's and the luxurious, top-of-the-line Beamers we had seen at the other church. Missing hubcaps, spare tires, dented fenders and rusted tailpipes were more prevalent here than the gold-plated rims, flashy hood ornaments and spotlessly detailed interiors that were noticeable before. But outside, more people begged for loose change, unfed, unclothed and uncared for. And the message within the Scripture remained the same.

Luke 12:22 Then Jesus said to his disciples:

Luke 12:33 Sell your possessions and give to the poor.

Now a man came up to Jesus and asked, "Rabbi, what good thing must I do to get eternal life?"

Jesus replied, "If you want to enter life, obey the commandments."

"Which ones?" the man inquired.

Jesus replied, "'Do not murder, do not commit adultery, do not steal, do not give false testimony, honor your father and mother,' and 'love your neighbor as yourself.'

"All these I have kept," the young man said. "What do I still lack?"

Jesus answered, "If you want to be perfect, go sell your possessions and give to the poor, and you will have treasure in heaven. Then come, follow me."

Wow! This isn't going to be easy. "Must I sell *everything*?" I asked, seeking council from my good friend Benny. "And give it *all* away?" I always have been a perfectionist of sorts.

"That's your own personal decision, your own free will," he told me. "Each individual will do what he or she thinks is required of them, perhaps striving to do even more. Some people have the desire to go above and beyond the call of duty, but the commands and advice of Our Lord and Savior remain very lucid and clear, albeit demanding and hard to meet. After careful consideration, you have to do what you feel is being asked of you."

Wait just a gosh darn minute! Did he say "OUR Lord and Savior?" Could it be that Benny is a.........

Okay, okay, back to my *own* salvation and judgment..."So the more success I have, the more will be demanded from me." At this point I was merely thinking out loud. "And the more money I make, the more I must give away and the more good I must do! That's quite a heavy burden for someone. It's a big load to carry, don't you think? But, I feel I can genuinely handle it." *Yeah, right. Who am I kidding? I'd have to be a magician among the likes of Harry Houdini and David Copperfield to pull off a stunt like that. Give away all my money? Impossible.*

"Good thing Christ died for your sins!" Benny exclaimed with a borderline smirk.

Was he serious? I couldn't be completely certain and I didn't want to ask for confirmation. Not just yet. One thing I do know, however, is that we both continued to crave more experiences, more lessons, more teachings and more sermons, as we were on the verge of uncovering a treasure trove of information.

"Let's go to Dallas," Benny suggested. "How 'bout a short road trip to see that well-liked pastor, T.D. Jakes. What d'ya say? Are you up for it?" We had both seen him on T.V. and were of the opinion that

An Adventure of Biblical Proportions

he was a very flamboyant, animated and charismatic character. One pre-recorded broadcast was all it took to convince me we should visit him in person. The very next Sunday, Benny pulled into my driveway at about four o'clock in the morning and just flat out laid on the horn.

"Whaaaaat? You don't think I have an alarm clock?" I asked while climbing into the vehicle.

"I was only making sure," he answered unsympathetically. "It's time to jet!" *Uh, oh, I don't like the sound of that.* I secured the lap belt snugly around my waist just in case this rocket ship of ours hit any turbulence and laid down in the backseat.

"Wake me up when we get there," I told him. "I'd rather sleep for a while than suffer through your bad driving."

He peeled out in reverse, squealing the tires and burning some rubber in what was probably an early wake-up call for half the neighborhood. And as the afterburners on the old cargo van fired up, we were on our way to the Potter's House as Jakes' church is called. Benny's blue & white Chevy Astrovan we had nicknamed 'The Mystery Machine' after our favorite cartoon, The Adventures of Scooby Doo and, in a way, I guess we too were unraveling mysteries about ghosts and spirits…the Holy Spirit!

> **…and to make plain to everyone the administration of this mystery, which for ages past was kept hidden in God, who created all things.**
> **-Ephesians 3:9**

> **the mystery that has been kept hidden for ages and generations, but is now disclosed to the saints.**
> **-Colossians 1:26**

> **However, as it is written:**
>
> "**No eye has seen,**
>   **no ear has heard,**
> **no mind has conceived**
>   **what God has prepared for**
>   **those who love**
>   **him**"
>   **-I Corinthians 2:9**

...but God has revealed it to us by his Spirit. The Spirit searches all things, even the deep things of God.

Surprised we could cover so much ground in so little time (256 miles in 3 hours and 47 minutes) I woke up just inside the Dallas city limits feeling well-rested and ready to praise the Lord! Pulling up in front of the church, I was shocked at the size of it.

"If this is the Potter's House," I joked with Benny, "I'd sure like to see where the candle maker lives! So...does this mean that Reverend Jakes is the potter?"

"No, man, don't by silly. It's just a reference to what has been written by the prophet Isaiah."

**But now, O LORD, You are our Father,
We are the clay, and You our potter;
And all of us are the work of Your hand.
-Isaiah 64:8**

"But, you're right David, this place *is* huge. It looks more like a mansion to me than a house. Do you think they'll even let us in like dressed like this?"

Benny was always a little self-conscious about the outfits we wore. Our suits were ugly, wrinkled and outdated and neither one of us could afford to purchase any new threads at this time. My light brown, fake suede sport coat and Benny's flashy plaid jacket and somewhat matching navy blue slacks would have to do. To tell you the truth, even if we had the *dinero,* it's not entirely certain we would choose to spend it on a new wardrobe. *There are better ways of parting with my cash,* I thought.

"See that guy over there? He's digging through the trash looking for something to eat. He must be hungry. Should I give him the dollar I have in my pocket?"

"Yeah, give it to him Benny. And don't worry too much about your outward appearance. There's no dress code where we're going, so I'm pretty sure they'll let us in. Come on and have a little faith, will you?"

An Adventure of Biblical Proportions

> **"Do not let your hearts be troubled. Trust in God; trust also in me. In my Father's house are many mansions: if it were not so, I would have told you. I am going there to prepare a place for you."**
>
> **-John 14:1-2**

Entering through the narthex of the church during the prelude to the benediction, we were welcomed at the door of the vestibule by a friendly greeter who, upon asking if we were first time visitors, handed us program bulletin detailing the exact order of service.

After squeezing into a front row seat in the upper balcony next to two hefty grandmothers in big, flowery hats, and after getting accustomed to the strong smell of Chanel #5, rose-scented lotions and fragrances and the globs of hairspray used to maintain that 'straight out of the beauty parlor' look, we sang a few hymns (our voices drowned out by the bellowing old ladies to our side), watched a couple of newborns getting dipped in holy water and readied ourselves for the upcoming sermon from Pastor Jakes.

> **Then Jesus said to them, "Watch out! Be on your guard against all kinds of greed; a man's life does not consist in the abundance of his possessions.**
> **And he told them this parable: The ground of a certain rich man produced a good crop. He thought to himself, 'what shall I do? I have no place to store my crops.'**
>
> **- Luke 12:15-17**

"You know what this man then said to himself?" a stern-looking Reverend Jakes asked the congregation in his usual animated fashion. "He said, 'This is what I'll do. I will tear down my barns and build bigger ones, and there I will store all my grain and my goods. And I'll say to myself, 'You have plenty of good things laid up for many years. Take life easy; eat, drink and be merry.'"

> **"But God said to him, 'You fool! This very night your life will be demanded from you. Then who will get what you have prepared for yourself?'**

> "This is how it will be with anyone who stores up things
> for himself but is not rich towards God."
> -Luke 12:20

Suddenly, everyone in the place began to get a little fidgety and we all started to perspire and sweat. Squirming around in their seats next to us, the two elderly grandmas reached into their handbags and pulled out a couple of small handheld fans trying to circulate the air and cool themselves down. It was getting very hot. *But, what does that mean?* I started to think. *Store up things?* Should I clean out the garage? Get rid of all those old pairs of shoes? *What does it mean to be rich towards God?*

> "What should we do then?" the crowd asked.
> -Luke 3:10

"Do what John said to do! Take John's advice!" The strong words screamed out from behind the pulpit with a certain dramatic flare, but with a truth so sharp they pierced the heart like flying javelins straight from heaven and, aided by the force of gravity, able to land down here on earth, penetrating into the chests of all believers in Christ and love.

> John answered, "The man with two tunics should share with him who has none, and the one who has food should do the same."
> -Luke 3:11

"Do this and your reward will be in Heaven!" shouted the fiery, black pastor. "And God will bless you! And He will bless your family! Of this we are assured! Can I get an Amen?" And the church responded with a resounding, "Amen!"

> "The King will reply, 'I tell you the truth, whatever you did for one of the least of these, you did for me."
> -Matthew 25:40

"Hallelujah! Praise the Lord!" they cried out from the gallery and all around. And after closing the service by singing one final hymn,

"How Great Thou Art", Benny and I and thousands of other parishioners exited down the stairs, out the open doors of the cathedral and into the warm sunshine of a bright Sunday morning in Dallas, Texas.

As we shuffled and skipped through the parking lot reaching the spot where the we'd left the van, the first thing that caught my eye as I slid open the side door was the large amount of clothes piled up high in the back, wadded up and wrinkled in an unsightly mess, not only just an eyesore and a Six Flags amusement park for lice and fleas, but a complete and utter waste of what, if properly cleaned and washed, would make useful jackets, t-shirts, pants, jeans, belts, coats and sweaters. *I've got an idea!* I thought, and decided to run it by Benny.

"Let's take this stuff to the Laundromat, wash it and then donate it! How 'bout it? You don't really need all this stuff, do you?"

"Uhhh, those are my clothes, dude. What do you expect me to wear?"

"Oh, come on!" I pleaded with him. "You've got a whole other bag packed. And, besides, you heard the sermon. Look here what I see, you've got two tunics, err, *I mean,* jackets. What do you say? I'll tell you what…instead of buying that new cd I was wanting from the music store, I'll donate the money, along with these clothes of yours, cleaned and washed of course, to the first homeless shelter we can find! Is that a deal?"

"You got it, man. It's a deal."

"Awesome! You won't be disappointed, I promise. There's a little washateria just a few blocks away. Let's go!"

And, like that, Benny and I spent our Sunday afternoon at the nearby 'Suds and Duds' doing laundry, washing and folding clothes that we would eventually drop off, along with twenty dollars in cash, at the local mission in Ft. Worth, not too far from where more than ten years ago I sat for the last class of my undergraduate college career, Mysticism 101.

"We've gotta strike while the iron is hot!" declared Benny. I could tell he had real soft spot in his heart and the sole act of giving and of being of service to others had triggered something deep down in his soul, producing a warm, fuzzy feeling inside of him and sparking a yearning desire to relinquish his selfish needs in exchange for becoming a faithful, humble servant of the Lord. He had not only accepted, but unabashedly embraced the doctrine of love, of Christ, and the message of the Bible.

> **Jesus replied, "'Love the Lord your God with all your heart and with all your soul and with all your mind.' This is the first and greatest commandment. And the second is like it: 'Love your neighbor as yourself.' All the Law and the Prophets hang on these two commandments."**
> **- Matthew 22:37**

Now that the back of the van had been cleared out and emptied of its stockpile of dirty clothes, enough space was created in Benny's 'Mystery Machine' for two moderately comfortable makeshift beds, one in the way back on the freshly vacuumed carpet and the other in the seat where I had slept so soundly on the way up there. Benny had only one remaining request; and with my restless, adventurous spirit, how could I refuse?

"I'm setting my watch to go off at 3:33AM," he said to me, upon which out of faint curiosity I replied, "Why would you do that?"

"Oh, well, you know…the Trinity…the three in one…the Father, the Son and the….."

Holy Ghost! He didn't have to say it. He'd been touched by the Spirit! And just when you least expect it, right? Nah, not really, I had suspected for quite a while that Benny was a…

"You're gonna love this church," he told me, "It's a good one. And the pastor is a fantastic motivational speaker, a real leader. He reverse tithes and gives 90 percent of his earnings back to the church! He's lived in the same house for twenty years. And he owns only two suits!"

"Well, maybe he should give one away," I interrupted. "You know what John said…" And before I ruffled any more of Benny's tail feathers, I let him know that, for the most part, I was only kidding. "Now where is this place?" I asked.

"Don't worry about it. Just get some sleep and I'll tell you in the morning. We've got a long drive ahead of us tomorrow."

A few hours later, at the precise time he had planned this pre-dawn departure, Benny's titanium metal Casio watch sounded off like that of a starter's pistol fired into the air, signaling the beginning of a much anticipated event. My friend then ignited the engine on the old Chevrolet, drove up the entrance ramp and onto the freeway and headed west down the Interstate towards....

"California. We're going to California," he said in a very satisfied tone as if we had some great intended purpose for driving there.

And we did. This may very well have been one of the most purposeful drives of my entire life, not quite so much for what occurred there in Orange County, but for what Benny revealed to me on the way home. To make a long story short, Benny had a plan to visit Pastor Rick Warren, best-selling author of The Purpose-Driven Life, at his Saddleback Church just outside of Los Angeles.

For twenty two hours straight we drove, stayed for two short hours, then turned around and drove it again. I'd spent so much time lately with my good friend Benny, one might even be tempted think that, instead of a church in Saddleback Valley, we were headed over to Brokeback Mountain to film the sequel about two gay Texas cowboys and their 'Summer of love' way out West. That was not the case, however. My sexual orientation, I can assure you, had not changed since the last time I checked. In fact, a few weeks prior, I had the fortune of meeting a nice, young lady, another *bella Latina*, Lizbeth Vazquez from Mexico City, by way of Chicago. *Could she be the one?*

"Lizbeth," I said to Benny. "Her name comes from Elizabeth, the House of Elijah! You *know* how my name comes from Jezebel, *don't* you? You know the story...Jezebel tried to kill the prophet Elijah. Now, almost three thousand years later, here we are the two of us, both Christians! Lizbeth Isbell! Sounds perfect, don't you think?"

"Yeah, yeah, whatever David, why do you try to do this with every girl you meet?"

"Do what?" I questioned.

"You make these silly connections, play these name games and stuff, trying to justify some kind of whirlwind romance written in the stars. What are you expecting? Fireworks...maybe a lightning bolt through the roof, a tingling sensation in your toes, an ache down in the marrow of your bones? What?"

I think my friend may have been a little jealous and feeling a little jilted, for he too was approaching his mid-thirties and still had not succeeded successfully in locating that special someone, his *amor verdadero.* He was right about one thing, though. "Give yourself up to God," he had told me.

Alright, alright, I said to myself, *if this doesn't work out, I'll just give up and quit searching.* To hell with all these stupid fantasies and dreams of meeting…her…my *alma gemela,* my twin soul. But, I knew deep down there wasn't a chance in hell of that ever happening. No, I would never give up on love.

We changed the subject, talked about how we would run the non-profit, formulated plans on how to fund different community projects.

"We'll clean up the city," Benny said, much to my liking, "And fix up all the run-down soccer fields, basketball courts and youth sports facilities! We'll serve the Lord by helping those in need, spreading hope to the poor and downtrodden, taking the Gospel of Jesus Christ to the streets, reaching people *wherever* they are, whether in a dark place or stuck in a rut. We'll strengthen faith, families and communities and make the world a better place!"

Even as the A/C ran full blast, spitting out cool air as we passed through Palm Springs, crossing the stark and dry Mojave Desert and into the arid zone of Arizona, I still felt dehydrated and in need of a drink. However, a couple verses in particular that Pastor Warren had quoted earlier that morning really seemed to stick out in my mind and kept repeating themselves inside my head…

> **Blessed are those who hunger and thirst for righteousness, for they will be filled.**
> **-Matthew 5:6**
>
> **Blessed are the pure in heart, for they will see God.**
> **-Matthew 5:8**

But I *do* hunger and thirst for it so *very* much! And if righteousness were a drink served at the local bar, I'd order up a pint of it, maybe a gallon's worth. "In a cold a frothy mug, please, Mr. Bartender," I would say.

If only righteousness were able to be acquired at the neighborhood convenience store, taken from the cooler, bought and paid for, I'd purchase an entire twelve pack or, perhaps, maybe a case or two to take home and pass out to all my friends. "Don't mind the tab, this round's on me!"

I'd ask for twist off tops and drink it straight from the bottle, "Bottom's up!" with a lime wedge chaser and a pinch of salt. "You are the salt of the Earth!" I would say as I gave a toast to all my fellow patrons.

And pure in heart? I can do that, too. I'll eat nothing but green lettuce and raisins, organic carrots and sunflower seeds. I'll purify this damn body of mine until my heart is as clean as a whistle and as pure as a freshly poured glass of artesian well water.

But, unfortunately, we all know that's not the way it works. Oh no, righteousness has a much higher price tag. It demands sacrifice, good deeds, penitence, prayers, supplication and devotion. It requires love, patience, kindness, humility and honesty. Like a good, hard, dry piece of beef jerky, you must grip it between your teeth, bite it off, tear and chew. It can be real tough, a struggle to swallow sometimes, but once you get it down it provides enrichment to your body and nourishment to your bones.

"I've got something important to tell you," began Benny, "But, first, let me ask you one question. Do you honestly think you can *prove* faith?"

Aw, shucks, back to this again?

"Well...I think I *have* finally proven it to myself. (With more than just a little help from above, I might add). But to others, I don't know? Have I proven it to you?"

Well, have I? Did Benny consider himself...? *Is he a......?*

"Maybe it can't be done?" I conceded, losing a tiny smidgeon of hope. But, just as quickly...

"Maybe it can!" replied my Anam Cara, restoring the faith I had momentarily lost.

"Maybe you *have* proven it to some people, maybe not to *all,* but to some. Look at it this way; at the very least, I think you've proven Columbus wasn't the first person to discover America." Benny continued, "You've proven that so many place names are Hebrew, Greek and Arabic in origin…Alabama, Alaska, Nebraska, the Bahamas… California, Brazil, Illinois and Iowa…Michigan, Missouri and, not to mention…"

He paused for a moment.

"You left one off the list. And I must say it's a doozie, a real attention getter. Should I tell you which one it is?"
Heck yeah. Are you kiddin'? What'cha waitin' for? "Please, if you could be so kind, I would love to know this top-secret, classified information of which you are aware. And if you could only find it in your heart to share with such a pour soul as I, the wisdom and knowledge held by such an esteemed and accomplished individual as yourself, I would be ever so grateful to you for divulging this precious gem of a revelation that you've been withholding from me for what seems like an eternity and…"
"Alright, enough of the sarcasm, you want to know or not?"
"Is the Pope Catholic? You bet your bottom dollar I do! What is it? Another state?"
"It's Massachusetts."
"Massachusetts?"
"Yes. Massachusetts," he said.
And traveling straight through Lordsburg and past Las Cruces, somewhere near El Paso on the *New* Mexico side of the newly erected, hotly debated border fence, less than half a marathon's distance from "Old" Mexico, that's when Benny decided to reveal to me the meaning of the word…
"*Mashiach*, of course, is Hebrew for Messiah or 'the anointed one.' The *Jews* are the Jews, obviously. And *etz* is the Hebrew word for 'tree', defined in the dictionary as a woody, perennial plant with one main stem or trunk which develops many branches. Massachusetts is Mashiach Jews etz, a branch of Messianic Jews who immigrated across the sea and planted themselves in the New World. *Capiche? Comprendes?*"

> "I am the vine; you are the branches. If a man remains in me and I in him, he will bear much fruit; apart from me you can do nothing."
>
> -John 15:5

MashiachJewsetz! I was speechless. "Ugghhh, yeah, I...." *Incredible! Truly amazing!* How were these things, hidden for so long, now starting to come to light?

Come to light. Come to light.

Come to light...

Come to...

Bright light!

Where are we?

Benny remained behind the wheel. The sun was now up and the car was getting hot again.

"Crank up the air, man, it's burning up in here," I said

"It's on low. We're almost out of gas and I've got absolutely *no* money left, not one red cent. And, don't worry dude, I already checked your wallet. Your poor butt is just as broke."

"You did *what?*" I really wasn't too alarmed at the thought of him rifling through my billfold in search of gas money. We had to get home, didn't we?

"Oh and, uh, you might want to open up the vent. I think you may have closed it last night in your sleep. It got kinda cold out there on the plains."

"You mean you drove all night...without stopping?" And before he could answer I recognized we were within half an hour of arriving home to Houston. "You in a hurry or something?"

"Just excited, that's all. Things are gonna get busy, you know. Here, why don't you take over now? I'm pretty beat."

But, we're only 30 miles from... "Alright, pull over," I said. And Benny swerved, darting across two lanes of traffic and into a Texaco filling station on the right hand side of the Interstate. *Whoa!*

We sure could've used a couple drops of gasoline as the needle on the fuel gauge was pinned all the way to the left, way past empty. We were running on fumes at this point. I thought about grabbing a nozzle from off the pump and shaking the hell out of it and the hose, maybe trying to force a few droplets of liquid to dribble out and into the tank of the Mystery Machine. Benny was bent down, hunched over and looking under his seat when I stepped around the front of the van.

"Hey, here's a quarter! And, look, a nickel, too!" he exclaimed excitedly.

This is pitiful. I reached down deep into my pockets and pulled out whatever I could find, one small coin and some lint. "I've got a penny." *That's better than nothing.*

"Thirty one cents!" Benny declared. "It's a sign!"

"Yeah, you're right. It's a sign that we both need jobs."

We paid the attendant for one tenth of a gallon of gas, accelerated back onto the highway and, luckily, made it home without the van stalling.

Three days later. Saturday.

As I opened the book, I was feeling well-prepared and ready to read from the text. My Hebrew I now spoke flawlessly, like a native citizen of Tel-Aviv, Benny's mom's hometown. Inside the synagogue, I stood at the altar before the congregation and began to recite from the Torah and, soon, followed with the reading of the *haftarah,* a selection taken from the *Tanach,* the Hebrew Bible, usually from the books of *Nevi'im* or "the Prophets."

Now, I really can't remember word for word exactly every single verse, but I know that my recitation came from the 53rd Chapter of Isaiah the Prophet.

Who has believed our message and to whom has the arm of the Lord been revealed? He grew up before them like a tender shoot, and like a root out of dry ground. He

An Adventure of Biblical Proportions

had no beauty or majesty to attract us to him, nothing in his appearance that we should desire him. He was despised and rejected by men, a man of sorrows, and familiar with suffering...he was despised and we esteemed him not. Surely he took up our infirmities and carried our sorrows, yet we considered him stricken by God, smitten by him, and afflicted. But he was pierced for our transgressions, the punishment that brought us peace was upon him, and by his wounds we are healed. We all, like sheep, have gone astray, each of us has turned to his own way; and the Lord has laid on him the iniquity of us all. He was oppressed and afflicted, yet he did not open his mouth; he was led like a lamb to the slaughter...By oppression and judgment he was taken away...for the transgression of my people he was stricken...and though the Lord makes his life a guilt offering...by his knowledge my righteous servant will justify many, and he will bear their iniquities...because he poured out his life unto death...For he bore the sin of many, and made intercession for the transgressors.

The next day. Sunday.

We had come to Memorial Drive Christian Church a good half hour before the sunrise service was set to begin. Benny had put on the customary white robe, draping it over his old, wrinkled suit, and was now standing waist deep in the lukewarm baptismal pool of water. The transparent tank where the baptism would take place was suspended high above in what appeared to be a loft built into the sanctuary wall, hanging directly in front of a pair of dramatically large stained-glass windows. Beaming rays of morning sunlight penetrated through the thick, jagged-edged cuts of glass creating spectacular streaks of color that shone in, illuminating the house of worship in the full spectrum of the rainbow.

The preacher, also wearing a similarly spotless white gown, gently placed his hands upon Benny's head, blessing him, saying, "I baptize you in the name of the Father, and of the Son, and of the Holy Spirit."

My good friend Benyamin, 'the right hand son of God', was thrust backwards, dunked in the tub, submerged in holy water, immersed in the spirit of the Lord and as he rose up out of the water, his wet garment clinging to his skin, I and the rest of the congregation could see a bright aura shining all around him, engulfing him in a soothingly peaceful and glorious light.

> **...and the Holy Spirit descended on him in bodily form like a dove.**
>
> -Luke 3:22

Epilogue

The janitor more than likely opened the sanctuary doors that very evening and with the aid of a stick broom, a dust mop, two flailing arms and a little sweet talk, succeeded in coaxing that fat, grain-fed Mourning Dove out of the church and into the dark of the night. But, you see...that's also what happened to my good friend Benyamin. He may have left the confines of the church that day, but the Holy Spirit, most certainly, did not budge from the boundaries of his heart, instead residing somewhere inside those walls, those chambers, those veins and ventricles, perhaps housed within the main aorta or maybe the atrium, opening up valves, going from room to room, resting inside Benny's blood-red cardiac organ as if it were the *kodesh kodashim*, the Holy of Holies, the innermost sanctuary of the *mishkan*, the temple of God in Jerusalem.

And like a symbol of peace, the little dove blessed with two able wings with which to fly, Benny also flew into the dark of the night as if he were an apostle, a saint, a 150-pound burlap sack full of mustard seed, untethered and unraveling, shot out the end of a loose cannon, "Old Glory" perhaps. My friend, a prominent Jewish Gardner, began sowing and seeding, watering and germinating, tending and harvesting, souls, sentient beings, the Word of Lord, the kingdom of heaven.

An agent wasn't necessary. We did all the printing and publishing ourselves, promoting and pampering the project almost as if this book were a manifestation of the Divine Christ Child himself, a newborn baby Jesus swaddled in warm woolen blankets laying in a manger or wrapped in a jacket cover and placed on a bookshelf beside the Talmud and the Torah, sandwiched between the New Testament and the Methodist Book of Hymns.

Wise men came from far away...said they had seen a star.

After more than a handful of author signings, visits to various book stores and book clubs and a few scheduled appearances on nationally syndicated talk shows, (the Oprah Winfrey Show, Dr. Phil and Larry King Live), we sat down to formally discuss the non-profit, formulate plans for moving forward and finalize the blueprints that had already been drafted.

Ever since the book first came hot off the press, our lives have been virtually non-stop. During the last four months, Benny has worked with the Zina Garrison Foundation, offering free tennis lessons to children of low-income families, and has also volunteered at Sports Quest, a faith-based organization providing coaching and instruction in youth soccer, running camps and clinics around town. (And, although he won't admit it, Benny spent his last $500 sponsoring twelve kids, handing out scholarships to those who would have otherwise not had the chance to participate.) He has even accompanied me on three global mission trips...to Estonia, to East Africa and to El Salvador, working menial odd jobs, standing on street corners with day laborers and migrant workers, picking up random shifts at Starbucks so as just to afford the airfare.

Just then the phone rang.

I picked up the receiver, unsuspecting of whose familiar voice would soon be heard on the other end of the line.

"This is the operator. You have a collect call from..."

Buzz. Click, click. Dial tone. Silence.

"Will you accept the charges?"

Who? "Ugh, yes, I..."

Click, click. Silence.

"Hola David!"

My God...Was I dreaming again? Had Benny spiked my coffee with a shot of concentrated cactus juice? It was Diego. He was calling from a pay phone in Panajachel. He, too, had seen the star.

"Tengo una pregunta." He also had a question for me.

I could almost hear in the background...the tiny waves of Atitlán lapping up against the rocky shore, the seething and popping of meat cooking on a grill, tourists and vendors, old women and children, shoeshine boys, little girls selling fruit. Thoughts flooded my brain. *How on earth did he find my number?* I wondered what he might ask. Had he called to confront me on why I hadn't...

"Are you going to translate <u>The True Love Messiah</u> into Spanish?" he asked.

What? Was he serious? Had he somehow managed to get a hold of a rogue copy that had made its way down to Central America? How did he know…?

"Yo creo que sí. I guess so," I told him. I mean…it seems this book would have a far-reaching audience…North Americans, South Americans, Africans, Asians, Europeans, Polynesians…I had planned on having it translated into 21 different languages and Braille. Yes, and Braille, too.

Diego interrupted, "Because there is something that has been bothering me for a long time." *Uh oh, here it comes.* He must be upset that in ten years I had failed to make it back to the tiny village of San Pablo, Guatemala.

"Yes…go ahead." I urged him to continue.

He cleared his throat and began to speak. "We are starting to think that maybe you're not coming back to see us."

I thought of a million excuses. None was acceptable. "I'm sorry, but I…"

"No worries," voiced Diego, "I will simply tell you what you need to know over the phone."

He had but one request.

"Meet me in Spain," he said, "And be sure to bring all of your friends."

"Okay. If you insist," I responded. "I'll invite everyone I know…but, might I ask *why*?"

And this is what he told me…

"My grandfather was a shaman. And his grandfather was a shaman. And his grandfather, too, and so on and so forth all the way back to the year 1524 when the first Diego de Compostela arrived in the New World, coming to Guatemala from Galicia in Northwest Spain. In fact, the town from which he hailed is named after one of our ancestors, the first Diego in my family line. The name 'Diego' actually comes from Saint 'Iago', a shortened version of the Latin name for 'Iacobo' or Jacob. Saint Iago or San Diego became known as Santiago."

I had heard of the town of Santiago de Compostela and was familiar with some of its history. It was indeed named after Saint Iago or Santiago, known in English as Saint James the Greater, an apostle of Christ. It was here in Spain where tradition has it that Saint James came to preach the Gospel of Jesus Christ shortly after the Resurrection. In accordance with local folklore, on January 2 of the year 40 A.D., the Virgin Mary appeared to James on the bank of the Ebro River, near Zaragoza. Following this appearance, Saint James returned to Jerusalem in Judea where he was martyred, beheaded by King Herod (grandson of Herod the Great) in 44 A.D.

> **It was about this time that King Herod arrested some who belonged to the church, intending to persecute them. He had James, the brother of John, put to death with the sword.**
>
> -Acts 12:1

By a series of miraculous happenings, the body of St. James was taken by boat to Northwest Spain and prepared for burial. His reputed final resting place, the cathedral in Santiago de Compostela, has become the destination of a major historical pilgrimage route since the Middle Ages and is considered by the Catholic Church to be the third most holy site in all of Christendom, behind Rome and Jerusalem. Millions upon, literally, millions of faithful pilgrims have trod the Camino de Santiago or the 'Way of St. James', traveling long distances, making the trek to visit the venerated shrine and pay homage to the patron saint of Spain.

"I am 64th in a long line of Diegos, all having descended from Saint James the Great, Santiago, the apostle and disciple of Jesus Christ. I am Diego de Compostela!"

"That's great Diego. And I admit I find it very interesting. But, what does any of this have to do with me going Spain?"

"Well, you see...the tomb of St. James, forgotten about for centuries, was rediscovered in A.D. 835 by a wandering shepherd who, as legend states, was guided by a star to where the remains and relics of the apostle lay buried in an obscure field in Galicia, Spain, in the exact location of the present-day city of Santiago de Compostela. A church was later built to house the bones and, after being destroyed by the Moors in 997, was eventually replaced with the famous cathedral upon which construction initiated in the year 1060 A.D."

Diego continued, "The origin of the name Compostela has always been attributed to this account of discovery by the wandering shepherd, owing its etymology to the Latin *campus stellae*, meaning 'field of stars.'"

He paused.

There was a brief moment of silence on the other end of the line that for a split second caused me to believe the call had been lost.

And then he began, "I feel the time is now ripe for me to reveal the true meaning of the name." Diego lowered his voice to just a whisper. "This knowledge has been passed down through generations in my family ever since James, the first *shamayim* in our genealogical line, communed with the heavenly realm, walking side by side with the Lord Jesus Christ."

"Alright, let's hear it." I would certainly, at this juncture, be captivated by any secret information that Diego might disclose.

"This is why you must go to Spain," he explained. "It is there where I will reveal the true meaning of Compostela for all the world to know."

There was no hesitation. "I'll be there," I emphatically stated. "Just set the time and the date."

"**July 25, 2010,**" he quickly told me. "This is the day of the celebration of the **Feast of St. James**. However, due to the fact the feast falls on a Sunday, it is considered a Holy Year, or Jubilee Year, in which a plenary indulgence is granted by the Pope, and all who make the pilgrimage are remitted of the existing temporal punishment due for sins previously committed."

Diego paused before continuing,

"There and then you will pass out pamphlets on which is published my written manuscript titled, '**The Coming Together of the Saints.**'"

Benny sat quietly on the couch hanging onto every word. He must have figured out by now with whom I must be speaking. After a few more minutes of listening intently, I received Diego's instructions and hung up the phone.

I started to think...*Compostela. compost stellae...*

> "I, Jesus, have sent my angel to give you this testimony for the churches. I am the Root and the Offspring of David, and the bright Morning Star."
>
> -Revelations 22:16

I informed Benny of the remainder of what was said. "Diego told me to, 'invite as many people as possible,' and that, as I should know, 'sometimes it's not necessary to physically travel in person.' He said, 'This is an invitation to join in the feast, to come to Christ, to make a pilgrimage of the heart, a journey of the mind and of the spirit.'"

My thoughts started to wander...*epistle, apostle, composite.*

"He told me to meet him in Salamanca, about 250 miles from Santiago de Compostela, that it would be less hectic and crowded there in the days leading up to the Feast of Saint James. He said the name of this ancient city comes from *Shalom*, the Hebrew word for 'peace' (*salaam* in Arabic) and *ankh*, the Egyptian word and symbol for life. *Shalomankh.*"

As Benny's eyes grew wide with excitement, I let him know that the instructions were to pick up the pamphlets sometime in mid-July, a couple of weeks prior to the Feast of St. James, and distribute them all along the route, handing them out to pilgrims as they enter the city.

Diego also presented a challenge to anyone who is fortunate enough to read The True Love Messiah...urging that they would pass out at least ten copies of the book, if not more, to friends, acquaintances, loved ones and strangers, handing it to them, saying,

"This is an invitation to come to the Feast."

When the hour came, Jesus and his apostles reclined at the table. And he said to them, "I have eagerly desired to eat this Passover with you before I suffer. For I tell you, I will not eat it again until it finds fulfillment in the kingdom of God."

After taking the cup, he gave thanks and said, "Take this and divide it among you. For I tell you I will not drink again of the fruit of the vine until the kingdom of God comes."

And he took bread, gave thanks and broke it, and gave it to them, saying, "This is my body given for you; do this in remembrance of me."

In the same way, after the supper he took the cup, saying, "This cup is the new covenant in my blood, which is poured out for you.

-Luke 22:14-20

THE TRUE LOVE MESSIAH:

An Adventure of Biblical Proportions

True Love Missions

True Love Missions is a non-profit dedicated to the funding of community projects for the betterment of society as a whole. Through the actions of the local, national and international charities and organizations it supports, **TLM** promotes the sharing of God's Word by actively volunteering in the service of others.

To donate to **True Love Missions** or to learn more about the dynamic ways in which we are working to change lives and what you can do to help, please visit **thetruelovemessiah.com** or send to:

True Love Missions
P.O. Box 430160
Houston, TX. 77243

* **Proceeds from the sales of this book go to True Love Missions and the charities and non-profits it supports.**

THE TRUE LOVE MESSIAH:

An Adventure of Biblical Proportions

Two sisters walked along the beach, cradling in their hands the clay-fired terracotta funerary urn, scattering fistfuls of ashes as they went. Some sifted through aged and weathered fingers, falling like powder onto the soft white sand and mixing with an infinite world of tiny grains and microscopic granules, they themselves mirroring an entire universe of pebble-shaped planets forming the woven fabric of a trillion galaxies. Some was tossed into the outgoing tide and washed out to sea, melting forever into the foam and the waves, quilting the shore a million times over with every effortless ebb and gentle graceful fluid flow. And still some of which the wind managed to take a hold was quickly carried away, all the way to heaven, pulverizing every particle and creating a rain shower of cosmic angel dust and prehistoric star matter.

The peaceful, soft and soothing sound of a four-stringed musical instrument played in the background, serenading the warm, salty ocean breeze and whispering through the stoic branches of a lone stand of majestic ironwood trees. The sand dunes were alive with many spirits. I could hear them laughing and playing. The heiau, the ancient stone temple, buzzing with activity, sat somewhere behind the misty veil of clouds, enshrouded in a mystical fog, snuggled up against the mountains on the far northern end of the beach. Polihale.

A voice echoed out for all to hear, sounding all too familiar with its hauntingly high pitch and perfectly mesmerizing tone. I knew exactly who it was...

"Somewhere over the rainbow..."

And as I looked over at the rivers of tears streaming down their sad, little faces, "Ahui ho," I told them.

"We'll see you later, Daddy," they softly whispered into the wind. "We love you, too."

The voice kept singing...

"I hear babies cry and I watch them grow
They'll learn much more
Than we know
And I think to myself
What a wonderful world...

THE TRUE LOVE MESSIAH:

…oh what a wonderful world."

An Adventure of Biblical Proportions

Please order copies at www.bookmasters.com, www.amazon.com
And visit us online at www.thetruelovemessiah.com

THE TRUE LOVE MESSIAH:

This may be THE END for some.
For others, it is only the beginning…

TLM Press